SUCCESS IN AMERICA

University of Massachusetts Press   Amherst   1976

✦

Success in America

THE YEOMAN DREAM

AND THE

INDUSTRIAL REVOLUTION

✦

REX BURNS

To Emily

Copyright © 1976 by Rex Sehler Burns
All rights reserved
Library of Congress Catalog Card Number 75–32482
ISBN 0–87023–207–X
Designed by Mary Mendell
Library of Congress Cataloging in Publication Data
Burns, Rex.
  Success in America.
  Bibliography: p.
  Includes index.
  1. Success. 2. Success in literature. 3. United States—Social
conditions. I. Title.
BJ1611.B877   131'.32   75–32482
ISBN 0–87023–207–X

CONTENTS

PREFACE

MOST OF the recent books on success in America define it as riches and the consequent social position bought by wealth. Often explicit or implicit is a belief in a concurrent spiritual impoverishment that accompanies the attainment of such success. Notable in illustrating the wide acceptance and application of this definition are A. Whitney Griswold, "The American Gospel of Success"; Robert Heilbroner, *The Quest for Wealth: A Study of Acquisitive Man*; Kenneth Lynn, *The Dream of Success: A Study of the Modern American Imagination*; Ephraim Mizruchi, *Success and Opportunity: A Study of Anomie*; John Tebbel, *From Rags to Riches: Horatio Alger, Jr. and the American Dream*, and Lawrence Chenoweth, *The American Dream of Success: The Search for the Self in the Twentieth Century*. But many Americans who today condemn the American Dream as materialistic are themselves speaking from a long tradition of an opposing concept of success that never quite died, one which for many nineteenth century Americans defined true success not as riches and fame but as a competence, independence, and morality. The emblem of this success was the American yeoman.

Sharing the materialistic definition of success, two fine works do offer focus on alternative concepts by discussing the moral and immoral means of attaining wealth: *The Self-Made Man in America: The Myth of Rags to Riches*, by Irvin Wyllie; and *Apostles of the Self-Made Man*, by John Cawelti. But the self-made man cannot be equated with the yeoman; indeed, as defined by Cawelti, this figure goes far beyond the simple desires of the yeoman and seeks social and financial eminence which has no room for the kind of mass application entailed in the yeoman dream. There are several other points of difference between Cawelti and myself toward which the specialist may wish to be oriented: the view of the Jeffersonian yeoman as inflexibly anti-industrial, versus the picture of the yeoman's urbanization in the mechanic periodicals; a society structured along economic lines and viewed as "open" or "closed" to the pursuit of riches, versus a fluid society which, in addition to the economic strata, is vertically divided into the moral and the immoral; the idea that in the late nineteenth century the aggressively self-made man was opposed to society, versus the belief that in that period aggressively materialistic success was the norm, and the yeoman dream was a weak conservative reaction. A third study, Theodore Greene's *America's Heroes: The Changing Models of Success in American Magazines*, omits the period 1821 to 1893, and, in addition, one may question whether the "hero" is a true model of success for the general population. Exemplifying the shadowy persistency of the yeoman dream well into the Twentieth Century and in the face of almost total domination by the materialistic concept are such varied works as the plays of Arthur Miller, the poems of Robert Frost, and Norman Podhoretz' tale of a lucky Willie Loman, *Making It*. Typically, Podhoretz senses an alternative to material success, but can offer no better definition of that alternative than the misleading "anti-success." Closer to the yeoman dream, though lacking historical knowledge of the idea, are myriad members of the so-called counter-culture.

Some comment on the evidence used in this study is called for. It ranges from popular literature to children's literature to labor periodicals to the novels of Nathaniel Hawthorne. The attempt has been to show in four kinds of evidence both the existence of the yeoman idea and its varying mutations.

The choice of periodicals appearing in the text is based on a wide reading, and an indication of its range can be seen in the bibliography of primary sources. Children's literature was selected as a point of beginning because in its didacticism this genre expressed in a simplified manner the outlines of the yeoman configuration. Samples from adult magazines could easily have been included—*Hunt's Merchant's Magazine* or the *Farmer and Mechanic*—but the area is vast, and one could easily be trapped by the desire to include more and more. Since the main configuration was already drawn in the juveniles, and since a reading of numbers of adult magazines added little to the existing

concept of traditional success, the decision was made to use the portrait of the yeoman found in the juveniles as the basis for evaluating
the fragmentation of that portrait in mechanic periodicals. It is hoped
that this method indicates both the range of the yeoman's appeal as
well as contributing some clarity to a very complex area.

The representativeness of a periodical was based on its longevity,
its apparent breadth of readership, and its role as a source of material
for other editors. The *Union List of Serials* and Frank Luther Mott's
standard history help direct the reader to these key periodicals, and
even cursory reading soon indicates who borrowed from whom.
Among the juveniles, Lydia Maria Child's magazine was chosen not
only because it opens the period 1825 to 1860, but also because of its
high quality, the wide popularity of its editor, and its position as a primary target of other editors' shears and paste. Samuel Goodrich was
a major figure in the development of children's literature in America,
and his magazines literally set the standard against which other periodicals were measured for a decade or more. The *Youth's Companion*,
which bought out Goodrich's publication in 1850, was the only magazine to span the entire period under consideration, surviving until
1929; it has received a chapter by itself. Other periodicals were not
included because the findings were repetitive: *Child's Friend, Boy's
and Girl's Magazine and Fireside Companion (Forrester's Boy's and
Girl's Companion)*, etc. In short, given the similarity of content of
children's periodicals during the age, and given the representativeness
of the above mentioned titles, quantity of citation was deemphasized
in favor of clarity of narration.

The labor periodicals did not offer quite the same evenness of
content; consequently, the reader will find not only such dominating
titles as the *Boston Mechanic* or the *Mechanic's Free Press*, but also
shorter-lived names. In Chapter Three, the attempt was to present
both regions and divergent attitudes toward the yeoman dream.

The selection of Nathaniel Hawthorne as the major literary figure exemplifying the effects of the yeoman dream is based on several
factors. First, he's one of the very few principal writers active throughout most of the period 1825-60. Secondly, Hawthorne has close ties to
Samuel Goodrich, having written many of his early works for "Peter
Parley's" publications. But more importantly, I wanted a serious thinker
whom the reader would not be likely to identify as an obvious choice,
one whose inclusion would carry some surprise and consequently indicate the breadth of impact of the yeoman dream. Melville would

have worked quite well (*The Confidence Man,* "Tartarus of Maids," etc.), but he comes late in the period. Cooper, who showed the yeoman in various stages in *The Prairie, The Chainbearers* and other novels, was not only an overly obvious choice but—I felt—lacked Hawthorne's sensitivity to the decline of the yeoman dream. The essayists Thoreau and Emerson were less interested in dealing with the mythic quality of the yeoman than was the novelist Hawthorne, and Poe was too peripheral to the issue. Finally, I hope that by approaching Hawthorne's work from this angle, some additional appreciation may be offered a writer whose attainments and struggles still deserve high respect.

Let me quickly express gratitude to the editors of *The Social Sciences Journal* and *Texas Studies in Literature and Language* who have cheerfully allowed me to use the following material published in their pages: "The Yeoman Mechanic: 'Venturous Conservative' " and "Hawthorne's Romance of Traditional Success."

An idea of my scholarly debts can be gained by a glance at the bibliography of secondary sources. Many thinkers have been teachers through their books, but a specific debt is owed to Henry Nash Smith's bench-mark work, *The Virgin Land,* both for the method and the vital discussion of the agrarian yeoman's movement west. And for personal assistance and guidance, I am grateful to Professors David Cooperman, Joseph J. Kwiat, and Herbert Eldridge. All errors of concept or presentation are, of course, my own. The library staff at the University of Colorado at Denver has provided unfailing help. For her patience and support, I thank my wife, Emily.

SUCCESS IN AMERICA

It is God that called thee to labour: And wilt thou stand still or be doing other things, when God expecteth duty from thee?

Richard Baxter

It is hard for an empty sack to stand upright.

Poor Richard

INTRODUCTION

PURITAN AND ENLIGHTENMENT VIEWS

✾

DESPITE THE assumptions of many Americans—and many non-Americans, too—the idea of success in this country has not always been equated with great wealth; indeed, it was not until the mid-nineteenth century that such a definition became a sanctioned code. Before that, beginning with the Puritans and modified by the Enlightenment, success was most often associated with a figure of middling income who worked his own fee-simple farm, the yeoman.[1] This kind of success had three major elements: a competence, independence, and morality. In brief, these elements may be defined as wealth somewhat beyond one's basic needs, freedom from economic or statutory subservience, and the respect of the society for fruitful, honest industry. Such success may be labeled "traditional" not only because of its roots deep into the sixteenth century and earlier, but also because of its use by many nineteenth-century Americans as a focus of defensive attitudes in the face of radical social change. The defense of traditional success and its related yeoman dream comprises the subject of this book, and the range of evidence cited is an attempt to show how widespread was that dream and its defense in our culture during the first half of the nineteenth century.

✾

For northern Europe, the seventeenth century was a period of opportunity for material advancement both at home and abroad, and, as Max Weber has argued, the Puritans incorporated this opportunity in their code of behavior now familiarly known as the Protestant Ethic.

Blamed or praised as a code central to the American mind, this

I

ethic was not new to the Britons who filled the separatist and non-separatist ranks in the seventeenth century. Its ideas already had the form of folk-sayings; its goals were likewise long known. A yeoman's child, if he were prudential, could rise in the world of church or trade, if not of state: Hugh Latimer had done it, as well as Harvey and Newton. But with the decline of feudalism, yeomen, like gentry, found their legal titles to be tenuous. A yeoman could lose his competence, and the land was no longer his forever. Without a title, without the land, without a profitable skill, the failed yeoman became a tenant farmer or even a laborer—legally free and possibly with a good income, but dependent on someone else for his land or wages. Yet rise or fall, yeoman and gentry of the seventeenth century were increasingly on their own, and they were convinced that their own foresight and industry would—always within the bounds of God's will—determine their success.

For the Puritans who came to New England, God's will was far more important than their own; but their anti-Arminianist beliefs did not slip into resigned fatalism. God had elected them to be His stewards and to exercise their wills and effort in the multiplication of His glory on earth. The doctrine of Plenitude has been discussed by E. M. W. Tillyard, the relationship between the Protestant Ethic and a developing capitalist economy has been dealt with by Max Weber and R. H. Tawney. Perry Miller has delineated the precarious balance in Puritan thought between man's will and God's.[2] All of these landmark studies emphasize the link between fruitful endeavor and religious faith, and this idea of Fruitfulness-as-Worship is critical for understanding the concept of a "competence." Since, for the Puritan, the material things of this world were but symbols of the spiritual things of God's larger world, the faithful steward would multiply these material things but always remember that the purpose of such fruitfulness was to reflect the glory of their real owner, God. An individual's public behavior, too, was a symbol of his spiritual state; any yeoman or gentleman who violated the code of fruitfulness raised serious questions about his fitness to be numbered among the saints. The result was that the fruitful *use* of wealth—great or small—was far more important in judging a person than was the mere possession of great wealth. Thus, despite the belief in predestination, the Puritan was duty-bound to prove his election to himself and his peers by leading a life of active worship—a life of endeavor fruitful for himself, his community, and most importantly, for God.

It can be seen that the second element of traditional success, independence, also had religious significance for the Puritans. Not only did their theology require freedom from existing forms of ecclesiastical ritual which interfered in the relationship between the individual and his God, but also the man who was not free to be fruitful was not free to worship through action. Man had to have the freedom to determine by his public success whether or not he was among the saints. Thus, "independence," while often based on money, was not to be thought of as a synonym for "competence"; and though freedom of the will might be a heresy, the freedom to be fruitful was a command.

But tension inevitably arose between private desires and public or even religious responsibility. One of the most critical tasks in the Puritan system of thought was to establish a balance between increasingly competitive laissez-faire economics and the idea of Christian brotherhood. In the words of Jeanette Tawney, the Puritans tried to construct a "Christian casuistry of economic conduct,"[3] and, with several variations, this attempt continued well into the nineteenth century as a defense for traditional success. Repeatedly, the Puritans stressed the difference between harmonious and competitive endeavor, the first being a natural corollary to the doctrine of fruitfulness, the second being a perversion of the steward's trust and a reversion to unfruitful chaos. "That common saying," William Perkins warned darkly, "Every man for himselfe, and God for us all; is Wicked."[4] And, for the loss of their paradise, Milton's Adam and Eve "in mutual accusations spent/The fruitless hours . . ." (9: 1187–88). Yet despite any tendency of the stewards to competitive strife, the worker in the vineyard was not to slacken; after all, God's kingdom was vast—and grossly underpopulated by the Saints.

The often strained attempt to unite incipient individualism and social harmony implies the kind of society the Puritans sought: one which was to be stable yet open to change for the individual. The dream of stability was, in fact, one dominant idea behind Winthrop's image of the City on a Hill; however, this stable society was not to be a fixed one. Because the individual was to have the freedom to exercise his faith and to worship by being fruitful, faithful stewards were to have opportunity to move up within the established social framework if God so willed. As long as the mobile person conformed to the behavior sanctioned at his new level, the social framework was not threatened, and harmony and individualism were compatible. A good deal of this feeling, of course, accounts for the Puritans' anti-communism.

Certainly, the desire of well-to-do Puritans to keep their wealth in the face of Leveller and Digger demands to redistribute that wealth was important; but the same anti-commune feeling was strong among many of those less readily placed among the "haves." Commonly owned wealth was a violation of God's ordinances, for by insuring material plenty to all regardless of effort (which man could see) or of spiritual worth (which God alone could see), it generated idleness, which was counter to the command to be fruitful. As William Bradford notes with some satisfaction about the early (and impoverished) Plymouth Colony:

> The taking away of propertie, and bringing in communitie into a comone wealth . . . was found to breed much confusion and discontent, and retard much imployment that would have been to their benefite and comforte. . . . Let none objecte this is men's corruption, and nothing to the course itselfe. I answere . . . God in his wisdome saw another course fiter for them. . . .[5]

That other course was the incessant and individual acquisition of material goods for the glory of God—a belief only tolerated in the Middle Ages, but which for the Puritans who came to the New World was divinely ordained.

In sum, the principal characteristics of—and the rationalization for—the Puritan's conception of a successful life was something like this: man, like everything else in the universe, belongs to God; God has given him duties and just enough free will to make him individually responsible to honor those duties; the first duty is to be faithful, and a major element of that faith is fruitfulness in a calling; there are virtues which will enable the elect to obey: industry, thrift, perseverance, charity, piety, patience, sobriety, honesty, marriage; man probably, though not necessarily, will receive earthly reward for his obedience, which reward will be in the form of wealth enough for self-sufficiency; this wealth is not to be loved for its own sake, but is to be used to further the Kingdom of God on earth; personal independence is necessary if one is to demonstrate grace by the exercise of his virtues; the social matrix which will best enable the individual to display his virtue should be stable—though not static—in which the home and property are secure, but individual mobility is still possible.

This configuration did not exist in a vacuum, nor was it engraved changeless on the White Stone. While the Puritan's concept

of success was lit by his ascending political star, the Royalist was faced
with darkness and ruin. After Cromwell's victory, the successful life
for the ex-courtier involved retirement into the primitive innocence
of pastoralism, and even with the Restoration, the pastoralism was not
surrendered. Rather it influenced the concept of success by becoming
the mark of a gentleman—one who was not involved in trade or ceaseless industry.[6] This "Gentleman Gardener" is not to be confused with
the English yeoman who also received homage in the neo-classic mind;
the latter was recognized in eighteenth-century England as a member
of a dying class which, furthermore, had tended to side with the rebel
Puritans. However, on a theoretical rather than political level, the
most salient difference is seen in the ideas of gentlemanly retirement
versus yeomanly industry. The former had the support of the gentry's
nostalgia and physiocratic beliefs, while the latter, especially in America, was supported by Puritan attitudes and economic necessity.

❁

The eighteenth-century world was seen as self-regulating, good,
and (as far as it affected man) complete; thus, there was no need for a
person to act the Puritan by assisting in the fulfillment of God's creation. For many Britons, their end and aim was no longer fruitfulness
for God but happiness for man; and in large part, this happiness consisted of obtaining enough wealth for secure comfort, and then retiring
from the realm of restless ambition:

> Know, all the good that individuals find,
> Or God and nature meant to mere mankind,
> Reason's whole pleasure, all the joys of sense,
> Lie in three words—health, peace and competence.[7]

This retirement often consisted of moving to a rural seat far
from the corruptions and turmoil of daily urban life. And though
perhaps industrious in his agrarian pursuits, the English country gentleman found the real value of his bucolic life to be its morally elevating
contact with Nature and with reflection. The relationship between the
country gentleman and the English yeoman is obvious, for the latter
was also termed successful on the basis of his competence and virtu-
ously independent pastoral existence. However, like the Noble Red
Man or Virgil's husbandman, the English yeoman seemed to be a rem-
nant of an earlier, better period. As Goldsmith laments in his *Deserted*

Village, urbanization and trade were seen as dooming this agrarian paragon, while the gentleman—with a far larger competence—could profit from the enclosure movement.

America, however, was different. There, the gentleman-farmer and the yeoman tended to merge. Whereas Goldsmith saw America as a "horrid shore" to which the outcast English yeoman was driven, many colonials were determined that their land would be a refuge for the yeoman dream; there would be no "landed aristocracy," no physiocratic estates which, though economical, were un-democratic. They tended to agree with Jefferson that workshops and their dependent ranks of laborers should remain in Europe, and that the small farmer, the American yeoman, was the basis of an ideal society. In the New World, every man could earn his own competence and independence, and the industrious agrarian life would insure his virtuous behavior. In describing the middle stage of civilization in America, later to be the Jeffersonian ideal, Crevecoeur wrote:

> Thus are our first steps trod, thus are our first trees felled, in general, by the most vicious of our people; and thus the path is opened for the arrival of a second and better class, the true American freeholders; the most respectable set of people in this part of the world: respectable for their industry, their happy independence, the great share of freedom they possess, the good regulation of their families and for extending the trade and the dominion of our mother country.
>
> Europe contains hardly any other distinctions but lords and tenants; this fair country alone is settled by freeholders, the possessors of the soil they cultivate, members of the government they obey, and the framers of their own laws, by means of their representatives.[8]

Modified by Puritan predispositions and the demands of an emergent nation, the idea of gentlemanly retirement came in America to mean a change in activity rather than a cessation of it. Cotton Mather stated it in familiar terms for early eighteenth-century America:

> There are *Gentlemen*, 'tis true, who live upon their Means; and some in their *Age* retire to eat the pleasant Fruit of the Labour, which they Underwent in their *Youth*. But yet it well becomes the

best *Gentlemen,* to study some way of being *Serviceable* in the world, and employ themselves in some good *Business.*[9]

That *"Business"* was the doing of good to others, and for Americans who attained their competence, fruitfulness was not retirement but a second career, as benefactor to fellow man. As Mather's quotation implies, the American Gentleman (including ex-yeomen who earned their competence as well as gentlemen who inherited it) had the opportunity for natural nobility, if not for titled rank. The claim to that nobility was found in the moral quality of one's public service; the most important service, Mather goes on to urge, was the gentleman's aid to the clergy.

By the end of the eighteenth century in America, there was little distinction between yeoman and gentleman since the virtues of the American country gentleman were identical with those of the American yeoman. The latter might have a smaller competence and little learning, but unlike his English counterpart, the American gentleman was not averse to yeomanly labor. Indeed the yeoman virtue of ceaseless industry offered a convenient foil to reveal the prodigality of the English gentleman as opposed to the American one. The confrontation between Mr. Dimple and Colonel Manly in Royall Tyler's *The Contrast* is only one dramatization of this popular belief. And it is only to be expected that the Revolutionary officers' society, made up of gentlemen by act of congress or the vote of their troops, should choose as their model, Cincinnatus—a military hero noted for his integrity, his frugality, and for plowing his own land.

In addition to the popularization of the yeoman figure in eighteenth-century America, the period saw other important changes in the related concept of success. The conflict between the Christian casuistry of economics and individual self-interest was not lessened, but it did become far more secularized. Self-interest came to be considered a universal law of human behavior which was not necessarily bad provided it was "enlightened":

> Thus God and nature linked the general frame,
> And bade self-love and social be the same.[10]

The problem arose in insuring that individuals would act in accordance with this enlightened self-interest, and many Americans were concerned with this problem in religious or especially political terms. Perhaps the most notable, as far as the concept of traditional success, was a man whose very name reflects his yeoman heritage and whose character was continually evoked in later defense of yeomanry: Benjamin Franklin. Strongly influenced by Puritan morality, he was nevertheless opposed to the otherworldly elements of traditional religions and, like other deists of varying shades, conceived of God in terms of man's common sense. The complex logic surrounding the argument that one's predestined faith was proven by good works which only the elect could do anyway, was readily replaced by the simpler logic of reasonable Divine Judgement for earthly actions; Franklin and his contemporaries were proud to be numbered among the "civil honest men" previously damned by Michael Wigglesworth.

In Franklin's eyes, a competence not only had value for social status, but it enabled one to do good deeds and thus work his way to heaven, "The most acceptable service of God [is] the doing of good to man; . . . our souls are immortal; . . . all crime will be punished, and virtue rewarded either here or hereafter."[11] His Arminianism put the source of grace neither wholly nor partially on God, but entirely on man. And one needed to be "free" in order to accept this responsibility; independence was thus also viewed from a more earthly perspective. Indeed, Lockeian epistemology made independence a psychological fact; the tabula rasa was atomistic, every person was a distinct sensate individual. This secularization and atomism had ramifications in the political realm where the superiority of groups or persons was seen as the result of superior environment and training instead of divine ordination or the inheritance of royal blood. Overlapping into the economic sphere, the ramifications emphasized the individualism already in Puritan thought; and man's freedom to pursue his own welfare became the standard by which the state was judged. In other words, for Franklin and many of his fellow Americans, independence became linked with individualism and shared both its materialistic justification as well as its increasingly intensified value. This, of course, put greater stress on the opposing vectors of enlightened self-interest versus selfish individualism. That stress is readily seen in Franklin's attitude toward the poor.

He believed that man's natural inclination to self-interest could be turned into profit for both the commonwealth and the individual by giving the poor neither prayers nor a dole, but the opportunity to work for wealth:

> I am for doing good to the poor, but I differ in opinion about the means. I think the best way of doing good to the poor is, not

making them easy *in* poverty, but leading or driving them *out* of it. In my youth . . . I observed that the more public provisions were made for the poor, the less they provided for themselves, and of course became poorer. And on the contrary, the less was done for them, the more they did for themselves, and became richer.[12]

The evil which Franklin found in idleness came from its waste of material goods designed for man's improvement. Benevolence for Franklin was no longer a duty to awaken souls to God nor the self-gratification of a refined sensibility through giving alms. Rather, the poor were to be given the opportunity for rewarding work which would redeem them morally and materially by the independent pursuit of self-interest. Assuming that Franklin needs to be defended in our own more enlightened time, let me emphasize that he saw material wealth, especially in America, to be as boundless as the Puritans viewed God's grace. His attitude toward the poor laws, as seen later in his letter to Alexander Small, reveals that he considered such opportunity for wealth to have been universal, albeit limited in the Old World by what came to be called Malthusian Law. Given the assumption that America had more than enough wealth for every man to have a competence, then the cause of poverty in the New World must lay with the individual, or with both. What was needed was a social environment conducive to virtuous industry. Such an exercise would result in every man having a competence and independence, and—Franklin's primary aim—a virtuous character whose self-interest was enlightened.

Like the godliness of the preceding century, virtue led to and was supported by competence and independence. The virtuous man was to act in accordance with the laws governing societies and universes. Since those laws were discoverable by anyone with common sense, the acts would meet the approbation of all reasonable men. As he lists it in his *Autobiography*, Franklin's method of achieving virtue reads like an extract from William Perkins (which it might have been): the exercise of temperance, silence, order, resolution, frugality, industry, sincerity, justice, moderation, cleanliness, tranquillity, chastity, and humility would result in the attainment of a virtuous character. Indeed, one would have little time to be other than virtuous. The point, however, is that the ontology of this code is far more secular than Perkins', its basis being the materialist Lockeian epistemology: the exercise of these virtues would strengthen them in the mind in the same way that a muscle could be strengthened in the body. The goal of the exercise, however, is not merely wealth; the eighteenth-century Franklin, unlike the later nineteenth- and twentieth-century views of him, was more concerned with a virtuous than with a wealthy society. The same method of instilling virtue is found in his very popular *Way to Wealth*, where the goal is ostensibly more material. As a youthful "Busybody" (1728–29), Franklin had preached conventionally, "Who would not rather choose, if it were in his choice, to merit [Cato's] character than be the richest, the most learned, or the most powerful man in the province without it?" He soon learned that many people would not—that such an appeal was to the already enlightened man, and that unenlightened souls usually preferred coin to character. In the *Way to Wealth*, Franklin fashioned an appeal to the unenlightened which led them unknowingly and relatively painlessly to virtue via the lesser pursuit of wealth. The pundit, given the Calvinistic name "Father Abraham," cites the following rules for earning wealth: industry, frugality, personal attention to the details of business, avoidance of debt, unlimited trust in God, and limited trust in others. Receiving special emphasis are industry, frugality, diligence, and piety. Obviously, the basic appeal of the article is to material self-interest; and the individual's well-being is the reward for following this behavior. Nevertheless, the preaching of these virtues had a moral level. The *Way to Wealth*, like much of Franklin's writing, demonstrates his use of the persona to assume a voice that speaks the audience's vocabulary and logic. Although Franklin's means were material, his purpose was to lead his readers to enlightened self-interest, and the promised material success is in reality only the first step in the attainment of a greater goal. Published with the almanac of 1757, the proverbs were, as Franklin later wrote, intended to inculcate "industry, and frugality, as the means of procuring wealth, and thereby securing virtue. . . ."[13] The sack was to stand upright, supported by a competence as one basis for moral rectitude; but, in addition, the exercise of the virtues would strengthen them in the mind so that the industrious person would also gain an enlightened character. Thus, the individual's outer and inner profits would contribute to the general social good.

To see this more clearly, one must remember the Lockeian epistemology universally accepted during the period: the continual practise of virtues would physically impress them so deeply on the mind of the practitioner that they would become habitual. Character would be reformed. The promised reward of wealth thus lured the reader to the exercise of this behavior, and the exercise was in itself morally elevating. It helped to insure that when a man did earn his earthly reward, his virtuous character would lead him to do good rather than evil with his competence. Where the Puritan saw the proper pursuit as a sign of granted grace, Franklin saw it as a method of attaining moral salvation both here and hereafter. "Employ thy time well, if thou meanest to gain leisure," Father Abraham tells yeoman and gentleman alike, and then goes on to define leisure, with an echo from Cotton Mather, as "time for something useful; this leisure the diligent man will obtain but the lazy man never."[14]

Corollary to Franklin's belief about the purpose of wealth and its proper pursuit was his theory that the direct source of wealth was not God but nature and society:

> All property that is necessary to a man, for the conservation of the individual and the propagation of the species is his natural right, which none can justly deprive him of; but all property superfluous to such purpose is the property of the public, who, by their laws, have created it, and who may therefore by others dispose of it. . . .[15]

In other words, a man has a natural right to a competence, but surplus riches are the creation of society and ultimately the property thereof. The real value of the surplus for Franklin lay in its promise of a man's ability to do greater good for humanity. How, Franklin must have thought, could he be wrong when newly discovered physiocratic economics so paralleled his religious and ethical beliefs? This economic theory taught that agriculture—God's gift of something for nothing—was the basis of all wealth. Therefore, the agriculturist was not only closest to God, but gain was inevitable wherever farm goods could be freely transmuted into other forms of property. Where society had the proper balance of productive farms and urban trading centers connected by good transportation, a competence would be available to every individual, and surplus property for the benefit of society in general would be plentiful. For Franklin, as for Crevecoeur, Jefferson, and countless other eighteenth-century thinkers, the closest approximation of this balance was an America dominated by yeoman farmers. Thus Franklin's vision of the virtuous social system found religious, ethical, economic, and even patriotic support.

In order for the model to work, society had to combine maximum individual freedom with a stable social framework; the creation of wealth by industrious and virtuous individuals would be urged, and that wealth, once existent, would be protected by and for society. This entailed freedom for each man to rise or fall to the place in life which suited his character. Franklin pragmatically recognized that numbers of men would lack ability and virtue and therefore fail, that many would have some ability and virtue and therefore attain a competence, and a few would have the superior ability and virtue to become a wealthy natural aristocracy. From this point of view, the ideal society was a Jeffersonian one of financially independent farmers and mechanics from whom the natural aristocracy would be drawn for each generation. And that ever-changing aristocracy would be marked not just by wealth, but by intellect and virtue, since, in Franklin's eyes, the proper pursuit of wealth and the attainment of virtue formed a dyad.

Though he did not live through the disillusion of the French Revolution, Franklin was concerned with pressures from the propertyless, but those pressures were conceived of less as a class threat than as disruptions caused by unvirtuous individuals. His solutions were drawn from his world view: religion served to protect the social structure from those who might otherwise upset the natural equilibrium through their ignorance or immorality; small entrepreneurs would be transformed by the virtuous pursuit into members in good standing of the established society; the poor, in his eyes, shared the same desires as the middle class and needed only to be shown how to achieve their goals. Through practicing what they were shown, the poor would lend their support to society. For Franklin, the safety valve of the American west supported this means of social and individual goodliness; as long as there was land and opportunity for America's surplus population, there was room for all in the yeoman society.

His conceptions of success, therefore, combined Puritan and Enlightenment thought. Optimism and benevolence, tempered by an awareness of man's fallibility, were the moods of Franklin's universe. In his world, God, working through natural laws, had made opportunity abundant; and every person, for the benefit of his soul as well as for his stomach, had to make the best of those opportunities. This required the development of a virtuous character according to guides which echo the Puritan homilies. Like them, Franklin emphasized God's command to do good works in an effort to overcome the tension between selfishness and enlightened self-interest; but unlike them he saw works as the way to heavenly and earthly salvation rather than as proof of election. Whereas the Puritan sought to establish the Kingdom of God on earth by discovering the few immutably predestined saints, Franklin's Poor Richard was obliged to labor with his reason to make himself and society conform to the few immutable natural laws leading to the best possible world. But, though every man was obliged to try, not every man could do it. The purification process was an arduous one, and man stood alone not only before a distant God and His unchanging laws, but also before his fellow men; in many ways, Franklin's Poor Richard was more terribly isolated than Jonathan Edwards's Sinner. Puritan and Enlightenment America saw independence and competence as integral elements of true success. But in the eighteenth century the meaning of independence expanded while a competence changed from the rationed use of God's ever-increasing stores, to become a basis for independence and moral behavior. In the two hundred years between the Elizabethan era and the death of Benjamin Franklin, independence and competence became more secular and more important for traditional success, and Godliness became Goodliness.

There is an elfin queen, named ENDEAVOR, who bestows wonderful things upon her humble followers.

Juvenile Miscellany, 1827

[Our hero] had started out to earn his own living with high hopes of doing fairly at once, and gradually working his way up to a good social and business position. He felt that he might still have done it but for the unaccountable enmity of John Wade. . . .

The Cash Boy, Horatio Alger, 1875

1

SPOKESMEN FOR THE YEOMAN DREAM

✾

AFTER THE war of 1812, the awareness of change was every-where in American life. Westward ran the course of empire with al-most frightening speed, and at the same time the eastern cities swelled with village youths seeking their fortunes in trade or the professions, and with immigrants seeking food and shelter. Change, hailed by opti-mists as Progress, either rattled through the valleys in a shower of or-ange wood sparks and acrid smoke, or came as silent, empty farms abandoned for the kinder soil of the west. The constant change of sea-sons, of shifting clouds and water, of trees in the cycle of life and death made up the landscapes of the Hudson River School; the growth and decay of civilizations formed the panoramic subjects of the popular Thomas Cole. Change was reckoned in numbers, and the new science of statistics developed from a national interest in cataloging growth. Change was also counted in votes, and a new concept of democracy soon strode down to Washington with Andrew Jackson. Old ways of doing things were quickly replaced by new, and the new ways them-selves seemed to last but a day. Technological change meant changing opportunities and taking those opportunities often meant social change. If a man had the will and a few bank-notes for a start, he could make a fortune for himself; it had been done by people no better than that brawling ferry-boat skipper, Van Derbilt, or by the penniless immi-grant, Astor. Yet change was not welcomed by all. Ideas and beliefs which worked in the past tended to remain constant. The definition of success as competence, independence, and virtue was one of these; and

17

the closely related ideal of the yeoman was another. These concepts were held by many Americans in all sections of the country—large and small tradesmen, merchants, farmers, professional men—but of chief historical importance was one group which maintained those concepts. Members of this group shared the same general heritage: Federal, Calvinist, and New England; because of their position in the publishing, financial, intellectual and population centers of the nation, their influence was strong. Their attitudes had a social prestige which, while more highly regarded in Boston or New York than in Springfield, Ohio, or Hannibal, Missouri, was nevertheless felt across the country. Added to the power and the prestige this group felt, was a sense of defensiveness about their values—change, which threatened as well as promised, had to be directed into sanctioned channels. One of the principal means of governing change and its effects was seen to be the education of children by various means. The attitudes and beliefs supported by this influential group are revealed by its spokesmen through one of the principal means of education: juvenile periodicals; thus, these serve as alembics for studying the yeoman dream.

The 1820s saw a burgeoning number of youth's periodicals. Their proliferation was due in part to improvements in the paper and printing industries, but a perhaps greater stimulus was widespread alarm about the growth of liberal political sentiments. Launched with full cargoes of doctrinal matter, most of the newspapers and magazines were conservative in politics and religion. Many were ephemeral, and the only traces remaining are the borrowings made by more seaworthy publications. But the sudden rise in their number indicates that the education of youth became a focus of national attention; moreover, the persistency of the genre—despite the short life of many individual publications—further indicates a continuing felt need for this education. The chore was shared by newspapers, farm magazines, workers' papers, and trade journals; but because of the widespread use of shears and paste, the overall result was a corpus of statements which has surprising consistency and which can be accurately sampled in a few major juvenile periodicals.[1]

The aim was to prepare youth to be successful in life, and both practical information and "moral philosophy" were offered in attempts to define that success and its pursuit. The "practical information" was general despite its appearance of explicitness; that is, "Be Diligent" could apply to a twenty-year-old store clerk or an eight-year-old factory operative. It was intended to, because this practical advice was to suit all occupations, and all occupations were viewed as capable of following it. The moral philosophy was in great part designed to fit in a world that had inherited Puritan and Enlightenment concepts of the successful life, and at times the concepts conflicted, at other times they supported one another. Usually, the moralist chose from either framework to suit the problem at hand; for example, in one paragraph an author could celebrate God as a kindly, rational mechanic, and in the next he would sorrow for the vast numbers of faithless damned. But consistent in all this minor or major vacillation was a view of American success as being made up of the traditional competence, independence and moral behavior. A survey of the *Juvenile Miscellany* will reveal the outline of traditional success at the century's beginning.

One of the first notable periodicals of this sort, the *Miscellany* was edited by Lydia Maria Francis Child. Directly descended from an early immigrant to Cambridge, Massachusetts, she was the youngest child of a strong-willed tradesman and a mother who had "a spirit for doing good." At twenty-two, she published her first novel, *Hobomok* (1824), and from 1825 to 1828, ran a private school. During this time she started the *Juvenile Miscellany*. In 1828, she married David Lee Child, lawyer and journalist, and together they became active in the anti-slavery movement. Among her several publications was the very popular *The Frugal Housewife* (1829), in which she cites "Dr. Franklin" as often as Father Abraham cited Poor Richard; and, in relation to the kind of success that Franklin advocated, it is revealing to note that the Childs retired in 1854 to a small farm in Weyland, Massachusetts, from whence they sallied forth to do good works on a modest competence.

The *Juvenile Miscellany* was a mixture of fiction and fact designed to inculcate good behavior. The facing page of volume 3 (n. s.) for September 1829 carries Wordsworth's lines:

> The child is father of the man;
> And I could wish my days to be
> Bound each to each by natural piety.

How natural Mrs. Child believed the infant's piety to be is a moot point, for she shared the eighteenth-century belief that good habits—more easily learned in childhood—fathered the good man. In the tale of William and John, for example, the former was dark, selfish, doubting, slothful, capricious, willful, anxious, and, of course, unhappy; the latter was open, generous, active, enterprising, firm yet yielding to the wishes and comforts of others, calm, and, of course, contented. The reason for such a difference was that William "had no seminal principles sown in his heart," while John was carefully brought up.[2] Occasionally, an epitome of good behavior is described as having "an instinct, which was a more certain guide in preventing any deviation from the strictest rule of propriety and good breeding, than the wisest maxims of a Chesterfield. . . ." But even such an apparently innate faculty turned out to be the result of a traditionally moral environment, for this particular creature of "instinct," Ruth Clifford, was the "daughter of a thrifty farmer, in one of our New England villages." The yeoman life and principles formed her "certain guide" while her opposite, Louisa Carey ("Louisa" was a dangerously Frenchified name), had been spoiled by parents who countered the salutary effect of bucolic surroundings with sloth and luxury.[3] In short, not only was the contrast between industrious yeoman and slothful gentry—faintly European, at that—still alive for Mrs. Child, but the Lockeian epistemology persisted despite the popularity in the colleges of the newer Scottish Common Sense philosophers. In viewing children as impressionable subjects without any predestined tendency to evil or to good, Mrs. Child and many other editors were empiricists relying on environment, experience, and sensation for the formulation of ideas; they saw the infant's personality molded by home and landscape, by eye-opening visits to the haunts of the sinful, by promises of the sensate pleasures of material reward. Such an environmentalism justified the need for the kind of exempla presented by the editors; and, seemingly, the readers agreed, for the editors' comments indicate a steady growth in circulation in and around Boston.

However, despite the importance given to early training and surroundings, the result was not a form of environmental determinism; the infant was not so easily relieved of self-responsibility. The meaning this epistemology held for traditional success lay not only in its philosophical materialism, but also in its strong emphasis on individual effort and the self-responsibility for the condition of one's own soul and body. Youth was to be drilled in the right habits so it could properly practice what the Mrs. Childs preached, and these habits were plainly spelled out in magazines that only the wilfully evil would ignore. Each child had the freedom to act or not to act, but failure to follow proper advice was depicted as leading to moral and material catastrophe. This individualism was clearly indicated in Mrs. Child's first address to her readers, found on the opening page of Volume One:

> If I am able to convince you that you *can* do, whatever you *try* to do, in the acquisition of learning; if I can lead you to examine your own hearts, and pray to your Heavenly father to remove from thence whatsoever is evil, I shall be very happy. . . . If you will *persevere*; if you will learn to think for yourselves; you can over come all obstacles in the path of knowledge; and if you really *wish* to be good, there is a kind Parent, in the heavens, who will help you in every endeavor you make, to be virtuous and religious.

As with her mentor, Franklin, the goal of this effort is not only wealth but, as we find out in later tales, the moral rectitude necessary for traditional success. Mrs. Child's interminable story "Happiness" portrays successively the rich man whose mercantile wealth is hollow in the "gilded desolation" of his materialism, the poor man who becomes rich and loses his contentment, the avaricious brother caught in the "wretched service of that master passion, Ambition," and a pair of sisters who fashionably flirt their real happiness away. Only brother Henry is happy; his maxim is "the resources stored in our own minds and hearts [are] the only treasures than [can] not be taken away from us." Henry uses the independence his inherited wealth brought to emulate Franklin and retire from work to pursue scientific knowledge for the benefit of mankind. This exemplifies the author's moral, "external gifts of any kind cannot create happiness, though when rightly used, they may greatly increase it."[4] Echoing Franklin, Mrs. Child urges that God is happy when His children are happy; and, like Franklin, she also found happinesss dependent upon virtue, and virtue dependent upon the proper pursuit of independence and competence, and the morality of doing good to fellow man. As in the eighteenth century, the resolution of the conflict between individualism and public harmony was wrought by enlightened self-interest.

Other tales emphasize the competence as a basic part of success. Franklin, praised as being among the most "useful to mankind," was presented for the children's emulation because of his ability to gather a competence through the virtues of industry, economy, perseverance, and "shrewdness and talent for business"; a "spirit of enterprise," readers are told, "was the first trait of his character."[5] However, to combat any tendency toward mere materialism, Mrs. Child continually mixed the idea of enterprise with large doses of Protestant Christianity; Franklin, the readers were wrongly told, greatly lamented his non-Christian youth.

Ruth Clifford's bucolic upbringing and Franklin's shrewd talent for business indicate the poles of occupational interest in the *Juvenile Miscellany*, as well as the elasticity of the yeoman image. The farmer is praised for leading the life most favorable to moral excellence, but the pastoralism is literary; the authors rarely depict a working farm. This country life while not opulent is seldom difficult, the weather is always sunny, the people are uncorrupted by fashion or ambition, and, though not rich, the farmer is always independent financially and politically. If there are problems in this Arcadia, the reader is not told of them. On the other hand, stories about the city often contain descriptive details which reveal the author's familiarity with that environment; actual streets are pictured, shops and buildings are tangible, and contemporary problems of town life do appear in the tales. Despite the hypothesis that there were no problems on the farm at this time, I suspect that urban life received notice because the writers and readers were more familiar with the town and its tribulations than with the farm. Slums, beggars, immigrants, and working mothers are some of the problems dealt with in the stories; and it is in these descriptions that the fiction offers its only realistic detail. Mechanical occupations are seldom described in the pages of the *Miscellany*, and when they are, their portrayal, like the pictures of farm life and for the same reason, lacks the weight of realism. But these urban occupations are not excluded from the yeoman dream. For example, Walter Armstrong, the son of a shoemaker, proved himself by industry and perseverance able to take over his father's position as a master craftsman and thus morally gain his independence and competence. However, this mechanical occupation, while praised for its material and moral achievement, was not viewed without some condescension; Mrs. Child admonishes, "Children, Walter Armstrong is worthy of your remembrance and imitation. He filled a humble station in life, but he filled that station well. . . ."[6] This story appeared during the year of Jackson's inauguration when few mechanics—particularly master cordwainers—considered their position to be a "humble" one. Consciously or not, the writers gave more prestige to business or the professions than to the so-called "true producers" of wealth. Such a hierarchy reflects both the place of publication and the commercial and professional values which the writers considered to be most important. And it further indicates that the writers believed that those values and the related formula for true success were the same for all "stations."

Mrs. Child's assumptions about the income of her readers are revealed in stories of poverty and charity. "The Little Beggars" describes a meeting between a poor boy and a protagonist who is not poor, and the author comments on economic distinctions and the benefits suitable to each class. "Poor children are just as happy as rich ones, except when they are suffering from cold, or hunger; and that seldom happens in America." They are happy because they are moral, "God has ordained that every body shall be happy, who is good; and he helps every one to be good who earnestly wishes to be so."[7] Obviously, the narrator is explaining the joys of poverty to those who are not familiar with them. At the same time that the poor are introduced to the reader, the theme of the unvirtuous rich who lack charity is often repeated. Many stories emphasize that generosity benefits the giver's soul as well as creating in him a pleasant feeling. Other tales make charity attractive as protagonist after protagonist learns that the virtuous humble are really better people than the proud rich, and that the rich can morally justify their wealth by giving away a bit of it.

Yet the major categorizing of humanity in the magazine was not along economic lines but into the virtuous and the unvirtuous. There was as yet no rejection of Franklin's belief that the moral pursuit of wealth resulted in a moral rich man; nor did Mrs. Child or other juvenile writers hesitate to depict an unvirtuous rich man to emphasize that true success was more than mere money. There were simply two images of wealth: the familiar ones of stewardship and enlightened self-interest, and of greed and selfishness. A character representing the evil rich is John Bates, who, though not yet wealthy, is on his way. He remarks wonderingly of the hero, "Walter is an odd boy.... He always thinks more of other people's comforts than his own; for my part, I shall look out for the first person singular."[8] John Bates' selfishness will make him unvirtuous and thus morally a failure despite his wealth. Most often, however, the unvirtuous rich in the stories did not work for their money but idly inherited it. Never having had to exercise moral virtues, these individuals lacked a strong character and their faults contributed to the portrayal of false success. Female inheritors were often exemplary representatives of this false success, especially if they inhabited the same world as the "fine" gentry—a world of

fashions and manners, of idleness, waste, and sentimental novels. A
poem by "A. M. W." describes the difference:

> Matilda decked in trinkets, silks, and laces,
> And early taught the fashionable graces;
> Yet wanted those which leave all such behind—
> The better graces of the heart and mind.
> Whils't Susan from her childhood taught to know
> The diff-rence 'twixt the substance and the show,
> And always forced to labor for her bread,
> Though *poor* in purse, was *rich* in heart and head.[9]

Like the rich, the poor were also depicted as either virtuous or unvirtuous. The former were those poor who saw themselves as the editors
saw them: godly, contented, and adhering to the traditional ethic despite its lack of material reward; though unsuccessful materially, they
were no threats to the stable society. "The Way to be Contented," we
are told, is to be occupied. Like Susan, the poor girls who must work
are thus more contented than the idle rich.[10] For an explanation of
why the poor could practise virtue and industry and yet remain unrewarded, the Puritan tradition was called on:

> But faith shall look beyond the rod,
> And trace the hidden hand of God.[11]

Poverty that was the result of unvirtuous behavior was punishment
justified; Hannah F. Gould was typical in arguing that debt was a personal weakness "like any other wrong indulgence."[12] Young readers,
then, were given two views of the poor: the sentimental one that poverty was no bar to moral worth, and the harsher one that poverty was
the result of moral failure. However, as later chapters reveal, by mid-
century, the balance between the two views became precarious enough
to weaken the appeal of traditional success as the yeoman dream frag-
mented under the impact of the industrial revolution.

Preaching contentment to the unfortunate was one attempt to
preserve social harmony, and the moral pursuit of a competence was
another means to this goal. Readers were indoctrinated with the belief
that the world was a good place as it was, and man must not upset it
by striving to be unjustly rich or by being discontented with mere
poverty. Institutions which helped to maintain the established social
order received the editors'—and hopefully the children's—support: in-

fant schools were good places that took poor children from ages two
to five and taught them "a regard for the property of others";[13] Sabbath schools were eulogized for instructing older youth in Bible reading and piety; criminals, the magazine was pleased to announce, were
incarcerated in prisons as a deterrent to further crime through fear of
punishment. The regard for property rights and creditor interests was
reinforced by constant reiteration of the virtues of industry and prudence, and by dangling the material and moral goals to which those
virtues would lead youth. As in Franklin's world, as with the Puritans,
the good society of the *Miscellany* was to be a stable matrix within
which the individual could earn his moral reward. If the world was
not perfect, it was because individual man was morally imperfect, not
the American social order that had been created under the direction
of a benevolent God. The way to achieve a perfect world was for everyone to seek traditional success and thus become morally reformed.
Those who were the most successful were not those with mere money,
but those who exemplified the values of the sanctioning group. And
movement into that group was welcomed. Not an exclusive body of
saints that had pulled away from the corruptions of England, nor an
aristocracy based upon hereditary wealth, the people who believed
in traditional success were making great efforts to be inclusive regardless of income, to insure that all the individuals in the society
shared the same morality. Despite their being inclusive, however, the
idea of success did not lead to a classless state. The view of the mechanic as "humble" indicates a continuing economic distinction within
the homogenous moral society. And though the most important division between men was the result of behavior, a moral man who was
wealthy was more esteemed than a moral man who was poor. Fortunately, it was believed, most men would attain the middle income of
a competence, and thus the great majority of virtuous Americans could
truly be called successful.

Society as viewed by the *Miscellany* was divided horizontally
by economic criteria into the poor, middling, and rich; and vertically
by moral criteria which distinguished between the virtuous and the
unvirtuous members of those three economic levels. Faith in the structure of society, plus a population of predominantly middle incomes,
would result in continuing universal progress toward harmony and
stability—conditions favored by the established members and favorable to business. Indeed, it is meaningful that when Mrs. Child began
to advocate the radical abolitionism which threatened social stability

and for which her society had not been adequately prepared, the subscriptions to her magazine were withdrawn and it died.

✿

Although the *Juvenile Miscellany* folded in 1834, the idea of traditional success remained quite healthy, and one of the century's most popular children's writers devoted volumes to its explication. Samuel Griswold Goodrich, known to numberless young readers as either Mr. Merry or Peter Parley, was born in Ridgefield, Connecticut, in 1793. His father, a Congregational minister, was not a yeoman farmer but did live in a community of small farms; his autobiography, *Recollections of a Lifetime* (1857), depicts a youth spent in rural surroundings peopled by both good and bad characters, though in moral New England, the former greatly out-numbered the latter. After a boyhood in this pastoral idyll, he entered business, but the enterprise failed through circumstances not attributed to him. Because of the War of 1812, materials were scarce and the necessity to smuggle raw supplies in from Canada made costs prohibitive. In addition, Goodrich reveals a lingering suspicion about the crassness of mercantile wealth, when he writes, "My connections were respectable: some of them eminent, but none of them rich; all had acquired their position without wealth, and I think it was rather their habit to speak of it as a very secondary affair. Brought up under this influence, how could I give my heart to trade?"[14] The eminence he sought lay in the field of letters, and, in 1816, he formed a partnership with George Sheldon to open a trade in books. Besides such lucrative favorites as Scott and Byron, they patriotically published the poems of the New England poets John Trumbull, James Percival, and John Brainard, usually, and perhaps deservedly, at a substantial loss. In 1823, Goodrich went to England and his literary Anglomania was greatly reinforced. There he dined with Scott, Blackwood, and Lockhart, and discussed Brackenridge, Brockden Brown, and Cooper; he was at last among the eminents. However, it was his visit with Hannah More which confirmed his inchoate desire to "reform" children's literature, and his praise of that worthy is revealing, "She was one of the chief instruments by which the torrent of vice and licentiousness, emanating from the French Revolution and inundating the British Islands, was checked and driven back: she was even, to a great extent, the permanent reformer of British morals and manners, as well among the high as the humble."[15]

With this model in mind, he sought to place the high and the humble of America in the category of the reformed. He edited and contributed to 28 volumes of children's periodicals; wrote, with Hawthorne and others, 31 school texts; sent 116 books into the world under the banner of Peter Parley. In all, he claims seven million authentic Peter Parley volumes sold, and many more sold by less worthy imitators. His most notable adult publication was a gift-book, *The Token* (1827–42), which presented such authors as Mrs. Child, Nathaniel P. Willis, Nathaniel Hawthorne, Mrs. Sigourney, Mrs. Sedgwick, Longfellow, and Holmes. This endeavor, he claims, ushered in the "age of annuals."

Writers and writing were not his only interest, for he was twice elected Whig senator to the Massachusetts legislature where he voted for the prohibitionary Fifteen Gallon Law. Although the rough and tumble campaigning of the period left him with a permanent distaste for politicking, he praises Harrison's log cabin methods, calling Van Buren's defeat "a most emphatic rebuke by the people." At the same time, he had an admiration for that western planter, Andrew Jackson. He further served the public as consul to Paris from 1851 to 1854, probably a political plum for supporting the Whig ticket. His private life was not without its misfortunes: his wife died early in life, he suffered from poor eyesight, a permanently crippling fall from a horse, and "nervous attacks" which he blamed on his sedentary occupation. Yet it is plain by the somewhat defensive tone of his autobiography that he considered himself to have been successful though not rich. On his own, he earned a competence, independence, and, if not outright godliness, at least a reputation for moral preachments and a kind of position among respected literary figures.

The Tales of Peter Parley About America came out in 1827; the first of the long sequence, it was very popular by the following year. *Parley's Magazine*, begun in 1833, was directed for a year by Goodrich himself until his eyes began to fail; occasional Goodrich items appear in later volumes. In 1841, he began a new magazine, *Robert Merry's Museum*, which absorbed *Parley's* by 1844. Eight years later, *Merry's Museum* claimed a circulation of thirteen thousand, a substantial figure for magazines of the period. Until 1850, when the *Youth's Companion* temporarily bought the title, he was the exclusive editor, then a frequent contributor through 1854; he died in 1860. The second editor, Reverend S. T. Allen, sold out to John N. Stearns, an avid temperance man; and eleven years later, in 1866,

Horace B. Fuller took over as publisher, signing Louisa May Alcott as editor. Her four-year term added little to a magazine already in swift decline, and in the early 1870s, the magazine collapsed.

Goodrich shared Mrs. Child's eighteenth-century empiricism and materialism; in reference to Wordsworth's statement that the child is the father of the man, he noted, "If it is meant that men fulfill the promises of childhood, it is not true. . . . If it is meant that the influences operating upon children ordinarily determine their future fate, it is doubtless correct."[16] At first, Goodrich simply imagined himself "on the floor with a group of boys and girls, and I wrote to them as I would have spoken to them." But gradually, from his reading of Locke and Watts, James G. Carter and Horace Mann, he developed a "natural" approach to learning: a child's "first ideas are simple and single, and formed of images of things palpable to the senses; and hence these images are to form the staple of lessons to be communicated to them."[17] He thus fed the children "facts, with truth, and with objective truth," and the result was an emphasis on history, biography, and geography, liberally illustrated with woodcuts to stimulate the visual senses. He has been condemned then and now for his materialistic crusade against romanticism and his consequent failure to delight the imagination of his readers. The materialism was not his alone, although he was particularly opposed to the nursery rhymes which, in his case, had tended to over-stimulate the imagination. One of his aims was to "purify and exhalt the imagination,"[18] and presumably this occurred when adventure was projected into the realm of the possible rather than into the world of unnatural fairy tales, and when the adventure had a clear moral lesson. Goodrich suffered no remorse for his campaign for fact rather than fancy; his was a crusade which matched Hannah More's and other Victorians' mingling of materialism and reform. Entertainment was acceptable, provided it did not violate propriety. The tales based upon Goodrich's own boyhood often transcend their didactic purpose in his enjoyment at spinning a yarn. Unlike Mrs. Child's, Goodrich's characters learned by action rather than by precept, and the result was greater narrative strength as well as a more accurate and detailed picture of early nineteenth-century life. He recognized the appeal of good stories for his readers: he admired Hans Christian Anderson enough to pirate several of his tales; Melville's *Typee*, liberally quoted, is recommended to children as "A very amusing book." A passage from *Jane Eyre* was also included, despite the novel's "Mr. Brockhurst" being a caricature of the Reverend Carus

Wilson, editor of a number of English Sunday School periodicals;[19] and even the growing penny-press phenomenon of Newgate literature was echoed in "Two Famous Rogues," a bowdlerized biography of Jonathan Wild and Jack Sheppard.

Goodrich also shared Mrs. Child's bias toward urban middle class interests and toward mercantile and professional occupations despite his conventional scorn for lowly trade. One of the more entertaining tales, an epistolary serial entitled "Billy Bump," presents the impressions of a western country bumpkin in worldly Boston. Its humor is based upon Billy's naivete, a method requiring the reader to be more sophisticated about a given subject than is the protagonist. That subject is town life:

> The most wonderful thing about uncle Ben's house is the stairs, which are a kind of ladder, to go up from one loft to another. These turn round and round . . .—and why they don't tumble down I can't say.
>
> I ketched a cold coming here, and it settled in my head; so I couldn't help hawking and spitting a good deal. Well, the floors are all covered with fine carpets, and when I spit on them aunt Lizzy rolled up her eyes; uncle Ben looked at me as if I'd been a rattlesnake, and cousin Lucy snickered right out. What it was all for, I couldn't tell. I saw that there was something in the wind. I felt a kind of perspiration all over; and to ease my awkwardness, I blowed my nose with my fingers. I expect I must have done it with considerable force, for every living soul rushed out of the room!

Unlike Huck Finn, Billy views civilization and its unnatural rituals not with alarm but with longing. "I . . . shall be very much obliged if you will tell me what is wrong and what is right," he asks of his Boston aunt. With Christian forbearance she emulates the Home Missionary movement; subsequent letters show increased gentility in grammar and deportment, and decreased liveliness and dialect.[20] The story clearly illustrates the self-perceived role of urban New England in schooling the uncivilized West, in bringing the moral element of true success to the rough frontiersman who cannot yet lay claim to the yeoman dream. Other tales treat the city as an object of interest and future importance for the readers; many stories, for example, illustrate that trade for profit is the basis of civilization. Robert Merry himself, the son of a small merchant, squanders his patrimony and goes to New York, where, because he "had not yet learned the importance of a precise and accurate fulfillment of a duty, and performance of promises," he has a long string of misadventures, each one serial length. These entertaining and useful examples illustrate the problems the unvirtuous lad is subject to: poverty, jail, homelessness.[21] Yarns like this teach virtues that will help the young man succeed in business and avoid the pitfalls of town life. As Billy Bump's mother had written, "[Boston] is full of great good and great evil. You will there find wealth, splendor, elegance, luxury, knowledge, refinement. These are by no means to be despised; on the contrary, it is lawful and it is laudable to strive to possess them. . . . But possession of them is dangerous."[22] Go east, young man, but go armed in virtue against the moral threats of urban riches and luxury.

At the same time that city life is viewed within the framework of traditional success, familiar praise for farmers helps fill the magazine's pages. The simple rural life of Goodrich's childhood was equated in his *Recollections* with youthful innocence, and this romantic view became a minor theme of his magazine. Often, with patriotic notes, America was sung as the last refuge of the yeoman dream; in the same language that Crevecoeur used a hundred years earlier, Goodrich asserts, "In England there is hardly such a class of persons as our independent, prudent, intelligent owners of the soil. . . ."[23] The life of the farm was praised for continuing to offer virtue, health, and contentment. The farmer, in other words, entered the pages of *Merry's Museum* as an unchanged convention, while the city was seen with a mixture of attitudes and an immediacy of detail that reveals it as being drawn from the life of the author. Although various manufacturing processes were described in detail, mechanics, like farmers, received a little conventional praise. It was believed they could readily, if vaguely, attain yeoman status and achieve the independence, competence, and morality that fruitful industry deserved. But a better form of success was for the mechanic to transcend his manual occupation for a business or professional career. Benjamin Franklin was, of course, the stellar example of this urban yeoman; his was the story of how "a poor boy, by diligence, honesty and good behavior, may grow up rich, useful, respected and happy."[24] Over half of his brief biography narrates his services to mankind rather than his mechanic endeavor. Franklin's greatness was that he did not remain a mechanic but left that occupation to enter the ranks of more gentlemanly professions and exercise

his benevolence. A story clearly celebrating this movement from mechanic labor to the professions is "James Wallace." By perseverance,
industry, honesty, and a thirst for knowledge, "The despised apprentice became the able and profound lawyer and was esteemed for real
talent and moral worth. . . ."[25] For Goodrich and many of his contributors, traditional success for the man who toiled with his hands at
his own farm or shop was increasingly a mere convention, while for
non-manual occupations—where men toiled with their brains in their
own firm—success meant both greater wealth and greater respect. Implied in this shift is a usurpation of the yeoman dream by business and
professional men, a usurpation far more evident to and painful for mechanics, as subsequent chapters will show. One typical middle-class
urban heroine was "Cheerful Cherry," whose father moved from the
country to Boston, "where he pursued the business of a merchant";
her home life was that of the average businessman's family, including
a two-week vacation at the seashore. The virtues Cheerful Cherry
reveals are those of traditional success.[26]

As might be expected, however, Goodrich demonstrated again
and again that virtue was no respecter of economic or occupational
classes. Even in an urban, mercantile world, virtue had to include the
way to as well as the use of wealth, and an inheritance was likely to be
a liability:

> for almost all that has been contributed to diffuse strength and
> knowledge and liberty among mankind—we are indebted to those
> who have been born and nursed in poverty.

And certainly, the unvirtuous pursuit of wealth in such an ambiguous
environment as the city would not lead to true success:

> The usual means taken to get riches are supreme selfishness or
> craft, or uncommon want of principle; and riches, when once ob-
> tained, tend to corrupt and degrade the heart, and stultify the
> mind.[27]

Even such an awesome figure as John Jacob Astor could have his
achievement questioned on moral grounds:

> It is highly probable that the great wealth of Mr. Astor of New
> York, which we have spoken of elsewhere, was in part obtained
> in this avaricious manner. It was certainly obtained—at least much
> of it—from buying and selling furs; and I suppose he bought and

sold as other traders are accustomed to do, without considering whether he was doing right or wrong by [the Indians].[28]

However, if Nathaniel Hawthorne can be believed in his description of his employer's penuriousness, Peter Parley railed against what Samuel Goodrich practiced.

A positive symbol of traditional success was again Franklin:

> As a boy of the middle class, successfully but laborously working his way upward . . . [Franklin] made [the *Autobiography*] at once the most attractive and most useful biography of modern times. All over Christendom, it has met with the sympathy of the working classes, as it has shown that the paths of ambition are open to them as to others, provided they be followed with Franklin's virtues—honesty, frugality, perseverance, and patriotism.[29]

"Patriotism" is something new in the myth, reflecting the nationalism of nineteenth-century America; but it meant to Goodrich, as it does to many Americans now, support of one section of society and its beliefs rather than the love of one nation with all its variety. Franklin, here linking the working class, middle class, and upper class, exemplified the moral division of society that contributed to the kind of nation Goodrich wanted America to be. And sanctioned behavior, or morality, was the most important element in judging the quality of one's life, "Success in life depends not on the vocation, but on the manner in which we pursue it."[30] The good man would conserve the virtuous society with his thought, his behavior, and his spirit, "Democracy may rave—radicalism may foam at the mouth, and these may get votes and appropriate the spoils, but still law and order will prevail through the supremacy of reason, rectitude, and religion."[31] Peter Parley's three-Rs dealt with behavior; conservatism, wealth, religion and right are all lumped together under the banner of patriotism.

Far more than Mrs. Child, Goodrich was willing to stem the tide of political vice and licentiousness. One method was to present explicit political and economic theories for the edification of his moppets. In the first number of the *Museum*, he wrote "About Labor and Property." The primary axiom is "All things we see around us belong to somebody; and these things have been got by *labor* and *working*." Since such ownership is morally earned, "It is very just and proper that every person should be allowed to keep his own property"—the poor as well as the rich. By knowing that property can be his, the poor man "will work to have things for his own use." In other words, industry and frugality, for Goodrich as it had been for Franklin, will be rewarded by wealth; therefore, property should be protected as the fundamental stimulant to those virtues which elevate man both materially and morally. A long serial which later came out in book form, "The Story of Philip Brusque," detailed Goodrich's theories on "the nature and necessity of government and laws" which would protect that property and insure its moral attainment. This story of a group of French castaways who try to set up a society illustrates the benefits of federalism. Communism and anarchy are seen as opposite extremes which destroy private property and with it civilization. On the economic level, the perfect government is the happy medium of freedom within the law; the freedom is to amass property, the law to protect that property. Such a government is the only one sanctioned by God, by nature, by reason, by Goodrich: ". . . man is made to possess things and to call them his, and to desire by his own efforts, to accumulate things to himself. To resist this principle is to resist Heaven and nature, and common sense." Idleness results in deserved poverty and vice, "Where the people are industrious . . . they are not only supplied with the comforts and luxuries of life, but they adopt good and virtuous habits, and are therefore happy. Where they are indolent, they are poor, vicious, and unhappy. . . . We must see that those who work are well rewarded for it." This reward no longer comes from God or natural law; its source is man-made government. Goodrich does argue, however, that government should be "natural"; that is, it should follow the plan of nature and of nature's god, otherwise individual wealth and consequent civilization are destroyed. During the villainous Rogere's communistic rule, Philip laments (like William Bradford), "The fruits [of the island] are fast diminishing, because they belong to no one in particular; and no one has any power or interest to preserve them." In the best tradition of classical economics, individual and national solvency are identified.

Yet, true to traditional success, Goodrich could not let the reader think that material wealth was everything. He inserts the story of a fisherman, M. Piquet, who found an axe—the only one on the island. The ownership of the axe was rightfully Piquet's for "he was entitled to the fruits of his luck"; he swam out a mile into the sea, and, by risking his life and making great exertions, brought his treasure to shore. Because he monopolized a property in great demand,

Piquet found it "unnecessary to work for his support [;] he grew idle, and then discontent." Then M. Piquet, the richest man on the island, ran for governor. His fellow castaways, knowing that his wealth was only luck rather than a properly won reward indicating moral ability, merely laughed at him. Mortified, he flung his axe back into the sea, "And from that day he quietly pursued the life of a fisherman, declaring that the intoxication of riches was by no means so pleasant as the content of attending a career of humble but useful toil." Because the good sense of an intelligent and industrious populace saw through the pretentions of this unvirtuous *nouveau riche*, the society was protected by its yeoman structure against threats from above as well as from below. Piquet's downfall, however, is farcical even in comparison to the rest of the narrative; it is as if Goodrich, despite the obviously serious thought he gave to presenting an ideal economic and political system, could not find a serious reason why the unvirtuously rich Piquet should fail. Apparently the evil rich, the lucky exploiter of natural resources, or the demagogue in a federal system, could be guarded against only by the moral enlightenment of an electorate made up of yeomen. Should that laissez-faire yeoman structure crumble, perhaps society's morality would follow and with it the only protection against demagoguery.

Goodrich places an interesting footnote at the conclusion of the tale, "The governor desired . . . that every person should love and fear God with sincerity. He maintained that no nation could be honest, virtuous, industrious, or patriotic, without religion; and that an enemy to religion was always an enemy to good government; always an enemy to the true interests of mankind, even if we only regard the affairs of human society in this world." Like Franklin, Goodrich had vast respect for the social utility of religion; unlike the Puritans, he believed religion supported the economic and political structure, rather than vice-versa. The worship of God had become primarily a social virtue and a badge of secular sanctification, and the utilitarian quality of this passage is typical of the magazine as a whole. While strongly Christian, it was non-sectarian and by no means "enthusiastic." Though little outright anti-Catholicism is evident, the Irish are portrayed as suffering victims of that benighted superstition; and other religions are discussed with all the objectivity of the following: "With the spread of light, the absurd and monstrous claims of the Brahmins are necessarily diminished."[32]

The economic system in "Philip Brusque" was presented in sim-

ple terms. Its definition of property was "material goods," and ownership was direct and individual. Although the business of the island was
interrelated by ties of trade, the industrious workers were independent
owners of their means of livelihood: yeomen tradesmen and yeomen
farmers. Merchandising was less a middle-man's occupation and more
the retailing of goods manufactured by the seller himself. Philip, for
example, "devoted his time to the manufacture of salt, and was thus
able to procure [what] he needed." This simple economic picture may
have been dictated by the magazine's juvenile audience, but it was also
generally held by many adults including Goodrich. Their economic
and political individualism was contingent upon an unsophisticated
economic model. With the increasing technological and industrial
changes of the period, with new marketing, manufacturing, and financial patterns, this simple structure became more and more idyllic
and less and less representative of actuality. When this simplistic view
of economics no longer seemed to fit the society, the related concept
of success also seemed anachronistic. By 1860, when Goodrich died,
the increasing awareness of the complexity in American economic life
carried with it the same sense of threat that cities, with their complexity and turmoil, held; it is in the tradition of American anti-intel-
lectualism that the simple is good and the complex is evil. Thus, as
shall be demonstrated in the next chapters, Americans whose vision of
success was based on a simple and consequently "good" economic
model were confronted with a complex and consequently "evil" economic society. The old success, the yeoman dream, had to change in
order to accommodate this complexity and its urban environment; but
while changing, it had to somehow maintain its goodness.

Goodrich's ideal political system had aspects other than the
purely economic. Brusque draws up a constitution "partly copied
from that of the U. S.," and not too surprisingly, the part Goodrich
saw fit to have Brusque copy contains the traditional axioms of representative democracy accepted, at least in theory, by Americans since
the Revolution:

1. All mankind are born with equal rights and privileges; all
are entitled to the same degree of liberty; all are equally entitled to
the protection of the laws.

2. All government should spring from the people, and have the
good of the people for its object.

3. That all government implies the abridgement of natural

liberty, and that the people ought to submit to such abridgements so far as the good of society requires.

The structure of the government is composed of an executive, judiciary and legislature. The only voting qualifications are sex (male) and age (21), a simple majority rules, property is protected, and "any citizen shall be competent to fill any office to which he is chosen." This constitution was rejected by a misled majority in favor of "perfect freedom"; but in the end, after an enlightening interim of benevolent dictatorship by good Governor Bonfils, the people accepted "without agitation or disturbance" a constitution similar to Brusque's.[33] Despite an interpretation of the constitution speaking of equality, liberty, and property, other articles show that Goodrich was unsure in his own mind just what equality meant. For one thing, not all men were equal: some were more industrious and therefore deserved more property than the lazy, some were born with more natural advantages, some were restricted from citizenship:

> Absolute equality is as impossible as absolute liberty. In the first place mankind are not born equal in respect to civil condition. Some . . . are born slaves. . . . Females . . . are never placed on an equality with men before the law. . . . All the members of society are born with a just claim to civil liberty. . . . Those laws which make one man a lord and another a serf . . . are violations of the principles of justice and the rights of man. [But] equality does not mean that a woman shall be equal to a man, or a child the same as a man; but that all women, all children, all citizens shall enjoy the same relative rights, privileges, and immunities.[34]

While Goodrich did not fear relative white male suffrage after the election of General Harrison, he nevertheless did fear demagogues (Rogere) and, like many others of his group, felt that tendentious education and religion would teach the future electorate to prefer the right kind of government.

Goodrich believed that he lived in the best of all possible worlds. It was not perfect, but it was part of the slow unfolding of the universe's gradual movement to perfection. Part of this belief in progress was that the individual could elevate himself without necessarily usurping the position of anyone above him. There was room at the top for everyone, and any inequalities were actually part of the cosmic benevolence. The belief in the essential goodness of the world received support from both Puritan and Enlightenment teachings, and reached philosophical status with Emerson. Firmly a part of early nineteenth-century traditional success, the belief in progress was to become more grim as the century passed and revealed the precariousness of the yeoman dream in an industrializing society. This precariousness was early felt in the familiar "problem areas" of poverty and reform.

Goodrich and those he spoke for were in possession of many of the things which society at large valued, but that possession was threatened from several directions. In one area were those who sought only wealth. In another were the "socialists," the Brownsons and Fullers and Owenses who advocated a radical social change which would violate the natural laws governing the moral society. In a third direction were the poor. Methods of defending traditional success varied; one was to offer the poor moral stature instead of traditional success, another was to enlist the idea of progress, still another advocated a gradual change from the concept of traditional success to the celebration of competition.

Generally the moral poor still consisted of crippled men, orphans, and widows who were nevertheless industrious, frugal, persevering, etc. The inability to work forced these people to violate their natural American aversion to accepting charity, a condition "not very common in our country . . . except in the large cities; and even there, the beggars are generally poor foreigners." For Mister Merry, the able-bodied American who begged was a moral outcast:

> To us in America, the idea of begging is very painful. We feel that the beggar is brought to his sad condition by some serious fault—by drunkenness, or idleness, or waste and folly. And such is the fact in our happy country. It is so easy to obtain a living in the United States, that all may have the comforts of life, unless some great calamity befalls them, and then they are taken care of, without the necessity of becoming beggars.
>
> But in Europe . . . the rich keep so much property . . . that . . . millions are reduced to misery and want.[35]

Though Europeans may be governed by economic determinism, in America, a man's fate was writ by moral determinism; and the correct charity toward the physically capable poor was education in moral

re-armament. Lessons generally consisted of urgings to industriousness or stories depicting the inspirational rise from rags to riches.
Joined with the homiletic approach to the poor was the sentimental
benevolence which grew out of the eighteenth-century sensibility cult
glimpsed earlier in Cotton Mather. It involved the gift of alms and
pity. The gift may or may not have helped the recipient to success,
but it did stimulate good emotions in the donor. Probably reflecting
the growing attention paid by the melodrama to the urban poor of
England and America is "Two Sides of a Picture" by "Peggy Betsey."
It describes the obscure poverty of New York City. While on a visit
to the city hospital, the interviewer asks a charity case:

> "But my good woman . . . is there nothing you can do? No labor
> by which you may earn something?"
> "Alas . . . the destruction of the poor is their poverty. . . .
> Since my clothes are so shabby, no one will trust me with work,
> and I must beg or starve."

But the point of the story is not that the poor escape responsibility
for their plight; instead, there is a reiteration of moral individualism
and a self-congratulatory emotion of diffuse benevolence, "I shall ever
remember, that in this world, things have two meanings, one for the
common observer, and one for the deeper, higher mind of him who
walks by the light of a love-illumined heart."[36] The one goal still
available for the economically hopeless was the familiar one of contentment with life through moral elevation. For instance, one poor boy
who was envious of a rich acquaintance happened to discover a fairy
of whom he asked wealth; " 'This is very wrong and very foolish,'
said the maid in green. 'You are born in poverty, and the boy
you speak of is born to riches, but it is not poverty or riches that
make people happy.' " The lad unvirtuously persisted in his demand
for upsetting the natural order, and after some unnerving adventures,
philosophized, " '. . . happiness springs from a contented mind. . . . I
see that the power which riches confer are [sic] not only useless, but
fatal to those who have not the training and wisdom to use them.' "[37]
In short, the readers—who had money enough to subscribe to a children's magazine—were told that the poor could attain contentment
provided they accepted the status quo of the American society; however, since this doctrine of acquiescence conflicted with the traditional ethic of industry and the concept of fruitfulness, Parley's and

other magazines came to associate acquiescence with "them" while industry and reward was for "us."

Paralleling the concern for the virtuous poor was, of course, concern with the unvirtuous rich. This type, when described as an exploiter of the poor, was generally European. A Goodrich article about the famine in Ireland depicts that colony as subject to "a constant system of grasping, which takes away its wealth, and leaves the country in a state of poverty."[38] Perhaps stimulated by the very popular English melodrama *The Rent Day*, Mr. Merry explains to little John that collection time is a sad day for the poor of Europe, "for if they cannot pay, and their landlords are hard hearted, they are turned out of doors." Indeed, little John, the child of a yeoman society, had to have Mr. Merry explain "rent" to him.[39] Since in Europe society was corrupt and merited censure, while in America it followed natural and divine law and could not be criticized, a rich American might be unvirtuous but he could never be depicted as an exploiter. Consequently, the American poor are told to be humble and content while foreign landlords are severely criticized.

The fictional poor of Parley's stories lived in the city, and often they pursued mechanical occupations related to one of the industries undergoing reorganization into factory production. Because such an environment was counter to the yeoman tradition, this urban-industrial poor was seen either as basically un-American or as unreal. "Romance of Manufactures" heralds this interest in the magazine, and the title is ironically appropriate, for Goodrich, copying popular writers who were discovering "themes of romance and rhyme" in the simple annals of the poor, urged the reader to visit the Boston Mill-dam plant and other well-known manufacturies. There they would find "ample materials for exciting the sentiment of wonder." A small part of this wonder is that human beings are employed in the factories:

> . . . If we go further, and study the conditions of the thousands and millions of human beings who are occupied in promoting these results; if we consider that here are men, women, and children, all possessing minds and souls, all having hearts, like our own, full of hopes and fears; full of joys and sorrows; full of wants, and wishes, and disappointments, —we shall find abundant occasion for the indulgence of the deepest and liveliest sympathy.

But Goodrich's greatest wonder is not excited by the condition of those strangely familiar factory workers; rather, it is the quantity of production which amazes him: two hundred thousand yards of print every week, two million nails per day, thousands of miles of thread each hour. This attitude is not his alone; the story which follows his prologue was lifted from the London (and New York) *Penny Magazine*, and deals with needle-making at Reddich, England. The concern is primarily with the steps of manufacture, and the only comment on working conditions refers to the grinders' refusal to wear filter-masks, "perhaps that their wages may not be lowered by rendering the work less injurious." Such avariciousness results in their being "killed by inches."[40] In general, however, *Merry's Museum* was almost unconcerned with operatives, preferring, like the *Juvenile Miscellany*, to focus on mercantile occupations and a mythical farm world. Labor saving machinery was hailed as a boon to man and a sign of progress, and if the morality of the factory environment is mentioned, it is to show that individuals could still be held responsible for their actions. Yet there was a certain awe in the depiction of machinery as the possible social impact of the burgeoning technology was felt. To judge by Goodrich's praise, a poem by George W. Cutter apparently expressed his own feelings:

> Harness me down with your iron bands;
>   Be sure of your curb and rein;
> For I scorn the strength of your puny hands,
>   As the tempest scorns a chain
>
>   .   .   .   .
>
> And soon I intend you may 'go and play,'
>   While I manage the world myself.
> But harness me down with your iron bands;
>   Be sure of your curb and rein. . . .[41]

To get a clearer idea of Goodrich's beliefs about operatives, it is necessary to turn to the autobiography where he describes Danbury in the early nineteenth century and notes that the hat factory operaives ". . . were foreigners, mostly English and Irish. A large part of the business of our store was the furnishing of rum to these poor wretches. . . . A factory workman of those days was thought to be born to toil, to get drunk, and make a hell of his home. Philanthropy had not then lifted its eye or its hopes above these ideas from England

and other foreign manufacturing countries. . . ." Fortunately in America the political and religious institutions reformed the factory influence, "It is a modern discovery that manufacturing towns may rise up, where comfort, education, morals, and religion . . . may be possessed by the toiling masses. This is not only a modern, but an American discovery, and refutes volumes of abuse that long-eared philosophy has leveled at republicanism."[42] The example Goodrich probably had in mind was Lowell, whose organization was intended specifically to change the reputation of factories so that a labor force could be found.[43] Though uneasy before the power of steam, Goodrich respected manufacturing as a force of progress tending, by its stimulus to individual industry, toward general moral and economic improvement, "When farming absorbed society, a large part of the year was lost because tavern haunting, tippling, and gambling were the chief resources of men in the dead and dreary winter months. Manufactures gave profitable occupation during this inclement period." Even by the 1850s, Goodrich does not seem to consider a labor force made up of women and children, nor does he consider that the traditional form of success could fail to apply to operatives, "law . . . comes from the people . . . farmers, mechanics, manufacturers, merchants—independent in their circumstances, and sober, religious, virtuous in their habits of thought and conduct."[44] If the yeoman dream was thought to be an actual possibility for all moral workers in the American society, then it is only logical to consider poor operatives in some personal way deficient and as a group alien to traditional success. And so they were to become.

Change, while it may have been dangerous, was not always thought of as bad; good change was called progress. Various influences contributed to the idea of progress in nineteenth-century America, and the idea itself was used to attack or defend other beliefs. It served to support both material and geographical expansion, and it provided an argument against radicalism by offering evolution rather than revolution. Two principal means were used to assist progress: education and religion. Together they meant moral reform.[45]

Goodrich saw progress as the orderly movement toward the greatest amount of prosperous happiness for the greatest number of virtuous people; such was the goal of Brusque's utopia, and such was the movement of the United States. This progress included "The multiplying and diversifying of the occupations of society . . . , transforming the condition of the people, by increasing their wealth, multiplying their comforts, enlarging their minds, elevating their sentiments: in short, increasing their happiness."[46] The impelling force behind this progress was obedience to the traditional virtues. In a passage which hints of Max Weber, Goodrich writes:

> The desire for improvement is inherent in the New England character. This springs from two principles: first a moral sense, founded upon religious ideas, making it the duty of every man to seek constantly to be and do better, day by day, as he advances in life. This is the great mainspring set in the heart by Puritanism. Its action reaches alike to time and to eternity.
>
>   . . . The other principle . . . is liberty, civil and social—actual and practical. . . . It is this moral sense . . . cooperating with this liberty, giving him the right and the ability to seek happiness in his own way which forms this universal spirit of improvement—the distinguishing feature of the New England people.
>
>   . . . It is easy to trace the operations of this principle in the humblest as well as in the highest classes. The man at the plow is not . . . a . . . servile tool . . . without thought as to the result of his labor.[47]

The progress toward the great society in which all worthy men would be truly successful regardless of class was to take place through the moral elevation of the individuals within the established political and economic framework. Although specific social reforms did not receive a great play in *Merry's*, the oblique influence of various movements can be glimpsed. The most obvious is temperance, although pacifism, anti-slavery (though not abolition) and Sabbath-keeping were also urged. The urban poor became subjects for benevolence in the 1840s, and a few stories about chimney sweeps can be found, wrought in great part by the wide popularity of the Dickensian novel of social protest. But in order to consolidate blocks of subject matter, let me defer the major discussion of reform until the chapter dealing with the *Youth's Companion*, a periodical which shows the reform movement in greater amplitude. What is important for the moment, is that Goodrich's attitude toward the poor and toward the factory environment reveals the growing division between traditional success and the permanent wage earners.

By mid-century, Goodrich's magazine showed increasing unease over the growing numbers of poor. More and more worthy people seemed to be unable to attain the traditional success by beginning as wage earners, particularly if the wages came from urban mechanic occupations, or if the occupations were subject to one of the periodic depressions that began to plague the economy. The literary result was a blurring of the moral division between virtuous and unvirtuous poor and a confusion of sympathy and rejection toward these unfortunates. At one instant their plight was portrayed in gushingly sentimental prose, and readers were emotionally called upon to aid the poor with gifts of food and money; the next moment, the poor were condemned for lacking the moral strength which could have enabled them to change their condition by themselves. In one angry breath, the rich were blamed for exploiting the unfortunate; while with a sigh, the downtrodden were told to persevere and to have faith. However, one idea remained constant: despite the suffering of individuals, the social structure was not at fault; neither cause nor cure was attributed to a belief so popular in our own time as "social forces."

A major motif which grows in volume from the time of the discovery of poverty in the American cities is the idea of competition. For the Puritans, men did not have to compete with each other for grace—the competition was with one's self and with Satan; for the Enlightenment, only those governed by unenlightened self-interest competed with other men or with beasts of the wild forest. For the yeoman, competition with fellow man was unnecessary because in America there was enough for all men to attain traditional success. But in the early nineteenth century, the idea of competition, while ultimately revolutionary, was used to support the existing social structure by finding the cause of failure to lie within the individual instead of in society. As mid-century approached, the goals of this competition came to be more and more material; though the pursuit of success was still supposed to be moral, a much more tangible reward made that success worth the increasingly savage struggle. This period also saw the theme "Persevere" become a major movement in Goodrich's magazine and, unlike Franklin or *The Juvenile Miscellany*, the only goal became immediate wealth and not distant virtue. Although industry, frugality, and temperance were still important, perseverance was given additional emphasis because it supported the idea of competition. It became increasingly popular to stress the difficulties to ma-

terial success; the only way the striving lad could, on his own, wrest
fame and fortune from a competing world was by persevering:

> 'Tis a wisdom you should heed—
>   Try, try again,
> If at first you don't succeed,
>   Try, try again. . . .[48]

The Enlightenment had conceived of progress as being within the
temporalized Great Chain of Being. There could be universal elevation in which one individual might raise himself without usurping the
place of another above him, providing that he kept ambition in check
and minded the goal of retirement from business. In the mind of
Franklin or Crevecoeur, for example, the struggle of man against
man was proper only for brutes—the Indians or the half-wild hunters
of the frontier. Civilization copied the harmonies of nature, and, in an
America of boundless plenty, there was little reason for a civilized
man of the sub-frontier or even of the cities to fight with his fellow
man for a limited amount of wealth. This idea remained long enough
to influence Goodrich, but it was not permanent. The idea of competition, latent in the Protestant Ethic and manifest in the tales of sharp
Yankee trading as well as in the humor columns of the newspapers,
intruded openly into the *Museum* by the mid-1840s. Goodrich, while
recognizing it, tried to soften it by reasserting the individual's moral
obligation to his fellow competitor in the terms of traditional success:

> . . . an admiration of excelling is one of the first and strongest
> principles of human nature; and we are especially pleased when
> the power of excelling is discovered to be in ourselves. . . . This
> desire to excel [is] at once the cause of virtue and vice, of success
> and failure in human life. . . .
>
>   We may strive to excel others, but never permit that strife
> to abate our love, or charity, or kindness, for them with whom
> we strive.[49]

Although no one yet asserted that "winning isn't everything, it's the
ONLY thing," the harsh slyness of a Sam Slick, the robust battling
of the Western giant Davy Crockett—as well as his war cry, "Go
Ahead!"—began to celebrate the idea of competition between all men.
Success as necessarily entailing competition began to rival traditional
success even in its very stronghold, and this change is evidenced in the

increasingly popular "life's race" imagery that depicts man struggling
for a goal which other men seek to wrest from him:

> Through life's crowded highways press,
>   Go Ahead;
> Earnest toil insures success,
>   Go Ahead.
> Let the Indolent delay,
>   Let the Haughty-minded frown,
> Up and doing by the way,
>   Bear the cross and wear the crown,
>   Go Ahead.
>
>   . . . .
>
> In life's contest—in life's race,
>   Go Ahead.
> Strive to win a noble place,
>   Go Ahead;
> With a free and willing hand
>   With a brave and cheerful heart,
> 'Mong the true and toiling stand,
>   Striving to enact your part.
>   Go Ahead.[50]

Such religious dedication to self-interest on life's crowded highway
enabled the lad to conquer others; parents are warned that "The boy
who cannot take care of himself . . . must be pitiably deficient in . . .
all the qualities of manhood."[51] And by 1857, Goodrich himself
praised the yeoman's rural upbringing not for its inculcation of virtue,
but because it raised boys fit to "triumph in the race of life."

In the mid-century *Museum* and other magazines like it, there
was no more retirement—not for the gentry, not for the yeoman; nor
did the editors urge withdrawal from business life to become
benefactors to mankind. Ceaseless industry was demanded by progress. The Great Chain was replaced by the belief that every one was
forced to race against the rest of mankind for a limited quantity of
success. Only those most fit to survive would finish, but somehow
their attainment would further humanity as a whole. Perhaps the
"life's race" imagery was popular because it portrayed a situation of
democratic equality in which all began the struggle together but only

a few made it to the goal. Perhaps the social upheavals in Europe during 1848 intensified the Americans' awareness of conflict as opposed to harmony. Perhaps the promise of California gold to be had simply for the digging (if you got there first and dug fastest) whetted the Americans' yearning for wealth. Perhaps the defenders of a competence capitulated in an attempt to have a log cabin hero of their own whose western opportunism and hard cider struck closer to the maintsream of enterprise-hungry America. Perhaps the inflated wealth of Astor and Vanderbilt, and a little later of Fisk, Gould, and Drew, made sheer riches more popular than a competence. Whatever caused the erosion of support for traditional success, the later nineteenth century reveals the defeat and not the victory of that idea. The struggle for riches became almost Darwinian and the morality almost forgotten; and as the century passed—witnessing a bloody struggle for the survival of the nation—an even harsher ethic of success placed the major division of society no longer along a line of virtue versus the unvirtuous, but between the rich and therefore socially contributive versus the poor and therefore socially burdensome. This is not to assert that the moral aspect of traditional success died completely: Carnegie voiced a platitude with his stewardship doctrine; end of the century Progressives had roots reaching into pre-Civil War traditional success; mid-twentieth-century writers ranging from Vance Packard to Arthur Miller have lamented in yeoman terms the purposeless materialism of the "affluent society" and the loss of Puritan "inner-directedness." Nevertheless, during the period of "the Great Barbeque," as Parrington called it, the traditional concept of success ebbed in popularity, and its withdrawal was marked by neither a bang nor a whimper, but by the shriek of steam and the moan of an alien poor.

Lydia Maria Child and Samuel Goodrich reveal the outlines of the idea of traditional success in the first half of the nineteenth century. Initially following closely the Enlightenment values, they believed that the competence and independence of a yeoman society could be attained by any American if he only pursued the goal in a morally acceptable fashion. However, by the 1840s, the viability of this success for factory operatives became an increasingly acute question. Repeatedly, Goodrich assured readers that there was no difference between the opportunities for operatives and those for apprentice office clerks; yet at the same time fictional themes in his magazine show a gradual restriction of the application of the yeoman dream to business and professional occupations, and a tendency to reject that dream's eighteenth-century values. The godliness of the Puritans and the virtue of Franklin faded, while the morality of Goodrich came to be a means of defending his group's assumed leadership of American society. Immoral entrepreneurs were typically excluded from membership in the group; but the poor, immoral or not, urban or rural, also began to be suspect or ignored. Under the impact of technological change, it became increasingly evident that competence and independence could only belong to the farmer of literary convention or to the businessman of the city. Consequently, in these urban-oriented magazines, success was depicted as the traditional possession of a mythical agrarian yeoman or as an increasingly competitive scramble for greater and greater riches. In farmer's magazines, the yeoman dream would persist until the end of the century, when the breadth of the land could no longer outdistance the strides of economic and technological change; and even in the twentieth century the family farm would be passionately (and expensively) defended as a bulwark of American democracy. In Goodrich's magazines, mercantilism, competition, and economic individualism—never very distant from the Protestant Ethic—were given free entry into the moral code by residual Enlightenment optimism and the new nineteenth-century belief in progress. At the same time, the vast material opportunity of the physical and economic frontiers, as well as the mythology growing from them, replaced the old warnings against "every man for himself and God for us all." This opportunity was supported by an increasingly widespread belief in the natural law of competitive self-interest as opposed to enlightened self-interest. The more harsh code also offered a convenient explanation for the embarrassment of the failure of great numbers of otherwise deserving people: they were individually incompetent. While this usurpation was never complete, the latter half of the century saw materialism and economic individualism predominate in the American mind.

Through all this, the Goodriches and Childs, their readers and their supporters, tried to keep what they considered to be their rightful national hegemony. One method was through reform movements, another was to embrace the concept of success as the result of harsh competition. Ironically, traditional success and its yeoman came to be defended in its purest form by the very people whom the Peter Parleys wished to console or to ignore: the growing proletariat.

He soon became a land-holder, then a prosperous cultivator of the soil, and shortly after a town-officer. By that progressive change in fortunes, which in the republic is often seen to be so singularly accompanied by a corresponding knowledge and self-respect, he went on, from step to step.

Cooper, *The Prairie*, 1827

He's an able man, Dilworthy, and a good man. A Man has got to be good to succeed as he has. He's only been in Congress a few years, and he must be worth a million.

Twain, *The Gilded Age*, 1873

2

THE EVOLUTION OF THE DREAM

❖

TRADITIONAL SUCCESS was defended by more than the Maria Childs and the Peter Parleys; spokesmen for other areas of society —rural, labor, intellectual, immigrant—supported their success. Famous novelists, anonymous labor writers, journalists of wide or narrow renown, all offered their definition of the truly successful man, and, early in the century at least, those definitions clustered around the yeoman. As the century passed, however, and the celebration of competition grew frenetic, many of these writers were forced to choose between the life's race image and the yeoman dream. One periodical, *The Youth's Companion*, reveals this conceptual drift not only in areas of business and the urban East, but also in the minds of mechanics and westerners. The *Companion's* editor, Nathaniel Willis, and many of his contributors represent a striving but far less prestigious element than Mrs. Child and Samuel Goodrich; nevertheless, they held to the values that these more established writers espoused. As with Peter Parley, the fundamental line between success and failure was one of symbolic behavior rather than wealth alone; but unlike Parley, Willis saw that this line was frighteningly thin, and that for him and those like him, it was buttressed neither by greater income nor by greater prestige. It thus had to be drawn with greater energy.

Willis was descended from seventeenth-century Puritans. His father, part owner of the *Independent Chronicle*, a strongly pro-liberty paper begun in Boston in 1776, served in the Revolution, and afterwards moved to western Virginia, where seven-year-old Nathaniel joined him as an apprentice. The boy remained with him until he

51

was sixteen, returning to the metropolis of Boston to seek his fortune while his father moved on to seek his own in Ohio. After serving as a journeyman for two years, Nathaniel married in 1803 and moved to Portland, Maine, to found the *Eastern Argus*. This paper was the organ of the anti-Federalist party, a vociferous left-wing minority, and the result was political turbulence, name-calling, and a ninety-day sentence for libel. Four years later, Willis was soundly converted to Christianity from agnosticism by the zealous Congregational evangelist Edward Payson, and, subsequently, religion so dominated the *Argus* that his party forced him to sell it. After a short and unsuccessful fling at being a grocer (unlike the more respectable Goodrich, he refused to sell rum), Willis returned to Boston and supported his growing family by publishing religious tracts. In 1816, he started what he called the "first religious newspaper in the world," the *Boston Recorder*; in serving God, he served himself, and, after a long struggle, he gained a competence if not great wealth. In a footnote referring to Nathaniel Willis, Goodrich wrote that he was "much respected for his industry, his good sense, his devotion to whatever he deemed his duty, and his useful services rendered to morals, religion, Christianity, and Philanthropy"; yet from his own Olympian heights, Peter Parley looked down on Willis's mechanic background, pointing out that though the latter had worked his way up to editor, he had been "originally a printer."[1] And Willis himself admitted that he had not been bred to a gentlemanly profession. Unlike Goodrich, he thought of his trade as a manual occupation on the same level as carpenters and shoemakers.[2]

The Willis home was a serious one, "its interests divided between 'business and Bethel.' " Willis's character has been charitably described as wooden: "His youth and early manhood had been full of hardship; his education was scanty, and he had the formal and narrow piety of the new evangelicals of that day, revolting against the latitudinarianism of the Boston churches. He was for twenty years deacon of Park Street Church, profanely nicknamed by the Unitarians, 'Brimstone Corner.' " Yet he was somewhat redeemed by a sense of humor, albeit a dry one, and an eye for a pretty girl.[3] Of his children, four escaped to New York and the publishing center developing there: Julia Dean Willis, who wrote reviews for the New York *Home Journal*; Richard Storrs Willis, who edited *Music World*; Sarah Payson Willis, better known in print and gossip as "Fanny Fern"; and the most famous of all, Nathaniel Parker Willis, New

York author, critic, and flaneur. Though not entirely pacific in his relationship with Nathaniel P., the deacon was nevertheless proud of his son's literary achievements; Willis may have bragged of his own mechanic beginnings, but he led or drove his children to the social advantages of superior education and professional rank.

In 1827, Willis founded one of the longest-lived juvenile magazines in America, the *Youth's Companion*; it made the fortunes of and outlasted at least two editors, and was finally bought by *American Boy* in 1929. The times and ideas presented by the magazine reflect one hundred years of the American mind, but the briefer span of 1827 to 1860 is the substance of this chapter. Born out of the "Youth's Column" in his religious newspaper, the magazine in its early years continued a theological emphasis which must not have been entirely repellant, for every decade or so, amid pleas for payment of subscriptions, Willis announced an increase of circulation which sometimes amounted to one hundred per cent. The number of subscribers at the time of Willis's retirement in 1857 is conservatively estimated at five thousand,[4] but the number of readers was probably far greater, as issues circulated among families and friends. The magazine quickly outgrew local readership, probably because controversial issues were avoided, and its appeal transcended jealousies between the various sections of the nation; an editorial comment late in 1827 notes that the magazine was being sent to fifteen states, one territory, Lower Canada, and Nova Scotia. Letters to the editor were continually received from such distant and often lonely places as a plantation in Georgia or a farm in "Belle Prarie, Minesota Ter."

The various departments were entitled Narrative, Nursery, Descriptive (travel), Sabbath School, Deaths, Natural History, Morality, Parental, Editorial, Poetry, and, to cover any remaining subject, Variety. In evangelical fashion, the first numbers stressed the ambience of death; but with the passage of time, Willis's earnest first-page sermon was gradually reduced in size, its lead column position taken over by equally earnest but more entertaining short tales and serials. Wholesome fiction began to supplant didacticism as the magazine reflected the demands for entertainment as well as utility, and although Willis was never reluctant to lift material from other publications, the later issues do have a greater number of original stories. After Willis's death, the magazine reached a relatively high literary level; edited by Daniel Sharp Ford, it moved into its golden era by presenting such writers as Herbert Spencer, Hamlin Garland, William

Dean Howells, John Greenleaf Whittier, and Jack London. The format changed occasionally either to attract new generations of readers or to take advantage of changes in postal regulations. Until 1841, it was a four-page weekly of quarto size crammed with minute type, and after the first volumes, woodcuts embellished the front page and banner, and smaller illustrations found their way inside. Very seldom did Willis stoop to advertising merchandise, although after Ford took over, commercialism in the form of notices and premiums began to appear. In 1834, the subtitle "And Sabbath School Recorder" was added, reflecting the wide interest in that institution; but it was dropped two years later, perhaps to preserve the paper's independence from an organized Sunday School movement, though much related material remained. In the early forties, the slogan "Devoted to Piety, Morality, Brotherly Love. No Sectarianism, No Controversy" was added, demonstrating a growing fear of radicals of all stripes (and also perhaps the resurgent belligerency of the American Peace Society); in addition, the new slogan shows the popular increase of sentimental benevolence, or, as one of the stories has it, "A Kiss for a Blow."

Although the established spokesmen for traditional success were well represented in even the earliest numbers of the magazine, Willis's own values were not submerged. The result was a blurring of social level. The earliest illustrated banner, for example, shows a seated mother holding a magazine and surrounded by two daughters and a young son just lured in from hoop rolling; all are neatly dressed and obviously happy, and the caption reads, "The Companion Has Come." It is appropriately a scene of middle class domesticity, for the urban middle class was the principal group represented in the articles and tales as well as in the homilies. Nevertheless, Willis ran a series of original articles—perhaps submitted by a relative—which praised the West and westerners for their economic promise and Christian behavior. The author tells his readers that the West is as genteel as the Northeast, and in "Scenes in Ohio," a Fourth of July observance is given highest praise for being "a proper New England holiday." This is in sharp contrast to a poem from *Parley's Magazine* describing an evening visit to an Indiana cabin:

Half a dozen "Hooseroons"
With mush and milk, tin cups and spoons,
White heads, bare feet, and dirty faces,

Seem much inclined to keep their places.
But madam, anxious to display
Her rough and undisputed sway,
Her offspring to the ladder leads,
And cuffs the youngsters to their beds.[5]

The urbane Hudibrastic poet, the author of "Billy Bump," the Home Missionary Society—all were far from praising Western morality and manners; for them, the West was a hot-bed of atheistic and anti-traditional ideas. While Willis agreed that the West witnessed a struggle against the powers of darkness, he saw it as being won and had the temerity to assert that more Sabbath-breaking could be found in Boston than in Ohio. Like McGuffey, Willis saw the best institutions and ideals in the West to be those based upon the traditional moral purity of New England; but also like him, Willis had been in the West and had respect and affection for the area.

The tales and articles, drawn as they are from a wide range of sources, have various audiences in mind: the obituary of Master John R. Hutchinson reveals that he attended the Boston Latin School; a letter from "Brainerd, Cherokee Nation," praises the magazine as a friend to Christian Indian children; Hannah More and other contributors to Victorian home periodicals are represented, as are items from American labor newspapers. The editor inclined toward the less well-off, while his contributors, pirated or paid, ranged from conservative English writers to radical American democrats. What is consistent is the reward for approved behavior: the *Companion* addressed those who owned and those who wanted to own the opportunity for yeoman success.

Unlike Goodrich, Willis did not consider himself to be a professional pedagogue and paid little attention to epistemological theories, being either unconcerned with or unaware of the difference between urging children to listen to their innate conscience, and demanding that parents be strict disciplinarians in "training up" their offspring. For example, one self-explanatory title announces, "The Rod Tingles but it Cures," while in the same volume, another essay points out the tenderness of the individual's own conscience and the necessity of trusting to it for infallible guidance.[6] However, as mid-century approached and more and more sentimental reform themes filled the pages, greater space was given to stories and articles which broadcast the romantic theory that the child was innately closest to

God; this tendency reflects the increasing belief that bad habits could be overcome by appealing to the goodness in every man's heart, and that children, as in the melodramatic stories of T. S. Arthur, were often best able to make that appeal.

The view of society in much of the fiction was like that of Goodrich and Mrs. Child: industry, perseverance, frugality, and study are the proper means of individual advancement within a stable social framework. Although there was much talk about the elevation of society as a whole, even in the West praised by Willis that elevation was to take place with the classes in their relative positions and with opportunity still open for moral individuals only. Any "leveling" was to be a moral leveling which, as is pointed out in prose and doggerel, would not disturb the structure of the perfect society:

> Says Jonathan "haply beyond the salt lake,
> Our notions of liberty people mistake.
> Both natives and strangers who here pass along,
> Have a right to do right—but no right to do wrong." [7]

The constant theme of filial obedience may be seen as an aspect of this desire for a harmonious society; the spirit of obedience was love and awe, and its basis was the Fifth Commandment. The characteristics demonstrating this virtue were docility, meekness, unassuming confidence, submissiveness under disappointments, and "tender anxiety" for the honor and welfare of the parents, characteristics which are required of society's unfortunate in the face of their sufferings. It is not surprising to see adults placed in relation to God as children are to parents.

Despite this submissive attitude on behalf of His subjects, the God of the early *Companion*, like that of Mrs. Child and Peter Parley, was more akin to the Enlightenment concept than to the Puritan image. It was God's establishment and not His establishing which was noted, for the plan, social as well as cosmic, had been revealed, and the religious man's duty was to search his own soul for weaknesses which would prevent his following this plan. The active follower of the plan would be rewarded with material and spiritual salvation; all that was needed in addition to the prudential behavior was faith. However, as the century lengthened, man was seen less as a passive follower of a fixed plan, and more of an active participant in progress's gradual unfolding. Coupled with increasing secularization and materialism, participation in such an organic unfolding was to become an element of the doctrine of competition: the belief that the struggles of each individual, successful or not, contributed to the health and development of the nation or race. But before this tendency became a doctrine, success as espoused by the early *Companion* was in great part defined by moral behavior in relation to a traditionally static social model. The pursuit of success had certain ritualistic acts, including the traditional virtues, and although everyone was welcomed—even urged—to join the ritual, to do so would mean the change not of society but of the individual. The morals and religion advocated by the magazine defended the structure of society approved of by Child, Goodrich, and Willis; the ladder of society matched the ladder of Jacob. However, despite the efforts of the spokesmen, a spirit of speculation and quick profit seemed to be abroad in the land, one which violated the precepts of true success by causing unfruitful labor and unjustified wealth. The magazine clearly shows the conflict between the desire for wealth in a world of opportunity and rapid personal gain, and a fear that too much is happening too fast: that the wealth and power of the newly rich speculators, merchant-capitalists, bankers—men whose profit came not from the manual production of useful goods, but from somewhere in the market or monopolies —were replacing the leadership of the virtuous and upsetting the moral society. Willis saw and wanted material opportunity, but he also saw people rising to wealth who did not do so by behaving in a way which justified their possession of that wealth. And there was the heightened awareness of virtue unrewarded among the poor at a time when morally suspect millionaires began to ride through the streets. Two more or less conscious fears about the coveted opportunity thus beset Willis: that the unjustified were gaining supremacy, and that the poor would become restless at growing economic divisions and violate the laws of nature and God which governed them. The answers found in the magazine in response to this drift toward the opulent and competitive materialism of the later century are two: an increase in the volume of messages praising the virtuous aspect of traditional success, and a preaching of benevolence to placate the poor while maintaining a fixed social order.

The praise of virtue was at first presented in familiar terms. One specific area in which the *Companion* defended traditional virtues was the apprentice system, and although there were differing ideas of the apprentice's economic role, there was unanimity of opinion about apprenticeship being an education for proper living rather than merely technical training. While it was increasingly obvious to parents and to youth that self-employment was sooner found in business or the professions than in manual arts, the flight from apprenticeship was still condemned as a betrayal of truly moral industry; it seemed to be a rejection of most of the things which made up true success: the fruitfulness so obvious in manual crafts, the traditional avenues of morality for the virtuous poor, and especially the ideal of the yeoman whose independent moral pursuit of a competence helped create his virtue and that of society. And perhaps there was a feeling of nostalgia (seen also in Goodrich's autobiography) for the village economy of self-employed craftsmen who, with a stake in the nation and a clear chance to move into positions of public responsibility, had not been foreign-born strikers or unionists, but stabilizing supporters of the proper American society. The *Companion* ran article after article urging "Give Your Boys a Trade" instead of professional training or an interest in speculation. It seemed too often that youths felt ". . . they must be something better, though only in appearance, than their father; and so they frequently turn their attention to occupations which to them look remarkably genteel, but which all the world . . . know to be superficial and unprofitable."[8] This is the point of view of the person threatened by people whose positions were gained in seeming violation of traditional morals, whose successes—even if they were material—could in no way be called justified. And the threat to apprenticeship, the lure of gentility, may have been very real, for after working a brief and unhappy time for Samuel Goodrich, young Nathaniel P. Willis migrated to New York and soon became a worldly and somewhat rakish editor whose idle ways led to excommunication from his father's church. Seen from this angle, it is not surprising that such a venturous citizen of the land of opportunity as N. P. Willis would conservatively condemn his fellows for taking advantage of that opportunity; the public moral dimensions of apprentice training are clearly evident when failure to obey this traditional route to success is equated with subsequent violations of civil law, ". . . A very large proportion of all the prisoners in our jails and penitentiaries are persons who were either never apprenticed, or who ran away from their masters."[9]

Though apprenticeship took three to seven years (and often longer), it was nevertheless seen as a benefit to the boy as well as to society, "It takes a lad at a critical period of life—when he has a disposition perhaps averse to steady employment . . . and puts him to a steady round of duties. . . . He comes forth a man, the master of a trade, of fixed principles and good habits, and a blessing to himself and to the community."[10] The moral upbringing entailed in apprenticeship would help conserve the spokesmen's vision of society by insuring that the man who remained a humble mechanic remained humble, and that a mechanic who gained wealth behaved acceptably. However, the apprentice system could not be maintained in the face of the industrial revolution, and as the possibilities for that kind of success lessened, the magazine became increasingly oriented toward business pursuits.

Here, too, the praise of the virtuous and the condemnation of the unvirtuous businessman was at first presented in familiar terms. The two faces of mercantile wealth are set side by side in a biography of "Two Rich Men": Samuel Terry of Botany Bay was, as his address might indicate, an example of "how illusive and worthless a thing wealth is, especially with a man like him, and if obtained in a low and even questionable way"; but American Jacob Lorillard was justified in his wealth, first because he rose from being an obscure tobacconist's apprentice by his own integrity, industry, perseverance, and love of books, and secondly, because when he was a millionaire, his moral pursuit of wealth led him to exhibit benevolence and generosity.[11] In fiction, a wealthy self-made merchant could say to a yeoman brother who had been content with a competence, independence, and the "better things" of art, music, and family, " . . . I have got enough to buy up the whole of your town, bank and all— and yet your life has been a success, and mine a dead failure!"[12] The miser and the morally weak heir were stock images of failure despite their wealth, and many stories showed that the only way for the immoral rich to regain a pure soul was through financial failure. Indeed, the decline from riches-to-rags was as conventional a theme as was the ascent; the hazard of new or old fortunes, if obtained in an unjustified manner, was the probable loss of heaven and the certain loss of one's earthly happiness. One widespread and troublesome belief in the *Companion* was that a business occupation by its very nature was a threat to traditional morality. With his mechanic bias, Willis was typical in pointing out the dangers inherent in buying and selling as opposed to honest craftsmanship: sudden failure, the lack of a "practical trade" to fall back upon, temptations to dishonesty, and uncertainty of reward despite one's moral deserts. Merchandizing was compared to the lottery whose rewards and losses fell to the virtuous and unvirtuous regardless of worth; the cyclic economic depressions and the first hints of the robber barons seemed to support these suspicions. By mid-century, the distrust spread beyond mechanics to include more genteel defenders of the yeoman dream, and the competitive pursuit of business riches was commonly seen as positing aggressive materialism against the simple spiritual pleasures of hearth and home:

> Why should business life destroy domestic life? . . . Why should a man, by excessive toil at his business unfit himself for the happiness which he may find in his family circle: He hurries to his place of business—he is eager all day to catch at every prospect of increasing his gains—he can scarcely give a moment to talk on any other subject. . . . —He continues these habits during the most vigorous years of his life, until they become fixed—often he has gained a competency . . . , then aims to be rich, even the richest![13]

In confronting the threat of an evil rich, spokesmen for traditional success had heretofore relied upon the exercise of virtue to create the moral wealthy; but now, frighteningly and increasingly, it seemed that such exercise could corrupt, that the self-made man could run riot, destroying his soul and endangering society. In money-making, he could become a Gradgrind; in politics, a Napoleon; in domestic life, a tyrant. By 1857, the new editor, Daniel Sharp Ford, could separate the pursuit of wealth from the moral life, and urge moral behavior not on the grounds that it was the inevitable result of the proper pursuit of wealth, but that it was an obligation men owed their fellows despite becoming successful, "My boy, I should not be sorry to see you, one of these days, a man of wealth and influence, and greatness—for it is not wrong to be a rich man or a great man—but I should be sorry to know that you did not make it one of your constant aims in life to be useful to your fellow-man."[14] He was apparently speaking to himself as well, for by building up the circulation of the *Companion* through advertising and bonuses, Ford built his own fortune. When he died a millionaire, he had philanthropically given a vast amount to bettering relations between business and labor in an attempt to maintain the harmony of society; characteristically, he worked through the offices of the established churches.

A corollary to the fear of the unvirtuous rich was the fear of the restless poor. For them, true contentment consisted not in wealth

but in being grateful for one's blessings, and the theme of contentment was designed to make sure those blessings fit the society the
spokesmen wanted. It is perhaps no coincidence that many tales
bearing this theme come from English magazines published by middle
class reformers to defend that social order by "elevating" (indoctrin-
ating) the lower classes; the English middle class was even more
concerned than the American with preserving the order of society
against operatives and navvies, for if their social order changed under
the pressures of mid-century revolutionary excitement, then the
middle classes' long struggle to usurp leadership from the aristocracy
would be meaningless. They advised the English poor—and middle
class readers were told to think thusly about them—that moral worth
greatly overshadowed mere money: "Happy Cottage Children" were
models of piety and filial obedience despite their humbleness; "The
Orphan Boy" was poor but repentant and therefore rewarded; "The
Listener" was overjoyed to hear an old and poverty-stricken woman
die happily in Christ despite her social level; "Blind Mary" was af-
flicted but faithful. The list of titles, almost infinitely long, shows
that English didactic moralism designed to defend the status quo
against a possibly restless poor took as much space in the *Companion* as it had in *Parley's*. Although its presence was in good part
the result of economics (without an international copyright law it
was far cheaper for Willis to steal from English publications than
to pay American authors), it was also the result of an outlook shared
by many American spokesmen. It is not by accident that this growing
chant of placation was paralleled by a growing demand for moral
reform, both spurred by fear. Yet unlike the English, the Americans
faced a dilemma generated by their highly defensive patriotism: if
virtue went materially unrewarded and there were no evil social
institutions to blame, where then did the fault lie? Perhaps youth
wasn't trying hard enough—or in the right direction.

As the Civil War approached, proper effort and direction were
indicated in the increasing number of articles that presented the "get
rich" idea. Generally, the arena of this effort was business enterprise,
and although the virtues extolled are familiar, the titles of the articles
change from "Advice to Apprentices," "Honesty the Best Policy,"
and "Industry and Idleness," to the more explicit and material, "How
to Get a Farm," "How to Make Money," and "How to be Rich."
The beginning of this celebration of opulent materialism is around
1844, with a noticeable increase coming in 1848 and after. California

gold, which stimulated business, apparently also stimulated interest in business pursuits; additional interest was probably related to the stories reflecting the increasing movements of population to the cities. Whatever the cause, wealth rather than virtue began to motivate the self-help advice of the mid-century *Companion,* and this wealth was not always, as the changing titles indicate, the traditional competence. In democratic America, this wealth was supposed to be available to all; it was not a matter of special talent or luck or birth:

> The great difference in regard to accumulation, causes many to suppose that there is some mysterious faculty of acquiring property with which a few are particularly endowed. . . .
>
> The increase of property is not primarily the work of man. It comes from those laws of Providence, by which the natural bush becomes a great tree, if its natural growth is not intercepted. . . . In the great current of human business, [money] will increase if it is not misapplied.
>
> We seldom find persons . . . suffering poverty, who have not in some way squandered enough to render them comfortable and prosperous. It was not their misfortune nor their want of faculty, so much as a want of compliance with these great laws of Providence which are written on the face of creation, and upon the whole history of the world.
>
> Some of the best financial lessons . . . published are to be found in the Bible: and if it were consulted more, there would be less distressing poverty, and more grateful competence, and cheerful contentment.[15]

This mixture of romantic organicism and laissez-faire is heavy stuff for youth, but apparently Willis felt that the subject and its treatment should be shouldered by his readers. For us, the implications are clear: the present order is best because it is in accord with the immutable natural order; economic failure is the result of personal shortcomings (despite the assertion that profit is not the work of man); the god-given laws governing the universe can be understood by any man through the study of revelation; and—most importantly—the reward for obedience to divinely sanctioned virtues is not morality but money. Even articles of a more traditional aim reflect the mid-century drift toward materialism. The Morality column of April 27, 1848, describes "How to Get a Living":

Industry should be expended in seeing to all the details of business. . . . Be economical. . . . Stick to your own business. —Let speculators make their thousands in a year or a day; mind your own regular trade. . . . Let your business be one which is useful to the community. All occupations possess the elements of profit in themselves, while mere speculation has no such elements. Never trade at great hazard. . . . Don't be in a hurry to get rich. . . . Never do business for the sake of doing it and being counted a great merchant. . . . That business will be most respectable which is most successful. Do not get deeply in debt. . . . Do not love money extravagently. . . .

The advice is straight from William Perkins, but the nineteenth-century goal is far more material; instead of the love of money being the sin of avarice or idolatry, the warnings now are primarily prudential: "The extravagant desire of accumulation, induces an eagerness, many times, which is imprudent, and so misses its object from too much haste to grasp it." By 1848, the other-worldly wages of religious sin have been wholly replaced by the this-worldly wages of economic sin.

A major facet of the spokesmen's increasing materialism is a shift in the praise of the self-made man from one whose strong virtue is the result of his pursuit of a competence, to one whose ability to compete depended upon the exercise of his muscles or his cunning in the world of business. The term "self-made man" may be of American origin—the earliest use of it I could find was in the 1827 volume of the *Companion* in an article entitled "A Self Made Man" by one "Professor Newman." Its application as a title implies its earlier existence as a popular phrase. What is important, however, is the use of the term to describe an epitome of traditional success, Roger Sherman. Sherman is pictured as an ex-yeoman mechanic, who, when his competence had been attained, retired to serve his fellow men in Congress. Only five years after this use of the phrase, Henry Clay applied it to a group of rich manufacturers whose success was less the virtuous manner of accumulating and using wealth, and more the mere fact of amassing—and continuing to amass—riches.[16]

Heretofore, business life was often distrusted on the grounds of its moral dangers; however, by the mid-forties, the business life was praised, and sharing that praise was the idea of competition, "You must throw a man upon his own resources to bring him out. The struggle which is to result in eminence is too arduous, and must be continued too long, to be encountered and maintained voluntarily, or unless as a matter of life and death. He who has a fortune to fall back upon will soon slacken in his efforts, and finally retire from the competition."[17] Inherited wealth was now condemned because it endangered not the moral sense but the competitive drive. Man's need to survive independently was compared with that of other animals, "By a universal law of nature, the young of all animals are thrust forth from the parental nest. . . . You are now called upon to assert your faculties in the noble object of self-dependence."[18] Nature as much as God (were the two separate any longer?) said that individual man must struggle, and this natural struggle was seen as bringing out his innate abilities; parents were warned, "If you wish your children to be industrious, independent, self-relying and happy, they must be taught to depend upon their own exertions."[19] Though the idea of biological evolution was still lacking, the ground was well prepared for the acceptance of Darwinism; and, anticipating William Graham Sumner, the new competitive materialism assured mid-century readers that America would not suffer from either an aristocracy of inherited wealth nor an ever-repressed poor, that the heir to riches was sure to fail from lack of exercise, while the lad who buckled down and showed true grit was bound to rise—any lad could do it, provided he was only put to the test. One is reminded less of Franklin and more of Horatio Alger or Teddy Roosevelt.

In the *Companion* of the 1850s, income and independence were still integral elements of the idea of success; but the income tended to be defined as riches rather than as a competence, and the old idea of retiring to practice benevolence almost completely disappeared. With this turning from the traditional content of success, the romanticized picture of the truly happy man was overshadowed by the idea of success as competitively won riches. Yet preachments to moral behavior did not die out, nor were they restricted to placating the hopelessly poor. Rather, the behavioral element of the yeoman dream merged with the reform impulse, and this merger is readily sampled in the *Youth's Companion*.

Being on one level a reemphasis of the moral aspect of traditional success in reaction to the growing doctrine of competitive materialism, the reform movements of the 1830s and 1840s also reflected the changing political and economic beliefs of the spokesmen of traditional success; on one hand, reform was to lead the nation back to the yeoman virtues, while on the other hand, it was to guarantee continuing leadership in a rapidly changing society by the spokesmen's class. The leaders of the reform movements which marched through the pages of the *Companion* most often represented an economic and social level higher than Willis's own and more in line with Mrs. Child and Goodrich, but I suspect their followers were dedicated not so much to the leaders themselves as to the way of life they represented. To many of the rank and file, the pursuit of wealth no longer seemed as morally safe as it had been in the time of their fathers: the power of the evil rich seemed to be increasing, the yeoman mechanic was becoming a forlorn hope, and the free market system in the city and nation was threatened by monopoly and the speculator. Perhaps worst of all was the threat to traditional morality seen in the growing celebration of competition and business endeavor. Something was terribly wrong and the American spirit had to be reclaimed by re-establishing true success as the American's proper goal; however, there was an uneven division between those reformers who advocated coercion of the morally fallen and those who tried to assimilate them into the realm of the morally acceptable. Roughly, the distinction was according to economic status, with the more elevated advocating coercion under their hegemony, while the less exalted preached assimilative reform in a return to the yeoman society. The leaders of the major national reform organizations were generally Whig, orthodox, and associated primarily with mercantile wealth,[20] but not all reformers were rich merchants, not all were orthodox ministers. Much of the work was done by co-believers whose names were only whispered in history, and it is doubtful that the organized movements would have been as powerful had there not been popular predisposition in their favor. The source of much of that popularity was the widespread feeling among all classes that traditional success was being destroyed.

☼

Two major reforms of the period, anti-slavery and the more radical abolition, had to overcome a great deal of early unpopularity and distrust. Willis, for example, as late as 1857, replied to a reader's query about William Lloyd Garrison, "I dislike controversy, and sectarianism, and Garrisonism, and Mormonism, and all other isms that are inconsistent with the Gospel of our blessed savior. . . ." In addition, both crusades were often unpopular among spokesmen who advocated other moral reforms. An example of early and unpopular abolitionist argument can be found in Mrs. Child's *An Appeal in Favor of . . . Africans.* In this 1833 discussion of "our duties," she pointed out that Negroes shared the universal human desire to be respectably human, but that the institution of slavery prevented the consummation of this wish, "There is among the colored people an increasing desire for information, and a laudable ambition to be respectable in manners and appearance. Are we not foolish as well as sinful, in trying to repress a tendency so salutary to themselves, and so beneficial to the community?"[21]

In this *Appeal,* she devoted little space to the uneconomic aspects of slavery, for the main attack was against the sinfulness of the institution. It is not surprising that her attack should have met with little support; even the American Anti-Slavery Society in that same year urged education of the Negro rather than abolition of the institution, since ignorance "enslaves the mind and leads to the ruin of the immortal soul."[22] Later, during the 1840s, the abolition cause broadened its membership in good part by changing to a more popular appeal. Whereas slavery had been previously depicted as illegal or immoral or cruel—and somewhat removed in its direct effects on the reader— support was now found by portraying slavery as an immediate threat to traditional success; attacking the institution of slavery was a way of attacking one of the forces eroding the yeoman dream. In the 1850s, Mrs. Child greatly expanded her earlier economic argument against slavery in terms of yeoman imagery. In *The Right Way the Safe Way,* a detailed analysis of slavery designed to present a "business-view" of the subject, the major theme is that the institution violates all that is moral and profitable in traditional success: "[Slavery] takes away the motive power from the laborers, who [therefore] naturally desire to shirk. . . . It makes them indifferent to the destruction of property. . . . It stimulates them to theft. . . . It kills their ingenuity and enterprise." And the moral effects on the whites were just as pernicious as the effects of inherited wealth, "[Slavery] renders labor a degradation, and consequently, it is a matter of pride with them to live in idleness. Extravagance and dissipation follow of course. . . . Intemperance, licentiousness and gambling, are fearfully prevalent in slave-holding countries."

Importantly, the danger threatened to extinguish the island's yeoman society; citing the *Edinburgh Review,* she tells her audience, "Plainly, the artificial, arbitrary interference of law with the freedom

of man, and freedom of trade, was bringing about the extinction of
the working-class, and was whirling their [West Indian] masters
along to utter ruin."[23] Her argument stresses slavery's violation of
those divinely ordained natural laws upon which traditional success
and its related goodly society were based. The punishment is moral
corruption and economic slavery for both blacks and whites, and the
reward for abolition is a harmonious yeoman society. Her description
of the West Indies after liberation makes them into another New
England: "The spirit of enterprise . . . had been roused since emancipation," with a resultant growth of "the middle classes" as well as of
individual and public prosperity. Most important was the moral regeneration which resulted in a return of the yeoman virtues to the
whites and a respect for law and a stable society among the blacks.
Mrs. Child, while she had not changed her stand on slavery, had
changed the emphasis of her appeal; and she found herself lionized
where once, because of her abolitionist views, the *Juvenile Miscellany*
had failed. A similar change in approach is seen in the verbal warfare
in Congress over slavery. Although prior to 1840, "radical" abolitionists and "rabid" Southerners debated heatedly, it was only a glow
until John Quincy Adams fanned it into a flame with his defense of
the right of petition. Northerners previously indifferent to slavery
were brought to the realization that the peculiar institution was a
threat to their own freedom[24]: the chains of slavery extended as far
north as the Canadian border. This realization was intensified with
the passing of the new Fugitive Slave Act of 1850, which brought
home to Thoreau and other New Englanders the knowledge that
America's yeomanly independence was under attack from the South.
Since the Northerner was being led to believe that the yeoman dream
could not exist in a nation where there was slavery, one major defense
by Southern writers was to deny that the possibility for yeomanry
still existed in the North—to depict Northern cities and factories as
populated by "wage slaves" while at the same time celebrating the
Southern life as the only one where the true agrarian yeoman could
survive.

Reflecting the period's arguments, the *Companion* treated anti-
slavery sentiment in four stages: 1827–33, 1833–40, 1840–60, 1860–65.
In the first issues of the magazine, a series of tales revealed that "even
Negroes" could find Christ: a nine-year-old British lad who tried to
pray with all the earnestness of a young slave he read about; "The
Pious Negro" who when dying said, "Me see Jesus in heaven holding

out his hand to poor Negro man . . ."; "Little William and the Sweep" urged "I hope People are now growing wiser than to frighten children, by telling them foolish stories about black people. . . ." One impetus for this concern with the religious equality of the races was, of course, the British abolitionist movement which culminated in emancipation throughout the Dominion in 1834. It is probable that the British abolition movement and stories like these influenced the generation of Americans who in the next decade led their own anti-slavery movement outside the more cautious approaches of their elders. But although these stories are implicitly anti-slavery, there is no agitation for the destruction of the institution. Rather, the Negro is pictured as a human being with a soul, one who achieves moral success despite his degraded physical condition. As examples of the power of Christ and as stimulants to the behavior of the whites, these virtuous blacks, like the white poor, could be successful in the moral realm though they were failures in the material. Thus both the idea of success and the stability of the social structure—including slavery— were preached at the same time. The second stage of anti-slavery feeling in the *Companion* was a brief spate of open condemnation, perhaps generated by the founding of the American Anti-Slavery Society in 1833. One of Willis's open letters to a contributor during that year states that the treatment of slavery had to be "suitable" for the magazine, and apparently this did not exclude tirades against whippings and enforced prostitution, for such was the content of "First Impressions of Slavery" published in March, 1834. What was not suitable is indicated by the article's silence on how to remedy slavery. The outspoken criticism was short-lived; the third stage was one of silence on the subject. Maybe militant abolitionism violated the magazine's new motto, "No Controversy," maybe Willis did not like the rising group of political and radical anti-slavery leaders, maybe the example of the *Juvenile Miscellany's* failure a year or two earlier convinced him that silence was indeed golden. In any case, after 1840, discussions of slavery were replaced by letters to the editor stressing the mutual love between the North and South. The one type of Negro still worthy of charity and pity was not a slave but the free chimney sweep, probably singled out because of his urban occupation and because of the current English middle-class reform movement urging a government clean-up of the sweeper's trade. At any rate, Willis was unwilling to fall in behind either the less militant anti-slavery movement or the abolitionists who were determined to get something done.

He waited until violation of the established social structure could be called for on familiar moral grounds—that is, when abolition could be described as a defense of the traditional social system rather than as a dangerous new threat to social stability. Like all modern wars, his war found its justification in the plea of self-defense, and during the Civil War the magazine's silence—like its motto—was broken. Abolition sentiment was patriotic now, slavery was a threat to "the American Way," freedmen and "contrabands" were depicted sympathetically, and old Deacon Willis himself came out of retirement to bitterly denounce the South for causing the war. "Our boys" and "our flag" were celebrated with a fervor not seen again until "the American Way" was threatened by Central European immigrants later in the century, when once again the *Youth's Companion* would fight back by inaugurating the now-familiar Pledge of Allegiance.

The rhetoric of the *Companion's* belated attack on slavery drew on the imagery of the yeoman dream to portray the evils of that institution. Slavery corrupted the human spirit through denying one of the fundamental elements of success—the independence which was both a moral alembic as well as a reward; a slave, for instance, could not be blamed for stealing (although he could be punished), because the institution had deprived its victims of the proper means of developing a sense of right and wrong:

> Nothing can be more demoralizing than the system of slavery to all who are so unfortunate as to be born and bred its victims. The great wonder is, that of the hundreds now fleeing from slavery every week at the South, there are so few who commit crime.

And:

> It is not expected that the slaves in the South can have a very high standard of morality. They have been wronged all their lives, their rights in themselves and the profits of their own labor stolen from them by the rebels, and now if in their turn they steal from their former masters it is but the fruit of the education they have received.[25]

Even slaves fortunate enough to be house servants were corrupted by the institution: "These children are treated well in some respects. Their bodies are fed and clothed comfortably, but the food for the mind, which you, my young friends, need and love so much, they do

not have."[26] Though a Negro may have a naturally endowed crafti-
ness, a proper education was necessary to overcome the effects of
slavery once the man was freed. A dialogue with an alert twelve-
year-old cabin boy on a river steamer ends, "Although these fugitives
do not know how to read, and of course are very ignorant, yet they
evidently understand human nature, and many of them read character
with remarkable shrewdness. . . . A good Sabbath-school gentleman
from Boston, said he wished he were in circumstances to take the
boy with him—he would make something of him. And if properly
educated, he will make something."[27] The reward of "A Young
Contraband" who made his way North was "working for fair wages
on a farm on Long Island;"[28] he was as close to the yeoman dream
as possible.

Despite the romantic belief in man's innate goodness, the influence of environment was still felt to be a major factor in the development of the person; consequently, even a naturally good ex-slave
needed the aid of traditional morality and worthy institutions if he were
to develop an acceptable character. Slavery, a threat because it corrupted the character and challenged the moral society, became a just
reason for war because it destroyed all the yeoman virtues. Fortunately, in the spokesmen's eyes, the freedman posed no threat to their
own society, being either at the bottom of the social and economic
scale or in another caste system. And, the spokesmen thought, experience had shown that those Negroes who did gain material prosperity were those who subscribed to the traditional virtues and who
thus supported the established society.

Significantly, those Northerners who continued to object to
militant abolition even after the beginning of hostilities were, in
actuality, (if not in wish) already denied the possibility of yeomanry.
Often new immigrants, afraid of competition from "two million
freedmen" for their low-paying labor, attacked the shops and stores
of notable abolitionists. Like the spokesmen, they assumed that the
ex-slave would be capable of competing for success in the open labor
market, particularly as strong-arms, dockworkers, servants, or factory
hands; thus they viewed the freedman with the same eyes as did the
abolitionists who thought that simple manumission was equal to freedom of opportunity.

Temperance was a second major reform given much support
by the *Companion*, and it, too, reveals the defensive use of the yeoman dream. In the late eighteenth century, temperance reform was

used against the irreligion and vice of the post-war period; and soon it became a weapon of the politically weak Federalist party. With the decline of that group, the movement slackened but then became resurgent in the nineteenth century as a means of purifying the uncouth frontier farmer or the propertyless but newly enfranchised rowdy of the eastern cities. The American Society for the Promotion of Temperance, also known as the American Temperance Society, was formed in 1826; its founders were leading ministers and wealthy New Englanders who approved of the temperance crusade's Federalist ancestry, and who readily admitted that their purpose was to make the nation safe by creating a moral climate that supported their political goals. But the movement did not long remain in the hands of these leaders. It became teetotal (much to the disgust of some of the founders) and less socially established participants used the idea not for its political aim but as a form of self-help and as a badge of business reliability.[29] Gradually, the temperance appeal, like many reform movements, transcended political lines as it grew in popularity. When the American Temperance Society had been founded, for example, Methodists in Western Massachusetts who were ardent Jacksonians warned their members against supporting this Whig-dominated organization. However, in 1838, the Massachusetts Temperance Union offered a new appeal that was more evangelical and teetotal than political and it gained the Methodists' support. At the same time, this new appeal was "deemed too radical by some of the old temperance workers and they stood aloof from it." One would expect the leadership of the MTU to have reflected the new members' fundamentalist beliefs and their less socially elevated position, but such was not the case; the officers were still drawn from the ranks of the well-established, though both Whigs and Democrats now participated. President John Tappan, the first secretary of the old Massachusetts Society for the Suppression of Intemperance, was a successful merchant who had also served a term as president of the American Tract Society, an organization receiving wide Methodist support. Other officers included John Reed (Whig congressman), Ebenezer Alden (medical historian), George N. Briggs (a self-made man who was a Democrat turned Whig; governor of Massachusetts), Henry Edwards (Democrat, governor in 1833), Walter Channing (Unitarian minister), Thomas Whittemore (Universalist minister and Federalist), and Harrison Gray (politician, also a Federalist).[30] Thus, leadership was based on social rather than political criteria, and the evangelical methods reflected not so much the attitudes of the officers and leaders, as of what those leaders thought their followers wanted.

To protect the status quo, radicalism in the defense of virtue was no vice: the Union was interested in both persuasive and compulsory reform. One method was the establishment of the Cold Water Army, a martial group of infant teetotalers which demonstrated the theory that early inculcation of youth would result in sober adults, and great was the rejoicing when a four-year-old would sign the pledge. Willis's magazine carried numerous accounts of Army activities, often noting with evangelical pride that many of the observers and even a few of the participants were Irish. The Union also sponsored the "Fifteen Gallon Law" (1836) which prohibited the sale of liquor in less than fifteen-gallon quantities, a move designed to strangle the low-income, penny-a-shot drinker, while leaving unscathed the more wealthy and virtuous imbiber who would be neither economically nor morally endangered by a bulk purchase. Though this particular law was quickly repealed—it was not only unpopular but unworkable—Union members George Briggs and Ashahel Huntington were later in the forefront of the "monster petition rally" of 1852 which pleaded for the prohibitionary "Maine Law." It may be remembered that Goodrich wrote with pride of having voted for the Fifteen Gallon Law while a Whig representative, and he implied that the repeal of the law was due to representatives listening to their constituents rather than to their consciences. But the quick repeal of the law indicates that the coercive-minded temperance workers were at this time a minority; and, in fact, the most popular temperance drives of the period were indeed assimilative rather than coercive. In the *Companion*, an easy link was forged between poverty and intemperance on the grounds that drunkenness prevented the exercise of the traditional virtues; whereas the poor man whose failure was not morally explicable could be offered only heavenly reward, the drunkard's reason for failure was obvious and in order for him to be reclaimed, he had only to exorcise the evil habit. Given the spokesmen's dedication to support the existing society and thus offer no real analysis of the Industrial Revolution's effect on traditional success, a certain irony emerges: the drunkard had a greater hope of assimilation into the patterns of traditional success than had the moral poor.

Assimilative temperance had two main themes: the first, springing from the less established members, was a self-help movement; the second, more closely related to the established members, viewed the righteous as helping to uplift the unrighteous through example and sentiment. Both saw the drunkard as the major threat to the yeoman dream, and both saw reclamation as having first individual and then social benefits. Neither conceived of drunkenness or the loss of traditional success as a result generated by causes psychological or economic, and one of the more famous alcoholics of the era, Edgar Allen Poe, held a decidedly unpopular opinion when he argued that drunkenness was an effect and not a cause. One of the earliest self-help groups, the "Washingtonians," who were organized in 1840, began as a group of Baltimore mechanics interested in reforming themselves and friends like them. Reclamation, not coercive prevention, was their program, and their activities generally took place outside the realm of the more "respectable" temperance groups. President and founder of this impromptu society was William K. Mitchell, a tailor, and other charter members included J. F. Hoss, a carpenter; David Anderson and George Steers, blacksmiths; James McCarley, a coachmaker; and Archibald Campbell, a silversmith.[31] Their names imply British background, though apparently none were immigrants, and all enjoyed the image if not the fact of yeomanry. But somehow, somewhere, their yeoman status seemed to be slipping away and with it went their independence, their competence, their moral standing in the community. For them the cause was immediate: demon rum. Aiming to recapture true success by moral reclamation of the individual, they were not interested in political leadership in society nor did they march forth to convert the unvirtuous perforce; rather, they invited friends and acquaintances to their meetings and exercized moral persuasion and example. Those who tried self-help reform did so in the belief that true success was still possible for virtuous men no matter what their occupation, and that the failure to attain the yeoman goal was not the fault of society but of personal shortcomings that could be remedied. Unlike the Massachusetts Temperance Union, they were not defending the hegemony of a particular group, but seeking a means of recapturing the lost yeoman dream. To make the gatherings more interesting, each member told of his battles with the bottle, of the moral and economic degradation resulting from drunkenness, and of the rehabilitation possible with sobriety. Their most notable confessor was one John H. W. Hawkins, who, according to his biography, early formed a taste for liquor because he was apprenticed to a hatter. The story of his reform sounds like one of the many temperance novels, but it was apparently true: the tender care of his wife, after he had been carried home drunk, "pierced his heart with compunction and soon he signed the pledge."[32] It was this sort of temperance movement, rather than that led by the coercive-minded agencies, which caught on among the people, Whig and Jacksonian, old light and new. With the power of lay leaders growing in local and national temperance organizations, the established members of the older groups became divided along the lines of types of reform and leadership: to many, it seemed dangerous to entrust such an important crusade to unknown, lower class leaders whose appeal was to the heart of the drunkard instead of to the laws of the land. One coercive member lamented that the evangelical effect of the Washingtonians on the Massachusetts Temperance Union was shattering, causing "revulsion in public opinion which deranged the operations of the Union and divided our forces into squads, cliques."[33] However, when a Washingtonian chapter was finally established in Massachusetts, familiar names lent their dignity: Walter Channing was president, while lesser officers included the highly respectable Charles Wade and Joshua Buffum. The established members were not to be left out, nor apparently, did the electors want them to be, since their joining was a symbol of coveted respectability—and regaining society's respect was one of the basic goals of the Washingtonian movement.

The self-help movement was in part an effort by mechanics whose yeoman dream was threatened by changing economic patterns, but genteel spokesmen also urged reclamation and expanded self-help in the business realm. Because any economic failure and loss of prestige could be blamed on the bottle, both could be regained through abstinence; such was the message of many of T. S. Arthur's stories in the *Companion*, and of the many confessors who stood before Washingtonian gatherings. In an attempt to bring back the lost into the fold, women formed "Martha Washington" societies to help the men, and members in high social standing gave their support to such organizations. The fundamental appeal was to the drunkard's sense of moral responsibility, for that was the kind of failing he suffered; but there was also the promise of wealth enough for a competence if the drunkard would reform. Poverty was a certain punishment if he did not. Thus, the moral and economic aspects of traditional success were united in this broadly-based movement. Despite the uneasiness of some of the displaced conservative temperance leaders, they had little to fear from this assimilative reform, for by its appeal, assimilation would reclaim only those worthy of being saved, while the irretriev-able, being morally deformed, would stay in the gutters.

In the *Companion*, temperance reform passed through two stages that reflected first the coercive approach and then the assimi-lative. In the first stage, the drunkard was often an object lesson for the child, a man who deserved not pity but aversion because his situa-tion was punishment for moral turpitude or poor upbringing (which were often thought of as identical). The first temperance narrative in volume 1 is about a fat and friendly lad, William, who died from dissipation and caused the subsequent deaths of his aged mother and grief-stricken girl-friend. Pity is elicited for the family rather than for the drunkard, since his failure was the sign of an inner flaw as surely as was his oversized neck, which "imparted something pecu-liar" about him. The flaw was that he was an exceedingly jolly chap, and apparently his thick neck had resulted from over-exercize in swallowing. William is an example of the results of moral failure for which alcoholism is just punishment. That such character defects should be prevented by strict laws or moral upbringing is the point of one of Willis's own stories. Henry, a youthful frequenter at the den of that wily confectioner, Mr. Shambro (a most non-Saxon name), spent all his allowance on sensual delights. Unbeknownst to Henry, the crafty candy-maker spiced his sweets with rum, and, because his parents had been too indulgent, Henry lacked the will either to break his evil habit or to confess his wickedness to his parents. The inevitable happened, "He [now] is scarcely nineteen years of age; but his face is red; his hands tremble; he is commonly sick and wretched one half the day and riotous or drunken the other half. . . ."[34] Justly punished for the sin of a weak character, cast beyond morality into hopeless damnation, Henry is a warning to Willis's readers of the dangers of any moral weakness—that the final fall begins with a slight stumble. Drinking, like gambling, seduction, murder, or tobacco chewing, was both sign and punishment; eco-nomic and social failure were certain to follow the slightest moral weakness, and all were permanent here and hereafter. A minor point to notice about Henry's sad tale is the demand for total abstinence a decade before the Massachusetts Temperance Union made it a formal code. This reflects Willis's evangelism, and the "horrible example" motif is closely related to the hell-fire-and-damnation tradition of Brimstone Corner. Total abstinence, emotionalism, and fundamental-ism were long interrelated by the non-elite members of the movement.

One reason for advocating total abstinence was the belief that small immoralities would lead to larger ones, but from a cultural point of view the real importance lies in the strictness of the morality and the harshness of punishment which indicate Willis's awareness of the seemingly thin division between moral and immoral mechanics—a distinction which was personal rather than public, one of closely observed behavior rather than one of readily seen income or status. Since the principal distinction was behavioral, its rigidity gave needed emphasis.

In the mid-1830s, the *Companion* showed the influence of a changing attitude toward drunkards. Their failing was still moral, but now they were seen as objects of pity and hope rather than of scorn and damnation. "A Visit to S—— Lane" desribes a Boston hovel where the parents had just returned from the House of Correction to which they had been sent as "common drunkards." Because their vow of abstinence showed a spark of morality, the narrator visited them; unfortunately, on a subsequent visit he found the spark drowned. Not another word is wasted on them, though as a parting admonition the children are urged to go to Sunday School.[35] Numerous other tales depict appeals to the drunkard's better instincts by his wife or child (preferably a little daughter), and repentance always brings the reform which results in rewards of income, respect, and independence. By 1843, pity far outweighed scorn for drunkards, and young readers were urged, "Don't Throw [rocks] at Drunkards. . . . The drunkard is an object of the deepest sympathy. Show him kindness, and you can reclaim him."[36] Even more sympathetic is Mrs. Stowe's "Somebody's Father." The story need not be suffered through, but one scene is striking evidence of the widespread equation of a position among the earthly moral with a position in heaven; the coach passengers, who have been scornful of the pedestrian drunkard, are given a mild reproof which makes them view the staggering man "more as Christians should look on the fallen creature they were leaving behind."[37] Whether scornful and coercive or pitying and assimilative, the *Companion's* attitude toward drunkards was often expressed in the mythology of an upwardly striving group which, although feeling threatened, still clung to the idea of true success. Perhaps all the diffuse and ambient fears of the city, factory, sectionalism, foreign immigration, unions, freedmen and plague were objectified in whiskey; the failure anticipated for scorned drunkards was banishment to a traditional hell of poverty, dependence, and immorality; while the formula of the reclaimed drunkard was a litany of sin, repentance and redemption into yeoman heaven. Noting that the epitome of natural nobility, divine blessing, and self-elevation—the American yeoman— seemed by the 1840s to be fast disappearing under a landslide of ill-defined change, the *Companion* shared the belief that his disappearance was caused by a widespread weakness for whiskey. Reclamation rather than coercion became a better way to save American society; if a man only willed himself to obey the pledge, he would find that true success still existed.

The shift from coercion or ostracism toward benevolent reclamation as a means of defending the yeoman dream can be seen in other areas of reform as well. The "fallen maid," for example, began to be pictured assimilatively rather than coercively, and this change of attitude surprisingly preceded a similar change in the American theatre by some two decades. The first seduction story in the *Companion*, appropriately entitled "The Seduced" (1831), was borrowed from the *Female Advocate* and depicted the victim as doing the only honorable and genteel thing: withering away from shame. Apparently the readers did not object to their children knowing the facts of life, for the following year saw another girl seduced by an "arch young lawyer" and this sinner quite properly died of melancholy and consumption while the lawyer escaped punishment. By 1836, however, sympathy began to be expressed for the victim of the libertine; "An Unfaithful Husband" describes a New York lawyer who became enamoured of a thirteen-year-old milliner girl and "in an unguarded hour, he accomplished her ruin" (one is continually awed by the single-mindedness of nineteenth-century lawyers). After his youthful mistress had given birth to a daughter, he abandoned her "destitute and penniless, herself and child without funds, in a house of ill-fame." However, anticipating part of the shock of William Gilmore Simms' novel *Beauchampe* (1842), the seduced maid is allowed revenge before dying: in a confrontation with the villain at his home, she lamented the now-dead child and her aged father, begged, "May God forgive the injuries I have received," and took poison while the lawyer's wife went gracefully mad. This seduced girl was shown as repentant of her sin by evincing love for the lost child and a sense of shame for her actions; the tone of the story indicates that she will be rewarded in heaven. About a decade later, one seduced maid was described not only sympathetically, but received gentle treatment from her employer and did not have to die—the reader was urged to forgive rather than to condemn.[38] Perhaps the new tone was captured best in Nathaniel P. Willis's very popular "Unseen Spirits" (1844), which ends:

> But the sin forgiven by Christ in heaven
> By man is cursed alway.

Sympathy for the seduced girl is, of course, part of the period's inclusive religious evangelism and sentimentality. But perhaps another reason lay behind this new attitude: many members of society became victims of circumstances beyond their control, yet to admit to a fatalistic attitude would negate traditional success. Failure was still considered to be individual and moral, but such social disasters as the depression of 1837 overwhelmed people who were honored and even loved; the wealthy and highly respected Arthur Tappan, for instance, went bankrupt in the early forties through no apparent fault of his own. The result was that the blame for failure was less focussed, the weight of censure was less absolute; a second chance could be offered to drunkards and ruined girls whose individual weakness or ignorance came into fatal conjunction with some vaguely understood fault of society. The increasing literary sentimentality of mid-century contributed to sympathy for the fallen, and stressed reclamation through a better environment and a strengthened will rather than ostracism from a heretofore infallible society. With a lessening of censure for the girls' moral failure came a lessening of reliance upon their inner strength alone. Accompanying the gradual increase of emphasis upon competition and the benefits of apprenticeship for boys, was an increasing reliance upon institutional aids to morality for girls caught in a harshly struggling society. Not that one's own moral strength wasn't still the main line of defense; the *Companion* under both Willis and Ford stressed that the city's temptation was felt most by the morally weak, and willfully listening to flattery was a girl's first step to death in a brothel. But in addition to having inner strength, the girl should locate herself in a moral environment by seeking upright employment and living snugly with a relative or at a family-approved domicile. Naivete as well as unsteady morals could cause harm in a city filled with lawyers, and for maximum safety a proper environment and good acquaintances were almost as important as individual integrity. After cautioning against moral weakness, Ford recommends a trustworthy employment service with an appropriately symbolic name: the Female Moral Reform Society, which also offered a boarding house that was "safe."[39]

The urban migration forced recognition of the fact that the children of country yeomen were flocking to the cities to seek their fortunes, and that these young people were subject to dangers against which the traditional virtues now seemed only partially victorious. The inevitable tragedies, the code of sentimental benevolence, and the desire for an emphatic restatement of true success, all resulted in a sympathetic view of those who, though fallen, were still reclaimable.

Unfortunately for many Americans connected with the urban or industrial world, traditional success was an increasingly ill fit, and factory operatives especially were seen more and more as heirs to the Southern slave's place. The English, having greater experience with factory conditions, strongly influenced American ideas about these "lower orders," and many American spokesmen who at first thought that bad factory conditions were endemic only to a morally corrupt Europe soon accepted a division between operatives and yeomen in America. Nevertheless, the operatives themselves clung tenaciously to the dream of true success, for those who gave it up were thrust into a station defined even by their peers in terms of pity or contempt. The mechanic magazines to be discussed in the next chapter display the operatives' attempts to retain the yeoman dream; the *Companion*, even with its voices ranging from mechanic to business and cultural leaders, reveals the gradual denial of traditional success for the operative. In its early appearance, as seen in the matter-of-fact tone of obituaries, factory life bore no pejorative connotation for either adults or children. William Gordon, a twelve-year-old cotton factory employee, "On Friday preceding . . . was caught by the machinery and carried with it until his arm was several times broken and nearly drawn from his body, and was otherwise dreadfully mangled. After suffering excruciating pain until early next morning, his willing spirit took leave of its poor mangled tenement." The author praises the lad for his belief in Christ during his last moments, "although able to say but little," and then asks if the reader's sympathies are stirred. If so, "Weep rather for yourselves than for this child, or that exemplary mother who has repeatedly met similar bereavements in a manner which bespeaks her confidence in the wisdom and goodness of her heavenly father."[40] Neither child labor nor factory conditions were condemned; William and his mother are pictured as poor but morally qualified members of approved society. Wheras slavery gave Ne-

groes an opportunity to show their faith—and their position outside
the yeoman dream—by the misfortune of their lives, the operative's
opportunity to show faith was in the manner not of his existence, but
of his death. The implication is clear: the operative's life was not seen
as a burden to him because his occupation—if morally pursued—did
not place him beyond the pale of proper society. Youths associated
with all mechanical pursuits were usually pictured as potential yeoman and were urged to follow the traditional virtues which would
lead to traditional success. Part of the virtuous behavior was to be
faithful to their master and not gossip about his household, an indication that the breakdown of personal relationships between master
and worker had not yet become overwhelmingly apparent. Young
mechanics were told that all labor was a blessing, not a curse, and
that spare time should not be thrown away on novels and romances
but spent on self-improvement. Self-education was a means of material self-elevation for every youngster regardless of occupation or
aim, and it would lead to yeoman success: an independent shop owner
whose honest labor offered a competence to the individual and added
virtue to the society. The ideal most often held up was, inevitably,
Benjamin Franklin, " 'O, you're a 'prentice,' said a stripling . . .
tauntingly to his companion. The addressed turned proudly round,
and while the fire of injured pride and the look of pity was strangely
blended in his countenance, coolly answered, 'So was Franklin.' "[41]
Franklin had moved on to higher things, as, seemingly, all apprentices should be able to despite technological changes in their trade.

By 1840, however, the term "factory boy" made its appearance in the *Companion* as a species clearly distinct from the idea of
apprenticeship, and this type was not greeted with such equanimity
as in the early obituary. For example, Alfred Stitson's "The Factory
Boy" tells how even a child from this environment could be converted
to Christianity through the offices of the American Sunday School
Union; it was the lad's overcoming the hardship of life rather than
death which made him, like the slave, an epitome of Christian resig-
nation and faith. A poem by "G." of New York City moistly laments
the fate of the "Little Factory Girl":

> I dream about the factory,
> The fines that on us wait;
> I start and ask my father,
> If I have not lain too late.

And once I heard my father say,
'Oh, better were a grave,
Than such a life as this for *thee*,
Thou little sinless slave!'

    . . . .

There was a man he looked at me,
With cold and cruel gaze.
He bade me go and do it o'er,
The task I just had done,
The wicked look he looked at me,
I tried but could not shun. . . .[42]

The effect is less poetry than propaganda, but it has meaningful ramifications: the protagonist is no longer in the garden where all is fair
and bright and free, but is trapped in a dark prison not of her own
making where independence is lost and poverty is at hand. Note, too,
that the kind of labor, equated with slavery, stimulates a longing for
escape rather than increased industry. Such work is unwarranted
punishment for a "sinless slave" whose loss of independence and
whose morally perilous position completely denies the yeoman dream.
This poem is part of the general sentimental benevolence of the era
stimulated by, but scarcely rising to the quality of expression found
in Dickens or even Thomas Hood. Seeing themselves as the dominant
group pictured them, these literary factory children are resigned and
gentle victims of humanitarian pity but not of social upheaval. The
distance between the writers and their new subject is much greater
than that between little Willy and the author of his obituary, for
now—and despite their innocence—the factory girl or boy was already
a failure in the race for success.

The most abject of such protagonists, however, were English
factory children. Unlike America, England had too many institutional
encumbrances to support the American route to success:

It has been objected by Americans [about] these free schools of
England, that the children have few or no opportunities of changing their sphere of life. It is true, ambition is not planted in their
breasts, and their education . . . is not calculated to make them
otherwise than good domestics or excellent husbands and wives
in an humble station. Whether in the present state of society in

England, they would be happier if ambition were to come among them is hardly doubtful.[43]

America, and no other nation, was the land of yeoman opportunity for all men: "America is the most free, and independent, and happy nation on the face of the earth." In short, at the same time that sentiment for factory children was being expressed in poetry and fiction, the evils of the factory system for adults were seen as especially alien to America. As in Goodrich's view, as in the opinion of European travellers in America at this time, England crushed the factory operatives while America offered them the sanctuary of a garden wherein the yeoman spirit could flourish; not only were American factories often set in wholesome rural surroundings, but the frontier "safety valve" offered agrarian yeomanry to the crowded urban population. An English immigrant writes, "I miss the grand houses, and the broad parks; but O: its the children of the poor. . . . At play . . . flocking to the school houses . . . little hearts free from care, and plenty to eat and to drink . . . a time for rest . . . for play . . . to learn, is children's natural right."[44] The actual operation of the safety valve was, of course, quite different from what the spokesmen imagined since it served either those native Americans who, in the early stages of industrialization and urbanization, could return to neighboring farms when factory work slackened, or it offered ready opportunity only to entrepreneurs who moved west with enough money to get a start in business or farming. But in the minds of many contributors to the *Companion*, it was the impoverished worker himself who was given this geographical chance to maintain his dream of yeomanry, and his failure to do so was seen as the result of individual moral turpitude, "I could not help rejoicing that I lived in a country where the poor could by enterprise and industry, make themselves so comfortable and independent. How different would have been the fate of these people . . . had they lived in England, and been obliged to work in a factory."[45] After 1840, the safety valve often failed to relieve urban conditions, and there was a continuous country-to-city undertow in the westward tide. It is possible that by 1870, the agrarian yeoman figure had substantive appeal only for European immigrants and Southerners who were still land-oriented, while in the rapidly industrializing North and Old Northwest, the new "yeoman" was the competitive businessman. Indeed, even in the South, the Snopses were soon to take their stand.[46]

In the *Companion*, Lowell factories received special praise, generally borrowed from the pages of the *Lowell Offering*. One article begins, "Much has been said of the industry, intelligence and energy of the Lowell girls," and goes on to add that one lass gave to charity one-third of her year's savings of three hundred dollars—of which fifty quite properly went to that bastion of morality, the Home Missionary Society.[47] "Working girls," bubbles another author, "are happy girls! Who can but love them?—With cheeks like the rose—bright eyes and elastic step, how cheerfully they go to their work. Our reputation for it, such girls will make good wives. . . ."[48] The writer attributed the development of moral girls to the American factory environment and to steady employment. As the mid-decades passed, the *Companion* tended to continue seeing the ills of the industrial revolution as foreign to American adults; Willis wrote in a preface to *Thomas Hood's Song of the Shirt*, "The following very thrilling lines can hardly be appreciated in this country; but in England, where they were written, their forces may be more adequately felt. We have been requested several times to copy them . . . though some of our readers have doubtless seen them before."[49]

Willis nowhere mentions the Lowell strikes of 1834 or 1836, or the cordwainers', carpenters', weavers', and painters' protective unions which rose and fell in the 1830s, or the unrest of the Philadelphia and New York seamstresses after the depression of 1837. The patient sufferer was the only object worthy of Christian benevolence, and, at the same time, the doctrine of competition tended to make even the patient sufferer as un-American as the radical.

Paralleling the sentiment for the worthy poor is the *Companion's* occasional distrust of the radical workers' organizations. Labor agitators, beyond sympathy because of their attempts to change the social order, are pictured in an article which reflects three often mingled fears, of "associationists," of atheism, of foreigners: "Tammany Hall," young readers are told, has degenerated from its original purpose of defending yeomen against the "aristocratic" Cincinnati into a place where "Fanny Wright, and Owen, and others belonging to the same class of infidels, have labored to overthrow the religion of the Bible." There, the workers are "shabby" and addressed by "a deluded Polish lady in broken English." Fortunately, the ranks of the misguided workers are thinned by tract distributors whose efforts counter the influence of the agitators.[50] Ordinarily, however, labor problems do not ruffle the overtly serene pages of the *Companion*, for they are manifestations of other "isms" and are too often involved with the "mental poison" of party spirit. At the same time, business avenues to material success were increasingly stimulated by the industrial revolution, by California gold, by national expansion, and by generally vast opportunities for vast gain. Where less than half-a-dozen millionaires had been counted at the Civil War, by 1900 there were almost four thousand. As in *Parley's*, the success story in the *Companion* became more associated with business pursuits despite Willis's distress at speculation and his fear of the city. The traditional virtues were still supposed to insure that when a man did earn material success, he would also have attained moral success; but the truth of this formula was being viewed with increasing skepticism as it was realized that competition generated not magnanimity and benevolence, but savagery and self-interest. Consequently, during the mid-nineteenth century many stories began to detail a specific business morality based not on the exercise of traditional virtues but on illustrating the ethics of specific business practices. "The Strawberry Woman," by T. S. Arthur, presents two matrons discussing a point of business ethics. The first, taking advantage of her secure position in the market, had forced a woman to sell her produce for two cents less than the fair price:

> "The person who sold them to you [admonished the second matron] may not have made a profit enough upon them to pay for time and labor. If this were the case, she sold them . . . too cheap."
>
> "Suppose she paid too high for them? Is the purchaser to pay for her error?"
>
> ". . . I think it would be more just and humane to pay her a price that would give her a fair profit. . . ."

This ethical advice was connected by Arthur to the traditional Christian attitudes: "Economy is a good thing, but it should show itself in denying ourselves, not in oppressing others"; and the villain is conventionally evil, her name "Mier" suggesting "miser."[51] What is new is the caution against harmful competition in a more complex and detailed system of buying and selling. By the end of the century, when William Dean Howells would be writing *A Hazard of New Fortunes*, advocates of traditional success would abandon the hope of controlling business ethics by the appeal of moral homilies, and would simply argue that no man could become rich without exploiting someone in the intricate economic system; for there to be no exploitation, there should be no rich but rather a society where even distribution of the wealth would insure a competence for all.

The mid-century *Companion*, however, followed the flow of gold, and numerous stories show success coming through business rather than agricultural or mechanics' trades. In "The Newsboy" the hero is one of the fortunate and deserving children who become a druggist's clerk rather than a factory operative;[52] in "The Merchant's Dream" Arthur contrasts that useful worthy with the drone-like scholar and the productive but limited craftsman: "If the merchant were not to engage in trade, the manufacturer could not get his goods to market. . . . All who are engaged in the various callings that minister to the wants . . . comforts . . . luxuries of life, are honorably employed. Society . . . is held together by mutual interests. . . . As merchant, your position is intermediate between the producer and the consumer."[53] The *Companion's* middle-man was no longer an evil speculator robbing the yeoman mechanic of his profits; rather, he was a necessary adjunct to selling the greatest amount of goods to the greatest number of buyers. His position, in God's utilitarian scheme of things, became as respectable in the *Companion* as it was in the pages of *Hunt's Merchants' Magazine*, and with Ford's editorship in 1857, the exclusion of the permanent wage earner from traditional success was total. The *Companion* antedated *Hunt's* in its attempt to instill both a code of business morality based upon traditional ethics and nineteenth-century economic theory, and a sense of professional pride in the middle-man's calling. As for the problems of the factory and the displaced mechanic, the new editor's answer was like Willis's on slavery: ignore them. Yet despite praising that Victorian gospeller of the new success, Samuel Smiles, Ford cautions that the one "great end of life" is the individual's salvation of his own soul, and neither earthly success nor failure is important beside this; but with time salvation became less and less a primary goal for the American businessman as earthly success gained in importance. When Spencer's social Darwinism came to offer philosophical support for the already existing belief in harsh competition, material success was exalted as a prize worthy of the struggle. Almost immediately after he took over, Ford began running advertisements, and within a decade he added subscription premiums to increase circulation.[54] Like the change in format and editorship, the emphasis upon sales represented an age in which business came ahead of morality. As one of his advertisers cautions, "Keep the bowels regular and your conscience clear, and you will enjoy life."

☼

Based on the prudential morality of William Perkins and Benjamin Franklin, success in the *Youth's Companion* was early defined as an individual, moral, financial, and religious achievement open to all regardless of class or occupation. More optimistic than Franklin, more inclusive than the Puritans, the magazine promised that anyone who combined the God-given opportunity with sanctioned behavior would be successful. And even those who were slaves or deserving poor—widows, children, or cripples—were offered otherworldly rewards and a position among the moral elect if they behaved properly. Those who ignored or forgot the traditional values had to be reformed through coercion or assimilation in order to protect the chosen society. Coercion was the method selected by the more established element, which was already inclined, like Goodrich, to see the wage earner as outside the possibility of traditional success, and to see business pursuits as an honorable means to wealth and virtue. Those who felt that traditional success was still possible for the fallen worker advocated assimilation of the morally regenerate and a return to a golden age of yeoman democracy. But there was also widespread fear of the unvirtuous riches to be found in speculation and in complex business practices. The defense against this threat was to increase the volume of homilies, to plead for moral as well as trade apprenticeship, and to offer for emulation portraits of the morally successful rich. However, the forces of industrialism changed the apprentice system just as it changed other economic patterns, and more and more mechanics were excluded from traditional success to become operatives (permanent wage earners). No longer could they hope to remain mechanics and still be successful in the conventional manner, yet no other viable form of success was substituted. Indeed, the *Companion* came to conceive of the factory boy, the seamstress, the operative, as, like the slave, outside the opportunity for success. The yeoman dream tended to become a nightmare; success as wealth and independence was becoming a professional or a businessman's goal for whom the factory was a symbol of progress and a source of profit. For the operative, the spokesmen offered religious placation or silence.

This development is seen in the *Companion's* gradual change from the early broad representation of economic and social levels to the mid-century emphasis upon business; portrayals of professional and merchant occupations changed from Willis's tendency to show them as unvirtuous, to Ford's depiction of them as defenders of traditional values. At the same time, the very concept of success changed in the magazine. Although many writers still preached contentment and humility, their purpose was to maintain social stability through placation of the wage earner rather than defining success to include a competence, independence and virtue. For the business-oriented magazine, the new morality was a code of competition and material reward, and this new code justified heretofore morally tainted callings as well as the old hegemony in a new industrial environment. The yeoman dream survived in great part as the standard by which satirists came to judge the Gilded Age.

His brow is wet with honest sweat,

    He earns whate'er he can,

And looks the whole world in the face

    For he owes not any man.

"The Village Blacksmith," 1844

The relations instituted among men, by the present form of Society, are those of individual Selfishness, which generates Indigence, Fraud, Oppression, War, Disease, and False and delusive Doctrines, and the effects of which cannot be prevented by any change short of a thorough social Reorganization.

Horace Greeley, 1850

3

YEOMAN MECHANIC AND WAGE SLAVE

❖

THE FIRST half of the nineteenth century saw an increasing number of business opportunities at the same time that the factory system made greater demands for a permanent labor force. While business occupations gained in appeal, labor conditions in general and factory conditions in particular worsened, and although real wages seem to have improved over-all during the 1830s and 1840s, they apparently went into a decline during the 'fifties. Even increased wages were not freely given: an 1840 survey of the cotton mills of America reported that although wages were higher than in Britain, the Americans' hours were longer and the machines ran faster; the Chicopee strike of 1836 was a demand for more money; and despite some improvement, Pennsylvania workers during the period did not share widely in business progress. Nor were wages the sole problem; increasingly, a feeling of degradation spread among factory hands as they felt deprived not only of a competence and independence but saw society place them among the immoral because of their occupation. The Lowell women's strike of 1834 was caused in great part by a sense of lost status; in Buffalo during the 1830s labor unrest resulted from the belief that traditional avenues to individual success were being closed to manual occupations. In other sections of industrializing America, the moral division of society was beginning to exclude manual laborers because of their permanent wage-earning status or national origin. Even as early as the 1820s, Lowell had its "English Row" of supervisory personnel, and by 1840, immigrant labor dominated there with the English and Scots taking the better paid jobs and the Irish the lesser. In some areas, the moral discrimination seemed justified by the crime and disturbances among immigrants who began to move into the proletariat.[1] As traditional success became increasingly difficult to apply to manufacturing occupations, more and more American mechanics were placed in opposition to what they saw as new and "radical" business power. Most disturbing, the promises heretofore restricted to yeomen seemed more applicable to these new businessmen. Merchant-capitalists who controlled wide marketing and purchasing areas began to overshadow the yeoman mechanic with his small shop and limited capital; and to defend themselves, mechanics formed a number of labor groups ranging from benevolent aid societies to trade unions. Many of these failed for several reasons: poor leadership, political affiliation which divided membership, general antipathy toward "foreign" organizations such as labor unions, loss of sustaining funds in various depressions. But one of the most important reasons for failure was that native American workers were reluctant to consider themselves as part of a class interest, especially one associated with the permanent wage-earning status that necessarily surrendered the independence of the yeoman. Even toward mid-century when the labor union idea became less "British" and more acceptable to Americans, organizers often spoke in the language of the yeoman mechanic who was defending his shop against the inroads of monopolists and speculators. Thus, their rhetoric and logic were incompatible with a class concept of bargaining, and it is not without reason that European labor movements of the later nineteenth century sullenly accused American workers of being "capitalistic."

Despite their recurrent political entanglements and quarrels over unions and tariffs, mechanic and labor periodicals could not reject the yeoman dream, and the associated virtues which were so necessary for social approval. The appeal of traditional success was strong enough to prevent the workingman from conceiving of himself as a member of the proletariat, and it led him to envision his future as hopefully progressing from "operative" or journeyman to the familiar yeoman mechanic or the new "technological entrepreneur." Traditional success also served to identify the villains, who generally turned out to be the familiar "speculators" or "middlemen," sucking the profit of others' labor (merchants, intellectuals, and financiers who were defended by the more established members of society). This attitude was not constant, especially among editors

who groped toward advocating the idea of the technological entrepreneur; but as widely held was the conviction that only labor which
immediately resulted in a palpably useful product could be called
truly fruitful. Moreover, mechanics, while often respecting the roles
of economic and social leaders, were far less concerned than those
leaders with protecting the individuals who filled those roles. Instead,
ambitious mechanics used the concept of traditional success for pur-
poses related to the needs and values of their own group. It was behavior which merited their peers' respect by contributing to general
progress while at the same time garnering a private competence; it
was a code which differed from that of Franklin by giving increased
emphasis to material wealth; it was behavior stimulated by the growing hunger for material opportunity and by the mouth-watering assurance that such opportunity lay just beyond the next invention.
Yet, like so many ideals held to in a mutable world, the old concept
of the yeoman mechanic entailed an aspect of tragedy; for workers
caught in a flood of technological and marketing changes, it became
a two-edged sword. True, it could be used to attack the middleman,
the speculator, the politician, and the professor as idle, immoral vio-
lators of true success. However, the elements of competence and
independence so fundamental to traditional success tended to deny
growing numbers of wage earners any possible hope of ever achieving the dream. This had two effects. It drove from the ranks of
manual labor those with a chance for traditional success; conversely,
it lowered the moral standing of those who did not have the opportunity for a competence or independence. Thus, even in mechanic
periodicals a sharp division developed between workers who could
still remain within the framework of traditional success, and those
workers who were beginning to fall into the "lower orders." For
reasons which will become evident below, I label the two groups the
technological entrepreneurs, made up of engineers and inventors; and
the operatives, the permanent wage earners of an industrial work
force. The former was a group which in the later nineteenth century
rose to the ranks of civil and mechanical engineers, complete with all
the paraphernalia of middle class professionalism: degrees of pro-
ficiency, educational institutions, fraternities, publications, annual conventions, and professional quarrels. The latter became wage slaves. As
mid-century drew near and the improbability of yeoman success for
operatives grew more obvious, native Americans deserted their ranks
to leave room for those who could survive in no other way or for

immigrants who had not yet learned the intricacies of business life in America. And yet, while women, children, and foreigners became a labor force increasingly distinct from and often inimical to the idea of traditional success, the yeoman ideal of their spokesmen still remained closer to the tradition than did the new businessman's version of that ideal.

The total number of magazines and newspapers dedicated to furthering the interests of the American working man in the first half of the nineteenth century is impossible to determine. To many editors, the term "working man" meant anyone who "worked for a living," and many general news papers hoisted the workingman's banner in that way. But the genre of American mechanic's magazines clearly begins around 1825. The *Journal of the Franklin Institute* (originally the *American Mechanics' Magazine*) started life in 1826 modeled on the *London Mechanic's Magazine*. Like the Institute itself, which began to emulate the new scientific schools such as Union College or Lawrence School, the magazine was less political than educational, soon outstripping its general mechanic audience to become a more gentlemanly compilation of advanced engineering and scientific progress, and to feature an annotated list of patents as well as more sophisticated articles dealing with experimental techniques and scientific theory. Eventually, with the move of its editor to the patent office in Washington, a list of patents-applied-for filled the magazine. Perhaps the first "labor" periodical, one which self-consciously furthered the political aims of the wage-earner, was the *Journeyman Mechanic's Advocate* (New York, 1827). In the same vein was a newspaper, *The Mechanics Free Press* (Philadelphia, 1828–1837), often described as the first labor paper with any longevity. Other mechanic periodicals more or less affiliated themselves with an audience of specialized craftsmen, such as the long-lived *New England Mechanic*, which became the woodworking journal, *New Jersey Mechanic* (1847–1911). Finally, reflecting the growing division between mechanics and the nascent engineering profession, 1845 saw the birth of *Scientific American*, oriented from the first to formally educated engineers, and later to the wide range of scientific and technical specialists who have given speed if not direction to the present century.

One of the earliest and most imaginative periodicals which concerned itself with expressing the workers' ideals was the *Young Mechanic*, better known by its later title, the *Boston Mechanic*. It is of interest not only for the representative configurations of mechanic success in its pages, but also for its growing concern with the effects of industrialism on mechanics. Founded in 1832 by an American printer, George Light, and an English instrument maker, Timothy Claxton, the *Mechanic* illustrates the early Victorian period's emphasis upon fact. It found readers, even at a subscription rate of two dollars per year, and letters to the editor reflect a lively interest in the question-and-answer column. One, to the editor's great delight, encloses twelve dollars collected at Lowell from new subscribers; but despite its affiliation with Boston's Mechanics' Lyceum and a slowly increasing circulation, the magazine continually lost money until it folded in 1835.

The editors spoke for the mechanic who considered himself to be, if not an actual, at least a potential member of bourgeois society. Success and its pursuit were made up of many of the same elements that Benjamin Franklin advocated for his young journeymen and shopkeepers a century or so earlier. It was, however, far more secular in its ultimate aims; the magazine defined "respect" solely as contributing one's mechanical ability to humanity while also earning a competence and independence. To help mechanics attain this goal, the editors state their object to be the diffusion of a "general elementary knowledge" which was to be coupled with the traditional virtues inherited from the Puritan past; success and failure were seen in familiarly moral terms, ". . . knowledge is power, wealth, and distinction; . . . industry and prudence will, in general, lead to independence and respect; while idleness and dissipation, will end in slavery and disgrace. . . ."[2] ("Slavery" means, of course, the poverty-stricken permanent proletariat rather than chattel slavery.) In addition, the material improvement of the individual mechanic was seen as leading to the improvement of society at large. In a statement echoing Franklin's theory about the beneficent social effect of the individual's proper pursuit of wealth, editor Light wrote:

> The character and influence of the well-informed man among and over his fellow citizens at large, will always be advanced in an equal proportion by those same efforts which go most immediately to promote his own interests. . . . He will become just so far the better husband, father, citizen, the more fit for office or honorable distinction of any kind, and the more likely to obtain them.[3]

The power of self-education to elevate the persevering and industrious mechanic is the dominant and typical theme of the magizine's first volumes; the position to which the mechanic was to be elevated was yeoman status. This theme is presented in a number of ways. Many issues, for example, had biographical stories such as that of Englishman James Brindley, a self-educated man who rose from apprentice millwright to respected engineer.[4] Other approaches were simply didactic statements about the duties of a good apprentice mechanic. Though religious homilies are almost totally absent from the periodical, there is a general moral tone: it was sometimes suggested that a mechanic's success was not to be solely material, and avarice and competition were condemned because they elevated money over mankind. Still, the true good was essentially material. Money enabled independence and served as a basis for the good deeds and public service which resulted in respect from mankind. These secular preachments were general in nature: "The industrious farmer or mechanic [should be] content with small and sure gain."[5] Such advice was intended for the protection of both the individual and society; ruinous competition or speculation was not only the downfall of individual fortunes, but was also blamed for the periodic depressions which convulsed the entire community. Because the magazine addressed an audience assumed by the editors to be success oriented, there were few placations of the poverty-stricken or warnings to the unvirtuous rich. It was assumed—and urged—that every mechanic reader was capable of morally attaining traditional success through gaining knowledge and exercising the prudential virtues.

The psychology upon which this belief was based is closely akin to that expressed by Mrs. Child and Samuel Goodrich. Because man is a bundle of habits acquired when the mind is impressionable, youth should take particular care to form good habits; the person with the best chance of success is "the man who . . . makes his life a regular piece of clockwork."[6] One of the intermediate steps in this Lockeian exercise is self-education, "the education that any body may give himself, *any body at any age*." Democratically, all could achieve traditional success through the constant exercise of prudential virtues, and the result was a picture of mechanic society that matched the Jeffersonian ideal of a nation of independent owners of small farms and shops. But whereas Franklin's Poor Richard had used the promise of material reward to exercise the individual's moral faculties and thus elevate the individual's entire being (as well as society) to a more moral plane of life, the *Boston Mechanic* made the lure the goal: the reward of exercising the moral faculties would not be primarily a higher existence, but material gain, "Are not the *master workmen*, the *owners* and the *employers* of other men . . . those who have made the best use, not of their *fingers*, but of their *thinkers?*"[7] When morality does enter the argument, it is most often restricted to economic behavior. It was immoral, for example, to gain property through changing the social structure by joining a union or advocating class supremacy. Property laboriously acquired by a mechanic deserved the protection of a stable society, and society deserved the moral citizenry that the individual pursuit of a competence guaranteed. The balancing mechanism of self-interest and guaranteed individual property rights was seen as the basis of this stability and happiness. Rather than altering society, the mechanic was to prove his worthiness by demonstrating his virtues for the continuance of the proper society.

The familiar advocation of this combination of individual mobility and social stability was typical of most American mechanic magazines, as was the *Mechanic's* condemnation of interference with the free market's operations either by unions or by anarchy; monopoly, whether by owners or by workers, was a violation of God's orderly laws, "A mechanic who attempts to monopolize business or to injure his compeers by underselling, is guilty of high treason against society, as he violates that integrity and good will, without which the social compact would soon be broken asunder."[8] On the other hand, "A Stitch in Time Saves Nine" is the motto which leads the editor to condemn the threat to social harmony from below, "When the rude hands of rebellion begin to pick the constitution to pieces, and shake the fist in the face of lawful authority . . . the rod applied to one man's back may sometimes save the throats of twenty good men from the knife."[9] Success, for the English and American editors of the *Mechanic,* was the traditional success of the eighteenth century, though with more materialism and less sentimentalism. Unlike *Parley's* or the *Youth's Companion,* the purpose of proper social behavior was not to protect the already established business and professionally oriented members of the middle class, but to protect the rewards and responsibilities of upwardly striving mobile mechanics.

The magazine, in its later numbers, is also typical in reflecting the growing restlessness among mechanics who saw traditional success becoming impossible for them but not for "idle financiers" or "unproductive storekeepers." As the factory system spread, the mechanics felt themselves being thrust away from their success by men in business and the professions; competence, independence, and respectability were, because of changes in technology, marketing, and finance, becoming more and more difficult for a mechanic to obtain. This restlessness expressed itself in several ways in the *Mechanic* as well as in many other periodicals. While Light and Claxton tried to convince readers that mechanical occupations deserved as much respect as business or the professions, querulous voices stated that the traditional way to success no longer worked because of villainous middlemen; and there were even writers who more or less timidly began to question the structure of society itself. Literary and professional pursuits were singled out for claiming more public respect than their idleness merited, and thus immorally lowering the prestige of mechanic occupations:

> It is evident that talent, among us, inclines . . . to literary and professional pursuits; and this can be reasonably accounted for from the fact that . . . public opinion, has not in our community exerted an influence decidedly in favor of the mechanic arts as objects of enterprise and intellectual research. This adverse tendency in the public mind may partly be attributed to the baneful effects which have arisen in England from the extensive introduction of manufacturing establishments. But it may be fairly doubted whether these effects must necessarily accrue in this country, differing as it does from the old world. . . .[10]

Progress and national expansion were seen as depending upon the sciences, and the fine arts upon the cultivation of the mechanical arts. "It is unfortunately the fact," the *Louisville Herald* was quoted as lamenting, "that too many parents look upon mechanical employments as degrading, and prefer that their sons should be quacks and pettifoggers, rather than useful and respectable mechanics."[11] An article attributed to those heavenward gazing sweet sopranos of the genteel tradition, the Misses Sedgwick, asserts, "Talent and worth are the only external grounds of distinction. To these the Almighty has affixed his everlasting patent of nobility. . . . But we must secure, by our own efforts, the elevations that are now accessible to all."[12] The difference in tone between the other contributors and the Misses Sedgwick points up the difference in attitude between the mechanics and non-mechanic moralists who felt sorry for them: for the ladies, virtuous mechanics should not be scorned in their attempt to raise their social level up to that of the business or professions; the mechanic writers, like the early defensiveness of the *Youth's Companion*, assert that their moral and social levels are already the equal of businessmen or professional men, but that the fact is no longer recognized either by income or by community respect. This attitude grew stronger during the mid-1830s, a period of considerable labor unrest.

As early as the first volume, a letter (possibly written by Editor Light himself) questioned the universality of the popular success formula in the sacred area of apprenticeship. The writer asserted that among the disadvantages of apprenticeship for mechanics is that:

> No provision is made for the intellectual and moral improvement of the boy. . . . In some manufactures and workshops an abundance of leisure is afforded, after the work of the day is ended, for mental cultivation; but in many, when the evenings are occupied by labor, little leisure is afforded.
>
> True there are none who might not devote an hour daily to [study] . . . ; but it is to be remembered that when the body has become wearied by ten or twelve hours labor, it requires a strong incentive to fix the mind upon any subject requiring close examination. . . .[13]

The very things about apprenticeship that Goodrich and Willis cheered, Light and Claxton found missing in the factory environment; and they were even less optimistic about the opportunities for operatives who were beyond the apprentice stage: whereas farm laborers and craftsmen had plenty of time in winter to elevate themselves, factory workers who labored "from sun to sun in summer, and from daylight to eight o'clock in the evening in winter" found no good season for improving the mind. Yet Claxton believed still in the traditional means to success, chiding those same operatives because all of them managed to find time for amusements.[14] Though the definition and pursuit of success were not profoundly questioned, the *Boston Mechanic* increasingly demonstrated a belief that mechanics were being denied success by the nature of their labor rather than because of their individual deserts. The feeling that, contrary to all moral and social teachings, industry was not being rewarded was politically manifested in the ten-hour movement supported by the magazine in its closing months: "Comparatively few men can be found who possess disposition or energy, after laboring more than [ten] hours, either to engage in their own intellectual improvement, or, if heads of families, to go through their domestic duties in a proper manner. . . ."[15] Not only the long hours and the competition with foreign and unskilled hands was to be blamed, but also the division of labor entailed in the factory system, "an occupation which exercises but few of the muscles, and especially one which leaves little or no employment for the mind, when pursued without cessation or relaxation . . . must have an extremely unfavorable effect." This effect was to bring man "down to the state of a mere machine"[16] and effectively close off opportunities for the independence and respect so vital to one's manhood.

Torn between the fact of growing wage slavery and the yearning for the yeoman dream, the *Mechanic* was unsure of its own attitude toward new inventions. Machines, though they brought "more within the reach of every one," were not an unmixed blessing. When increasing automation did not put men out of work, it limited their adaptability in the changing technological environment, "the degree to which the division of labor is carried renders this matter still worse; for so far as the room for the exercise of skill is confined to a few operations, so far will the ability to change easily from one species of labor to another, in which skill is to be exercised, be lessened or destroyed." The remedy was for the worker to retain adaptability through a self-education which would enable him to take advantage of technological change not just by securing a job, but by mastering the machine and moving out of the ranks of wage earners into the ranks of shop owners or technological entrepreneurs. Mechanic apprentices needed only to "*read* and *think*" to be turned into "intelligent master workmen, fit to fill any station. . . ."[17] From this station, they could exploit the new technology and profit from it as moral businessmen rather than as laborers by making the machine produce respect and independence rather than mere wages. In short, the mechanic would become "more independent in his business, and better able to command his proper share of influence in society. . . ."[18] The trend of laissez-faire was also increasingly questioned in the magazine, although unlike the end of the nineteenth century, the purpose of such questioning was to defend rather than to attack individualism. That which threatened social harmony was the workers' lack of opportunity to attain traditional success, a lack caused by an imbalance of power; but the "power" which mechanics sought was not conceived of in terms of class interest. For example, although the practice of slowing the factory clocks during the day to keep the workers longer is soundly condemned as a violation of the individual's contract with the employer, the remedy is not to form an association and to strike, but to appeal to the "highly honorable character of those whom we . . . particularly address," the mill owners.[19] "Nothing is more unnatural and destructive," Light cries, "than war between the different orders of society." One of the principal aims of the ten-hour movement and the education it would enable would be the protection of the existing social structure against the lock-out and the strike, against the chaos of excessive self-interest in owner or worker. Education would enable the worker to better defend himself individually within the existing political and social framework, for when ignorant, he is "constantly liable to have his rights trampled upon, and to be injured by the competition of foreigners, whose increase ought to be checked by prudent legislation." Light perhaps naively assumed that the "more elevated of our community" would be enthusiastic about operatives starting competing shops or gaining the vote; but the alternative, he warns, is revolutionary danger "from the great mass of un-educated minds, whose restless heavings are felt in every part of the land."[20] Light was typical in his trust in education as an acculturating force, in his hostility to an immigration which threatened the status of mechanics, in his appeal to the middle class fear of disharmony. Rather than placation or a doctrine of class competition, Light (and most labor editors as well) urged equal opportunity for success as the remedy for an aggressive radical capitalism and a threatening lower class unrest. In the ten-hour reform movement, as in other movements strongly influenced by members of mechanic trades in the first half of the century, the desire for assimilation into, rather than the rejection or coercion of, the existing bourgeois society formed the basis of argument. And that desire was in turn based on the belief that mechanics could attain the same yeoman dream that they thought their grandfathers had enjoyed.

While he urged assimilation, Light was painfully aware of class distinctions hardening along economic lines. He was worried that if, disregarding traditional success, the workers endeavored

> by combination of forces, to secure the rights and privileges which they claim as their due, [then] a stronger counter-combination might be brought to bear like an overwhelming sea. . . . And though the merchant, and the professional man, and the indepen-

dent landholder, may not organize under the banner of a constitution, to bear down the struggles of the operative. . . , the *effect* of a combination may as truly take place . . . from that self-interest in which men must be expected to act in bringing their resources to bear upon their own private emolument, without regarding the general good.[21]

Note that merchants, professional men, and independent landholders, who in *Parley's* or the *Companion* saw the permanent wage earner as immoral and alien, are here described as the unvirtuous rich because of their wish to exclude the operative from yeomanry. That is, both sides of the rising economic and occupational barrier recognize that American society is beginning to consider a large number of mechanics to be failures not because of moral shortcomings but because of their wage-earning occupations. As might be expected, mechanic magazines paid far more attention to the factory environment than did the business oriented publications. More and more, American factories rather than English were described as unhealthy and degrading because they separated the operative from his aspirations. Even the showplace of factory life, Lowell, became suspect by American mechanics at the same time that European travellers were praising its bucolic cleanliness and high moral standards. To Light's way of thinking, assertions that health and manners were unaffected or even improved by such employment "would be more satisfactory, if the witnesses were not directly connected with the establishments." The morality of the female operatives, rather than being a result of the factory environment as so many writers asserted, was attributed by Light to the fact that they were of yeoman stock, the daughters "of farmers and mechanics, such as formerly would have employed themselves . . . in the domestic manufacture of articles similar to those now fabricated by machinery." The subsequent influence of the factory on characters which had been molded at home "is a question on which we are not informed," and, consequently, young ladies interested in such work should "make a little inquiry" before going down to Lowell.[22] The girls' span of employment was expected to be but a few years, after which they would return home, or "form new connections of their own"; that is, the girls' occupation was an interim one before achieving the female's traditional success of marriage. What factories might do to someone who could not escape through marriage is left unsaid. Like many other critics of the new ways, the editors of workingmen's periodicals questioned the effects of factory labor; in these magazines there is no sentimental depiction of the patiently suffering operative, nor is there any longer a denial that American conditions could become like the worst English ones. But despite questioning the factory, there was no questioning of the value of the yeoman dream.

Light's faith in American democracy as the bulwark of true laissez-faire and his trust in the efficacy of individual elevation through education remained unshaken. Summarizing a basic tenet of his beliefs is "Trust Yourself," which asserts in the philosophy of Adam Smith, "Nothing can give so good a *general* assurance of well doing as the personal activity of the individual . . . exerted in his own interest."[23] Like many another man of the time, Light was torn between the desire to support traditional success and the vision of a shrinking application of that ideal; it seemed that those for whom success was the most necessary both morally and materially were no longer being given a chance at it. For him, Jacksonian Democracy, with its image of the proud yeoman and its attack upon freedom-restricting monopolies, was a conservative code because it promised the extirpation of those new immoral forces—an economic aristocracy, rampant speculation, and selfish monopoly—which were upsetting the natural laws of harmonious enlightened self-interest. Offering a return to the old promise of traditional reward for individual virtue regardless of a man's occupation, Jacksonian democracy had the same appeal for Light as for Goodrich: the appeal of the old yeoman dream.

Machinery and the factory were thus seen in two ways: as offering a field of new opportunity and serving as instruments of oppression. The determining factors for the individual mechanic as to the type of force they would become in his own case were education and effort. A youth could still be as successful as Fulton or Watt, but if he did not exert himself, the penalty was wage slavery; the conflict between traditional success and the new technology demanded that the apprentice decide between being an operative or a technological entrepreneur. Eventually, from the point of view of even the *Boston Mechanic*, the right choice was the latter. Timothy Claxton made enough money to return to England and open his own manufactory of scientific instruments to supply the burgeoning demand in the area of technology, while George Light moved beyond such entrepreneurship to embrace an even more business oriented life. After the failure of the *Boston Mechanic*, he published and edited *The*

Young American's Magazine of Self-Improvement, a compendium of familiar homilies and paeans to merchant success. Enthusiasm and optimism mark the articles and poems, and perhaps Longfellow's stanza best summarizes the dominant themes of endeavor and patience:

> Let us, then be up and doing,
>   With a heart for any fate;
> Still achieving, still pursuing,
>   Learn to labor and to wait.

The first page bears an engraving of the young Benjamin Franklin from Sparks's *Life of Franklin*; he is no longer a mere mechanic, nor does he wear his leather apron and display the symbols of his trade. Instead, dressed in somber Quaker clothing touched off by lace and his neatly curled, shoulder-length hair, Franklin has become the sober burgher of a business oriented world.

Mixed with the enthusiasm and belief in the universal capability of all individuals, black and white, for self-elevation, comes the harsher note of competition and the soft tones of religious placation. Man must "wrestle, like an athlete, with all difficulties," and the shortcomings in those who fail is not social but personal, "Whether [a man] is to be a drone or a laborer, a curse or a benefactor, rests with himself." At the other end of the spectrum, James Russell Lowell's "Above and Below" taught, "For meek obedience, too, is light, / And following that is finding Him." Other homilies were more vaguely virtuous: Lyman Beecher advised "intellectual self-control," while Elizabeth Oakes Smith filled columns of print to urge the striving apprentice, "Be Chatty."[24] Speaking from a position shared by Goodrich, Mrs. Child, and Daniel Ford, the magazine presented the doctrines of sentimental benevolence and competition. It is perhaps important that one article even contained praise for the "higher meaning" in the publications of Peter Parley.[25]

Yet despite his public conversion to the newer concepts of business success, Light seemed not altogether convinced that his own lack of money, prestige, and a place in literary history were the results of moral shortcoming or stunted competitive drive. Many of his rhymes published in the *Young American's Magazine* celebrated the familiar aspects of traditional success as applied to the mid-century world, but when they came out in a separate volume in 1851 after more illness and another financial set-back, they were marked by some significant changes. "Keep Cool," for example, had several stanzas added similar in tone to the following:

Can't you find your quondam friends?
Keep cool;
You have only lost your cash:
They will all come dancing back,
When they see the dollars flash,
Keep cool.

A new poem shows an even more bitterly ironic mood:

When poor people want assistance,
Blink inquiry—pass them by;
And, at a convenient distance,
See the sorry rascals die.

. . . . .

Should they hint at bread and butter,
Cant of heavenly food the best;
If they mention shelter, mutter
All about celestial rest.

Show that they may mend their breeches
Pockets, if they'll heed advice;
Bid them bite like hungry leeches,
Scratch like cats among the mice.[26]

In the face of past beliefs about true success and the more recent support for placation and competition, Light expressed his doubts by ironic denial of those same shibboleths. This disillusionment was caused not by a change of abstract theory, but by the brute fact of personal experience; and as a result, Light leaned toward that small querulous group who questioned the materialistic tide that became a flood in the latter half of the century.

One of the first things that strikes the reader of the period's mechanic magazines is the apparently universal interest in inventions and improvements of unbounded variety. Ostensibly designed to save labor and time or to increase quality or safety, they are clear evidence of the technological entrepreneur's appeal. Ranging from new steam cars invented by English engineers to new methods of tanning submitted by an astute journeyman, the wide range of inventions and inventors shows that the craze was not limited to a few mechanically educated artisans but infected a large number of Americans. True, interest was boosted by the British embargo on exporting English machinery and by the relative ease of applying for patents in America, but one of its principal stimuli was the promise of wealth earned independently and —importantly—for a service that benefitted mankind. The whole purpose of a patent, of course, is to enable the inventor to make money from his idea; and if acquiring wealth and perhaps the independence of one's own manufacture or company were linked to benefitting mankind through invention, then both the moral and the material elements of traditional success were achieved at one stroke. Consequently, long and hot are the letters to the editor when a report misrepresented a claim or a claim was similar to an earlier one. The belief of Franklin and Jefferson that all men should freely benefit from a person's inventions could not survive the hunger of those who sought the yeoman dream by the commercial exploitation of inventions and improvements—the technological entrepreneurs. But whether or not this large number of participants represented all classes is another question. Most of these inventions were seldom the result of pure science, i.e., designs or processes based upon radically new theoretical concepts. Characteristically, the patents were improvements to existing mechanisms, usually of a minor nature, and seemingly in answer to the pragmatic question, "Given this gimmick, how can I make it work better?" The radically new inventions tended to come from the emerging corps of professional engineers who, well-trained by experience or schooling in both the practice and theory of mechanics, were able to translate their own or others' speculations into machinery and to find financial backing to exploit their invention. Robert Fulton epitomized the new trend by studying mechanics and engineering in England and earning a number of other patents before returning to America to design and find financing for the first really successful steamboat. In short, at the same time that factories were accused of limiting the education of mechanics, broad mechanical education was more necessary than ever if one were to be other than a mere hireling in the industrializing world.

In the early nineteenth century, increasing numbers of manual labor schools as well as schools designed to produce teachers of elementary science were founded to answer this demand for a broad scientific or technological education. Colleges developed courses in the applied sciences and were producing such alumni as Count Rum-ford, Eli Whitney, and Laommi Baldwin, who later in the century became known as the "Father of Civil Engineering in America." The demand for trained engineers in the years 1802 to 1835 was met primarily by the Military Academy at West Point, assisted by such schools as Norwich University and the Gardiner Lyceum. However, increasing industrialization made greater the demand for engineers, and Americans, unlike the English, placed successful inventors and technologists on a very high level of prestige. The result was a growth of schools that opened up "mechanic occupations" not only to the greater material opportunity found in industry, but also to the coveted bourgeois respectability previously reserved for "gentlemanly" callings; Rensselaer Polytechnic Institute, Union College, the Lawrence Scientific School at Harvard, and, not to be outdone, Yale's Sheffield Scientific School all produced graduates who had practical as well as symbolic importance for America since they proved that a yeoman figure could triumph in the world of machines and steam. The culmination of a widespread movement for equal opportunity in this area for most Americans was, of course, the Morrill Act of 1862. Prior to that Act, mechanics whose formal schooling was limited were served by a number of magazines. Typical is the *Mechanics' Magazine and Register of Inventions and Improvements* (New York, 1833–37) which aped the London *Mechanic's Magazine* in format by concentrating upon engineering and invention rather than on mechanics' social and political problems. Published and occasionally edited by D. K. Minor, it merged in 1837 with another Minor endeavor, the *American Rail Road Journal*. This, in turn, survived as *Railway Age, Mechanical Edition*. Most of the inventions listed are by men who made changes while on the job, tinkering in their spare time to improve objects in everyday use. In this category are numerous "improvements": a spring-action cap for oil reservoirs, intended to replace the threaded cap which was slower and often skittered out of slick fingers; a quick-disconnect safety hitch for teams and cars; changes in railroad axles, road beds, wheels, and bearings, all of which "inventions" have the stamp of being made by men who, familiar with the object, saw a need for and a way to improve it. Inventors in a second category were often professional men ranging from civil engineers to supervisory mechanics in limbo between certified engineers and practicing engineers. These inventions were often of a more ambitious nature: a new steam camel by "John L. Sullivan, C. E."; Harkness' Newly Invented Brick-Making Machine, steam powered and capable of 200,000 bricks per week; a farm machine designed by James D. Woodside, who was noted for also having "devised and superintended the work of placing the collossal statue of Washington on the summit of the monument in Baltimore."[27] Occasionally, as later with the Negro inventor Elijah McCoy (who has entered American folk parlance as "the real McCoy"), fortune and fame were demonstrably won when a professional inventor overcame the handicap of race or class to inspire generations of other Americans.

A conclusion which may be inferred about the type of democracy represented by this technology is that although it was widespread, its base rested primarily among those who had the time and ability to tinker, and who, if not already technological entrepreneurs, submitted their patents in an effort to climb into that realm. For instance, inventions which were the result of long familiarity with a problem most likely came from mechanics skilled in the area or from professional inventors like McCoy who sought their opportunity in improvements to machinery. Less likely was any notable contribution from apprentices or unskilled operatives. Moreover, except for tools with a limited function, much factory machinery required a knowledge of the overall production sequence, which knowledge was increasingly beyond a laborer whose job it was to turn a crank or feed a spindle. Perhaps this helps explain why the Lowell millgirls, whose publications indicate a high level of education, made no known mechanical contributions to their factories. The relationship between invention and status or desired status also accounts for the intense interest in "general knowledge" by mechanic magazines; such knowledge enabled inventions, which in turn brought traditional success. There is no question that a major hero in these magazines was the inventor who, by his own persevering efforts and entrepreneurial acumen, made a contribution to mankind which resulted in wealth, independence, and respectability for himself. While many mechanics were being forced into wage slavery and the loss of the yeoman dream, the technological entrepreneur captured it and fitted it to his industrializing world. In the words of T. B. Wakerman, the contributors to an 1835 New York trade fair were, ". . . the middling classes, our city yeomanry, the steady supporters of order, law and religion. . . . We have nature's noblemen. They have shown their devotedness to *our* and *their* cause. . . . They are not untaught operatives, but an enlightened, reflective people, who not only know how to use their hands, but are familiar with principles."[28] A magazine which, even more than the *Boston Mechanic*, followed the metamorphosis of the yeoman from mechanic to technological entrepreneur was Joel Munsell's *New York State Mechanic*. Like most others of its sort, the *State Mechanic* offered inventions, discoveries and practical knowledge, as well as general praise of mechanic arts. In its early issues, however, it also concerned itself with the mechanic's economic and political problems. "With politics we shall have nothing to do," wrote Editor Munsell in the opening number, and then proceeded to announce his affiliation with the New York State Mechanic Association and voice their political aims. What Munsell, like many other mechanic editors, meant was that he would not identify his periodical with either major political party.

Descended from seventeenth-century New Englanders, Munsell, the son of a wheelwright, decided to become a printer. His apprenticeship was marked by industry, prudence, frugality, Deism, and a few hi-jinx; and he was justified in later comparing himself to Benjamin Franklin, for he followed—apparently without realizing it at the time—most of that gentleman's advice on success. Becoming a journeyman in 1827, he moved to Albany and subsequently had a variety of printing, editorial, and clerical duties; his twenties were spent travelling, but he seems to have had little trouble finding day work wherever in New England or New York he wandered. These years also saw him enamoured of the theater, an evening's tippling, his scrapbooks, and reading "scientific facts." Self-education was a constant endeavor with him, and he took advantage of lyceums and self-improvement organizations wherever he went. His interest in party politics was slight; when a group of Albany mechanics celebrated Jackson's election, he complained that the noise disturbed his reading. In 1834, his twenty-sixth year, he married and settled to steadier employment, determined to make something of himself. Shortly thereafter he formed a partnership for an independent printing shop. Eventually, under his name alone, the Munsell Press became the second largest in Albany, employing about fifteen men. He had become independent and was on his way to a competency through his own industry. But traditional success also requires community respect, and Munsell's life reveals an abiding concern with morality and public service. As a youth he disliked an acquaintance because he was avaricious and "not content with independence alone"; despite his estrangement from formal creeds and a lifelong dislike of dogmatism, he supported organized religion for its social utility. As a man with a large family, he was interested in proper education, and in 1848 published *Select Stories for Children, Designed for their Moral and Religious Improvement* which stressed thrift and honesty. His advice rivals Chesterfield's prudence, ". . . if you regard anyone unworthy of your esteem, while you resolve not to be intimate with them, treat them with civility—for you do not know how soon they may be of some use to you."[29] His most famous services to mankind, historical publications and antiquarian interests, were undertaken not for the sake of profit but "because no one else took it up." Though he continually lost money on these projects, he considered them to be "very decent contributions to American History," and indeed they are.

As spokesman of the State Mechanic's Association, Munsell ran long series on the benefits of associationism and the necessity for support of that idea among all kinds of workmen. But he also published many articles decrying strikes, praising self-elevation, and urging the mutual outlook of employer and employee. This conflict of opinion marked other controversies such as the tariff question and the effects of machinery on labor. There was even, in early issues, distrust of the possibility of traditional success for operatives. One familiar theme concerned the mechanic's intense feeling of lost independence and prestige, "The learned professions are *over stocked*, and *lazily* riding on the backs of the producers, the *farmers* are living by their 'hired man'—the capitalists have taken to 'bossing' all mechanical trades, while the practical mechanic has become a journeyman, subject to be discharged. . . ."[30]

However, despite support for associationism, Munsell saw the fault to lie in grog and prison labor rather than in the social system. What was needed was not less laissez-faire, but more of it; the monopolies and ungodly combinations had to be broken so the individual wage earner would not be robbed of his opportunity to become an independent shop owner. The remedy was the ballot-box, education, and, as a last resort, associationism. This final step, however, should not be confused with the ideas of Brisbane, Greeley, Brownson, or Fourier. Instead, Munsell saw it take place somehow through the mechanics "asserting their rights, to which they are entitled as men on an equality with all others."[31] Both anarchy and socialism are soundly condemned; rioting hand-loom weavers of Philadelphia were told, "It is the most absurd thing in the world to resort to violence for relief. The progress of invention cannot be checked by any such means."[32] Indeed, inventions and improvements were depicted as the means to traditional success for the threatened yeoman mechanic: "The catalogue of illustrious mechanics affords instances of men who are venerated for, and immortalized by, the labor saving machines they have produced." One need not be a technological entrepreneur to benefit by the new inventions, for they were agents of inexorable progress and peace for all mankind; the reader is told that steam—perhaps like gunpowder earlier or, later, atomic energy—"will [pacify] the world by making war so obviously ruinous, and confounding victory and defeat in general and inevitable destruction . . . that there can be neither motive nor object in the contest."[33] Though temporary hardship could result, "the march of improvement is onward, and nothing can arrest it"; therefore, the mechanic should join the march through the traditional means of education and self-elevation.

After the fist volume, the querulous voices grew less distinct; and the magazine, following the trail of success, first celebrated the inventor and then the businessman. The operative was unfavorably contrasted with the mechanic, the value of riches was stressed, sentimental benevolence was urged toward the unfortunate (and separate) urban poor, and competition explained their failure. E. G. Squier pontificates, "If any class of men do not hold that position in our social organization which they should . . . the fault is in themselves."[34] The individual struggle became a "law of the race" as Emerson wrote, and its result was general progress.[35] So much for that rascal, the starving operative. Now it was the "business Men of New York," eulogized by Freeman Hunt, who offered entrepreneurial inspiration to the mechanic; they became a "perpetual stimulus to the mechanic and artisan to earn a similar reward by similar frugality, industry and perseverance."[36] An increasing number of ominous news items made plain the reasons for this strident shift toward business pursuits. English operatives were described as starving by thousands, while in Europe, workers suffered "sorrow, disease, poverty and starvation." It was not long before the same conditions were pictured in America; in 1842, many Massachusetts factories shut down, but fortunately, "the operatives mostly have found employment on the rail road which is now progressing between this place and Great Falls." Others were said to be not so fortunate: ". . . there is a great excess of laborers in [New York] . . . arising from two prominent causes—the decrease of employment and the increase of laborers. . . . Some are in great distress. Their distress must increase, as 10,000 emigrants are preparing to embark . . . to the United States." Threats to laborers from immigration continued to make the news, as did notices of riots and strikes against wage reductions. Factory closings and bank failures were reported to be numerous in the summer of 1842, and the editor advises shop employees that if they would "turn out and assist in bringing in the harvest they would find it the best remedy for the evils which beset them." Another item stating that 20,000 mechanics were out of work in the United States offered the solution of the safety-valve—coopers were needed in Mississippi and Missouri; but the article does not say anything about transportation costs, experience, or wages. A relieved note is sounded in August with the statement that of "over 200,000 persons out of work in the manufactures and workshops of New York and New England," many will be re-employed. But September did not bring peace. At the same time that the banks "were never more ready or able to lend on good notes than at present," Philadelphia weavers were reported to have attacked a fellow worker who "refused to join the present turnout" as they rioted against machines replacing their home looms. In New York state, workers struck to protest "a reduction of 25 per cent on their wages." Other strikes were attributed to factory regimentation—when the Lowell mills temporarily cut their speed by a third to reduce production, "their poor people were kept in the mills twelve or fourteen hours, to do what they could as easily have done in eight or nine."[37] By January, the paper pleaded for contributions to support souphouses because "the extreme dullness of the times renders it impossible for many of the laboring classes of the city to obtain even the necessaries of life. . . ." Into the Spring of 1843, strikes and turnouts, generally caused by wage reductions, punctuated the news column. And worse dangers threatened the "Daughters of the Poor": "Without education to give them knowledge, without religious experiences to make them estimate truly the value of life that now is and that which is to come, they too often become giddy, thoughtless, and indifferent, and finally sink under their numerous trials and temptations."[38]

The reporter is careful to point out that they are sometimes crushed by their employer's failure rather than by their own turpitude. And, always, there was the horrible example of the English operatives. The indications were there for all to see. Mechanics who in the last generation had a better opportunity for yeomanry or who had supplemented their incomes by part-time farming, were undergoing radical changes. The poor were made up of workers who often suffered for their employers' failures and had no recourse; the inevitable technological advances displaced skilled men in numbers of trades; wages and employment were subject to sudden cuts from causes only partially understood, and wholly without relation to an individual's merits; the factory life was a regimented one which changed men into machines. As described in the daily news, the mechanic tended to become a permanent journeyman, a mere operative, an unskilled laborer, with no independence, no competence, and little or no respect from society. Those men who believed in and who wanted traditional success would have to become technological entrepreneurs or businessmen, and the *State Mechanic's* shift in identification from the associational interests of the mechanic to the individualism of the market place was only natural.

Many editors did not follow the trend of the *Boston Mechanic* and the *New York State Mechanic*. Rather, they moved away from the new technological entrepreneur as an impossible dream, away from the businessman as morally suspect, away from celebrating competition and sentimental benevolence. Usually the pleas for associationism and political action by mechanics and operatives were still based on the dream of competence independently arrived at which would have the public merit of supporting the existing social order. These aspirations were often expressed in periodicals published at manufacturing centers whose audience was made up of operatives. But only a few of these publications had long life, most being poorly supported by the workers themselves and subject to extinction when wages were depressed. They do, however, offer insights into the beliefs and attitudes of their mechanic audience. Many of the papers appeared in New York, Boston, and Philadelphia, and other locations such as Albany and Lowell are not uncommon. There has as yet been no detailed study made of the circulation or effect of these periodicals, and often the editor is known only by that title; nevertheless, like the youth's magazines, their length of life and their range of "borrowings" offer an indication of their audience's predispositions.[39] A reading of several of the more well-known papers shows that traditional success was far from dead in the minds of the editors and in the hopes of the contributors, but whereas the goal was generally the same, the means to that goal varied with different editors.

The yeoman mechanic was pictured by hundreds of writers, often aggressively, occasionally with the anger and puzzlement of a lost dream:

> The fact that we who labor place ourselves for the time being in subserviency to the will of others, is often lost sight of. . . . If we voluntarily place ourselves in what others deem a position of dependence, it is our duty . . . to acknowledge a higher authority and be governed by it; for in no case do we surrender one iota of our personal rights, or degrade ourselves in the eyes of the wise and just.[40]

More often the picture was conventional, as in the "Mechanic's Song," "I am Nature's own nobleman happy and free. / A peer of the realm might well envy me,"[41] and perhaps the most famous yeoman mechanic is the one celebrated by Longfellow, reprinted almost everywhere, and forced into the minds of school children ever since —"The Village Blacksmith." There beneath the spreading chestnut tree stands a semi-agrarian figure independent and free at his forge, brow wet with honest sweat, mind pure with thoughts of heaven and apparently not much else. Longfellow uses the lengthy description of this ideal to preach a moral about effort and reward which at mid-century he and his rapt audience considered to be applicable to all competitive Americans regardless of occupation:

> Thus at the flaming forge of life
>   Our fortunes must be wrought;
> Thus on its sounding anvil shaped
>   Each burning deed and thought.

This yeoman mechanic was admired by Longfellow and by the many editors who reprinted the poem because he showed honest labor winning a competence and independence, and moral behavior earning the respect of society. And yet, there is something false—the stylized sentiment of convention—about this figure. As much as the famous painting of "Pat Lyon at the Forge" done by Neagle in 1826, this 1844 village blacksmith is a thing of artifice. In addition to being posed, he reeks less of sweat than of nostalgia. The poem might even be said to be patronizing in its picture of a mindless creature in his bucolic world. Compare Longfellow's sentimentalism with an 1833 abstract of the mechanic's life by Eli Moore, the trade union organizer:

> We, in order to guard against the encroachment of aristocracy, to preserve our natural and political rights, to elevate our moral and intellectual condition, to promote our pecuniary interests, to narrow the line of distinction between journeyman and employer, to establish the honor and safety of our prospective vocations upon a more secure and permanent basis, and to alleviate the distresses of those suffering from wants of employment, have . . . formed ourselves into a General Trades' Union.

Associationism, not sentiment, was his cure for the many ills in the mechanic's life.

But Moore, while attempting to form a confederation of journeymen whose interests were opposed to those of the employers, did so on the promise of traditional success. Note the similarities between, say, Peter Parley and Eli Moore: for both, self-love is "one of the elements of life and is essential to the welfare of society"; the aim of forming confederations of journeymen was to lessen the distinction between employer and employee, not only in income but also in independence and respect; and although confederation might have seemed un-yeomanly, Moore used the imagery and rhetoric of traditional success to show that his was the way to that dream:

> There never was a land under heaven where the intellectual powers of man had so fine a field and such fair play as they have in our own country and in our own times. If our march, therefore, is not onward to honor, competence, and fame, the fault is all our own.
>
> Will you meet me with the excuse that your early opportunities . . . were limited: . . . no time for improvement? . . . too late to enter the lists for distinction? . . . Such are the common apologies of the indolent, the spiritless, and the dissolute

He goes on with a familiar roll of men to be emulated: Franklin, Roger Sherman, patriot and jurist George Walton, General Knox, General Nathanael Greene, and the sculptor, John Frazee. Ironically, the success of these "artificers of their own fortune" came after they left the ranks of mechanics; seemingly, even in Moore's eyes, the trade union was not to elevate the class of mechanics wholly and at the expense of society, but was to provide a "fair field" for the individual to exercise his talents for traditional success, ". . . be diligent, be honest, be firm, be indefatigable. Pursue knowledge with a diligence that never tires and with a perseverance that never falters; and honor and glory and happiness will be your reward!"[42]

Even in periodicals with a proclaimed class interest, the yeoman dream was fundamental to the editors' position. The *Philadelphia Mechanic's Free Press* came out early in 1828 directed by "a Committee of the Mechanic's Library Company." Politically, it agitated for the ten-hour day, a mechanics' lien law, a new militia law, unionism, a bankruptcy law, and free public schools. Mechanics were advised to elevate their class by electing their own men; they should not be divided by the presidential election "which has nothing to do with our present object."[43] There was little disagreement that society was made up of the rich and the poor, the exploiter and the beleaguered worker. That part of America represented by Goodrich or Ford or Munsell was viewed with suspicion and jealousy, while established religion and Dr. Beecher were seen as agents of an "aristocracy" determined to place mechanics in ignorance and poverty while elevating business interests. A constant theme is the degradation of the worker caused by "the spirit of trade in its excess" which creates avarice and destroys the desire for rational esteem."[44] The ideas of sentimental benevolence and beneficial competition are scorned:

> We are told, that the idea of essentially ameliorating the condition of suffering humanity is hopeless, and the only thing we can do is hire men, at good salaries to preach RESIGNATION and ECONOMY and INDUSTRY. . . . *Resignation*—what stuff! . . . Economy . . . to those who may have, perhaps, sixteen dollars a year . . . for food for two or more mouths! Industry to those who were willing to work for such generous paymasters as the Provident Society![45]

Yet despite the periodical's condemnation of owners and capitalists, conventional apprenticeship is championed because it contributes to the proper goal for mechanics—to become a shop owner, and the names used to instill pride in workers are the familiar ones whose success transcended their original trades: Franklin, Arkwright, Greene, Sherman and Fulton. In an attempt to retain the old moral division rather than the new economic distinction between classes, the degrading term "lower classes" is summarily rejected as an insult to the "laboring and industrious part of the community"; it should be applied "only to the ignorant and vicious."[46] The moral coherency between the economically higher and lower sections of society would mean that mechanics still had a justified claim on traditional success despite their low income or "temporary" wage status; and, not unexpectedly, the symbol used to represent true success was the familiar yeoman, "There is no more honorable character . . . than . . . the independent and industrious American Mechanic. . . . His mind is free and his heart is unwarped by prejudice . . . [saying] 'give me neither poverty nor riches.' . . . He appears to stand forth to the world, the *nobleman of nature*, independent in mind, and honorable in feeling."[47]

Though the loss of opportunity for such success created ire, the *Free Press* was as fearful as Goodrich or Munsell of revolution or redistribution of property among the morally unworthy. There was constant denial of the charge of "agrarianism"—the equal redivision of wealth in society; what the editors sought was equal opportunity for limited wealth. Although the French Revolution of 1830 received praise, as did movements for unity among English workingmen, the right way to success in America was still knowledge on behalf of the individual mechanic and freedom of opportunity on behalf of society. These were to be gained through inaugurating public education and by anti-monopoly legislation which would reward the individual effort of mechanics.

The *Voice of Industry*, edited by a member of the Working Man's Party, W. F. Young, was published by an "association of Young Workingmen" from Fitchburg, Massachusetts. Like the *Mechanic's Free Press*, its avowed purpose was to support the Workingman's Party, although party spirit and sectarianism were decried. Associationism was the means of conquering "unfeeling capital and destructive competition"; the goal was a harmonious society in which everyone would be rewarded in proportion to his industry; the great fear was of the European order of society in which true success was impossible for laborers:

> As population increases, and [America's] towns and cities are seen to rise, as its conflicting and heterogenous elements approach each other, the result can but be, a constant increase of monopolization

and anatgonism to that deplorable degree witnessed in the old
world. . . . The workingman must be disenthralled from the power
of avaricious monopolization and isolated competition, and reinstated into the bonds of nature's brotherhood and union of
interests. . . .[48]

The use of "reinstated" indicates the feeling of a lost position and the
desire to return to it through traditional means; the socialism of
Greeley's *Tribune* was examined and found wanting because commonly owned property would enable the evil lazy to sponge off of
the industrious—and there seemed to be too much of that already.
What was needed was not Greeley's socialism or anyone else's, but a
return to the God-ordained world in which the rewards of industry
went to the morally industrious.[49] With the right kind of associationism, "The poor boy of yesterday . . . [becomes] the talented and
honorable young man of today, by the power of his good right arm,
and the potent influence of his principles. . . ." [50] Some vague kind of
associationism, along with education and the ten-hour day, were the
cures for ills besetting mechanic occupations. But by 1846, the *Voice*
did not sound so optimistic. Monopolies were accused of crushing
farm laborers, mechanics, factory operatives, day laborers, seamen,
small farmers, and small traders—an indication of the contributor's
conception of the division of society. Factories were regarded with
increasing hostility, and the Lowell girls' flight from the mills was
attributed to mechanistic conditions and poor pay. The *Lowell Offering* was attacked as a pro-employer publication: "Its influence has
proved detrimental to the interest of those it professed to protect,"
and the *Voice* accused the Lowell owners of being "slavers."[51] Other
New England factory workers were described as worse than slaves,
for they had no security. The argument that American factory workers were superior to Europeans was accepted by the *Voice*, but not
on the grounds that American factories were better environments
than the European mills. Rather, like the *Boston Mechanic*, they attributed the superiority to the Americans' yeoman upbringing, which
the factory now threatened, "They are the sons and daughters of the
husbandman and artizan, whose minds were nurtured in the Common
School or the Village Academy, before they left their homes to be
shut up fourteen hours per day. . . . Improved! What chance, what
opportunity is there for improvement under a fourteen hour system
of soul-crushing toil?"[52] Not only were the long hours and lack of
opportunity complained of, but also the blacklists and the strictness

of factory regimentation and barracks living. The idea of a stock-sharing plan is rejected since the workmen were too poor to buy shares; the surplus of laborers is blamed for forcing wages down, a situation supposedly brought about by the monopolies that drove country populations to the cities and prevented the city surplus from moving to farms to live as agrarian yeomen. Those who blamed the laborer for the safety valve's malfunction received Young's scornful reply that the whole society was at fault.

Nevertheless, even this strident periodical dedicated to a class-conscious view of the workingman tended to follow the drift of the yeoman dream into the world of business. In 1831, for example, the *Lowell Mercury* became a general news sheet. On most political issues it followed the Democratic party line, but nullification was an uncertain topic, and the paper was oddly quiet on local labor questions. One of the last items pertaining to the laborer was Nathaniel P. Willis's poem, "The Contented Poor Man" who was rich in religion and nature. The *Mechanic's Free Press* followed the same trend by 1834, becoming a general news and literary paper, the *Philadelphia Times, People's Friend, and Mechanic's Free Press*. Advertisements for credit, loans and cheap clothes were replaced by business school advertisements stressing bookkeeping and penmanship. (It was not until much later in the century that such writers as Melville, in his "Bartleby the Scrivener," saw that the aspirant clerk was as subject to mechanization as the operative.) While the *Voice of Industry* bucked the trend, it was at the cost of its survival; a new editor, supporting the local Work Men's Protective Union, plead for funds in 1848: "We tell the laborer all this, but he won't hear it; we picture it to him; but he is blind . . . we start a paper to advocate his rights and interests, but he lets it go down, and patronizes one in favor of, and pleading the interests of capital and aristocracy."[53] Editor Jaques was discovering that American workers were less interested in general social reform or the elevation of the entire working class than in joining the class of "capital and aristocracy."

Even periodicals whose editors advocated reforms far grander in scope than those considered above shared the self-defeating aim of trying to create a yeoman society out of an industrial proletariat. *The Working Man's Advocate*, founded in 1829 by the English printer George H. Evans, was the organ of the National Reform Association and formed the nucleus of a group of dailies and weeklies dedicated to advancing Evans's brand of agrarianism. Politically, he supported the Workingman's Party, the paper at one time being called *The Sub-*

terranean united with The Workingman's Advocate. The *Subterranean* was the publication of that party's candidate, Mike Walsh; after the elections, it lived up to its name and sank from sight. From 1845 to 1849, the *Advocate* shared the general nationalism as *Young America.* The most striking aspect of Evans's editorship is the tenacity with which his paper presented a single economic theory. A reader of Paine and a disciple of Jefferson, Evans believed that the millenium would arrive when every man, farmer and mechanic alike, had his own 160 acres of fee-simple estate. He wished, in short, to "return" to the ideal of the agrarian yeoman and to apply that ideal to an industrializing society. This could be done, he believed, by using the vast unsettled west—if land speculators could be prevented from blocking the workers' migration there. Had the land been equally parcelled to start with:

> The mechanic, instead of being confined, during the day of ten to fourteen hours to the four walls of a dusty factory, or dirty workshop, and at night returning to his half-starved family in the garret or cellar *of some other man*, would have worked four or six hours a day in his own workshop, or his own premises, in his own house, surrounded by the beauties of nature extracted from the soil by the agreeable and healthful application of his leisure hours.[54]

It is the eighteenth-century dream of a "shop and farm united," of the mechanic whose life is blessed with competence, independence, and the old yeoman association with the soil. It was a dream, Evans believed, that could become a reality in bounteous America if only the speculators and monopolists could be curtailed.

Unlike merchants, engineers, and inventors, Evans did not distinguish between the mechanic and the operative in his use of the terms—they both worked for wages in the factory of some other man, and that dependency equated both titles. Like the reform he called for, this equation implies an assumption that the industrial revolution was still compatible with a yeoman society. Not surprisingly, Fourierists are condemned by Evans because they are outside the morality of true success in denying the right of labor to "stand upon its own ground" as yeomen.[55] Phalanxes were not the answer; despite his admiration for Robert Owen and the praise of associations, Evans preferred to see the land divided up and individually owned. The unstated reason for his insistence upon such ownership derives from the eighteenth-century belief in basic self-interest, and a Franklin-esque faith in the moral results of a virtuous pursuit of a competence; his condemnation of certain types of labor and certain types of reform stems from his attempt to reclaim his goal from the idle and avaricious speculators. Thus, it is not surprising to read Evans' statement that "to us it seems that the proposition of the National Reformers is truly *conservative*,"[56] for in relation to the lost dream of yeomanry, it was.

Even some of the most thoughtful advocates of Fourier and Owen supported those socialistic systems in the hope of returning to the yeoman dream thereby. A figure who expresses this area of reformist thought in the first half of the century—and who foreshadows the broader Christian Socialism of the end of the century—is William Henry Channing. He was brought up by his widowed mother and, in good part, by the advice of his uncle William Ellery Channing. In his biography of his uncle, Henry says of the elder's reformist urge, "He thought that no work of substantial, sure, progressive reform could be effected in the community, without establishing new relations between the more privileged classes and their less fortunate fellow-beings."[57] Like his uncle, but in opposition to many of his peers, Henry saw competitive laissez-faire as increasing selfishness and social turbulence; and at the same time he believed that the laboring class would remain poverty stricken unless it could be led to "virtue, intelligence, and independent conditions."[58] He believed, as many after him believed, that middle class Americans were turning from the worship of God and the respect for humanity to the worship of property and the reduction of fellow man to an object of barter. Both Channings supported Orestes Brownson, and only infirmity prevented Ellery from accompanying his nephew to New York in 1836 to establish a Free Church among the "industrial classes." After the failure of his Free Church, Henry became a Unitarian minister in Cincinnati where he translated Joufroy's ethics and edited the notable *Western Messenger*. At this time he was willing, in spite of or because he lived on the Ohio sub-frontier, to sacrifice some civilization and art to regain the golden pastoral age of independent yeoman mechanics:

> I do not desire to release the laborer from his toil, for work is a
> good school of man. But labor in excess does great harm. The
> division of labor, which distinguishes civilized from savage life,

and to which we owe chiefly the perfection of the arts, tends to dwarf the intellectual powers, by confining the activity of the individual to a narrow range. . . . Perhaps to the heading of pins, the pointing of nails, . . . so that . . . civilized man treads a monotonous, stupifying round of unthinking toil. This cannot, must not always be.

Though he was later to change his mind, in this magazine, Henry was close to his uncle's opinion that the perfect society would come through elevating the soul rather than by changing social institutions. After the revolution in the hearts of employer and employee, the state would wither away and, as Thoreau was soon to call for in *Walden*, leave every man truly successful in a world where political institutions would "shrink into narrower space."[59]

In the 1840s, Channing resigned his ministry and returned to New York where he led a reform society and edited *The Present*. His aims were to wed the church and state, for "Love is the Law of Liberty," and he still believed that the source of corruption in the world was selfish, immoral acquisitiveness. But he shifted his appeal from reforming the individual soul to reform through some type of social change which would eliminate competition. Redistribution of wealth, rather than the rejection of it, would come about through association-ism. The medium of reform was now society rather than the individual, for poverty and the consequent loss of competence were society's failings which corrupted the soul and spawned countless other evils. To support his argument, he turned to statistics, and in March 1844 catalogued in New York City twelve thousand families assisted; four thousand paupers and criminals under city care; one tenth of the population engaged in prostitution; and one sixth financially ruined. All this was caused, he argued, by an avaricious and competitive desire for material riches; but his remedy, social reform, was anathema to the Goodriches, Munsells, and Lights. Like George Evans, Channing lamented the extinct yeoman dream and sought to revitalize it through institutional means. Associationism would lead to independence and competence for all, and, as in Franklin's world, morality would result when honest men had a fair field and a full belly. Channing's view of reform was even vaster than Evans's, for in his attempt to aid operatives, he also tried to redirect the spokesmen of traditional success from their drift toward opulent materialism, sentimental benevolence, and rejection of the class of permanent wage earners. His was the reform of a whole society, not just the elevation of a single class.

Because his magazine found little support among either the middle class who thought his moral preachments superfluous, or the workers, who thought his socialist remedies suspect, it collapsed. He then spent a few months at an active association, Brook Farm, and following that, moved to Boston and presided over the Religious Union of Associationists whose purpose was to spread the reign of love among men. In 1849, a year before that group's dissolution, he began his *Spirit of the Age*. This obscure magazine is a carefully thought-out foreshadowing of the Christian Socialist thought so important later in the century. "Heaven and Humanity demand that Christians and Socialists shall be one," he exclaimed, and went on to explain the magazine's name, "May the *Spirit of the Age* be a herald of hope. Its end is *Peaceful Transition* from competitive strife to organized cooperation, from isolated selfishness to associated interests. Its watchword and countersign are Universal Unity."[60] Those associated interests were not to do away with private property, but in some vague way were to insure the just distribution of property among the "producing classes" who had morally earned it. Like the early Puritans, he sought to institutionally insure God's plan of a just reward for labor; like them, he was not denying the moral value of the proper pursuit of individual wealth. "Throw a man on his own resources," Channing writes, "and give him a chance to make money, he will behave pretty well, as the world goes."[61] The trouble was that an anarchic, materialistic, competitive world seemed to prevent too many a good man from having a chance to "stand upon his own soil": "the producing classes who create the wealth . . . possess comparatively none of it, and live in poverty, while the non-producers and idle rich, revel in luxury. . . . Commerce which . . . should be carried on in the interests of production, has become the master of labor. . . ."[62]

In a lengthy article entitled "The Middle Class," Channing divided society into four levels: the "Privileged," who, living off their capital, were idle and therefore evil; the "People" who lived on marginal wages; the "Poor"; and the "Ruling Power in the Republic," the middle class who "combine capital with their labor." Both great riches and sinful idleness are (or should be) spurned by the middle class. It is made up of "a large proportion of the Professional, Commercial, Manufacturing, Mechanical, Agricultural orders throughout Christendom. . . . The Middle Class is legatee of past success and guardian of germs of good, . . . an elder brother charged by the Privileged to protect the family estates, and to provide means of education, till the People come of age." In our terms, Channing defines the middle class as those who through their own work seek competence and independence, and he adds the necessary moral dimension of true success. On them devolves the responsibility of propagating the yeoman dream and maintaining the society in which that dream can be viable. Ironically, Channing also reflects the drift of his middle class toward secularism and materialism; they are no longer stewards of God but of the privileged, and their goal is no longer heaven but proper society. Though perhaps unintentionally ironic, Channing was not blind to the opulent materialism that seduced the middle class: "By money it has gained, by money it holds honor and power, and money is it stimulated to heap together. . . . Bankers and owners of real estate are the transition between this class and the Privileged, and tradesmen, by economy and keen bargains try to rise to be merchants, mechanics to master manufacturer, farmer's sons to law or politics. . . . Mercenariness tempts the Middle class to join the party of reaction." The middle class, no longer content with competence, must also be rich; no longer content with independence, it must also have power. Nevertheless, Channing believed that the class still had the redemption of virtues gained in the moral pursuit of wealth, and these virtues formed a reservoir of yeomanly morality:

> Habits of self-help, and memory of progress earned in the rough schools of labor give healthy appetite and vigorous digestion; and refinement, learning, skill, grace, breeding are rapidly assimilated. . . . The Middle Class, while over-cautious is earnest and capable, while distrustful of dreamy philanthropists quick to aid substantial plans of benevolence, while tenacious of right is just in purpose, while by habit mean is at heart magnanimous.

The finer things of life which mark the attainment of social prestige can also be sought and attained in the same manner as a competence; self-elevation based upon prudential morality is seen as the force which has molded a virtuous character in the best Franklin manner. Channing depicted a traditional character whose disappearance he mourns. It is time, he urges, for this best of all classes to reassume its civic duty and protect the peace and stability of the state in such a way as to "curb the Privileged and free the people by Peaceful Economy."[63]

But not only did Channing find himself in agreement with the Goodriches by aligning the moral and and the economic criteria for classifying humanity (though unlike Peter Parley, the less wealth the more virtue), he also inherited the age-old conflict entailed in the yeoman dream. Voiced centuries before by William Perkins, it was brought to the stage of a cultural crisis by the rise of industrialism: Channing called for the redistribution of property through institutional means as a way of reconstituting the yeoman society, but the image he praised was the product of the individual pursuit and possession of property. As a result, he could not identify wholly with either the "People" as a proletariat or with the middle class in its drift toward opulent materialism. He remained a spokesman for an intermediate position whose followers were fast diminishing.

After this jeremiad for traditional success, the *Spirit* featured major European and American thinkers and columns of general news; but Channing was not entirely silent. Such problems as race riots in Philadelphia, railroad strikes, New York milk scandals, and opium addiction were discussed. He opposed the Mexican War and renounced Fourierism in favor of a freer type of associationism. The militia system and "industrial feudalism" were both condemned, along with the "aristocracy of wealth." As the magazine closed, Channing found himself in the same predicament as others who clung to the yeoman dream: caught between the unvirtuous rich and the desperate poor, he saw more and more people deserting traditional success in the chase after riches, and at the same time traditional success was deserting more and more workers. Having followed his intellectual heritage back in time through Franklin and Mather to Perkins, he turned to retrace his ancestors' migration; settling in England as a preacher (where Nathaniel Hawthorne noted having heard him), he spent the remainder of his long life cherishing traditional success and contemplating the eternal verities in a society that still had room for the non-materialist and the uncompetitive:

> To live content with small means; to seek elegance rather than luxury, refinement rather than fashion; to be worthy, not respectable, and wealthy, not rich; to listen to stars and birds, babes and sages with open heart; to study hard; to think quietly, act frankly, talk gently, await occasions, hurry never; in a word, to let the spiritual, unbidden and unconscious, grow up through the common—this is my symphony.[64]

❖

Traditional success was not solely the property of the Peter Parleys; labor magazines and papers shared the idea and presented their readers with the image of a competent, independent, and moral yeoman mechanic. Yet during this period, changes in methods of production, marketing, and finance made the image increasingly difficult to hold out as a goal for the urban poor or for factory operatives. The result was a growing division in the magazines between the mechanic who had the potential to attain the dream through taking advantage of these changes—the technological entrepreneur—and the one who could not—the wage slave. Like others who supported traditional success, mechanic editors reflected a fear of the growing numbers of unjustified rich and felt threatened in their social position. Yet unlike the established business and professionally oriented traditionalists, that threat was not only to their prestige and social leadership, but also to their livelihood and independence. Consequently, mechanic magazines showed far more concern with maintaining the material benefits of life than with defending the behavior code of the established element, and by mid-century they contributed to the general drift toward opulent materialism. This concern with wealth and individual mobility seldom entailed the desire to radically change the social structure. What was wanted was what Jacksonian democracy seemed to promise: the fair and free field of individual opportunity that had been America's in the golden age of yeoman farmers. That meant the restoration of widespread opportunity; it meant the destruction of monopoly and combination; it meant just enough government to insure that virtue would be rewarded, as well as the freedom from government to make sure that every individual earned his reward by himself. The new society was to be one of harmony and true success for moral man.

However, it was increasingly obvious that a growing number of mechanics, through no fault of their own, would never achieve the yeoman dream. Journeymen who had been raised on the idea of eventually becoming the masters of their own shop saw ownership going to men who had never been laborers. They saw themselves and their peers denied the possibility of ever becoming anything but toilers for wages in other men's factories. The flow of capital was no longer from consumer to producer but from "the market" to "the backers," or into new manufacturing techniques that further reduced the need for workmen with old-fashioned skills. The result was that mechanics, while often clamoring for the same things as businessmen—a fair price, respect, and the promise of independence—became divided between technological entrepreneurs capable of profiting from a complex financial and industrial society, and a proletariat whose ranks were invaded by women, children, and immigrants, all viewed more and more as a class of aliens inimical to true success. There was, of course, a need for skilled mechanics in the factories which produced various labor-saving machines, yet such jobs required retraining and probably geographic mobility, not to mention involvement in the politics of a rival trade. And, as technological knowledge increased, these jobs were also subject to automation or simplification. The result was that in a number of trades, the journeyman's wages tended to be depressed and his employment insecure in the face of unskilled labor; these results, of course, form the principal complaints of the Trades' Union. In addition, a ceiling was being placed on upward mobility within the craft or trade as the new professional schools began turning out well-educated engineers to step into top positions. Loss of prestige, loss of wealth, loss of independence, loss of mobility all combined to negate the mechanic's dream of yeomanry.

The idea of traditional success also had its effect upon reformers and radicals, many of whom saw the direction of the industrial revolution, but who could conceive of no alternative other than their inherited concept of the truly successful life. They attempted to find some way of counteracting the effects of what they considered to be a new and aggressive capitalism which bred a socially disruptive competition and selfish individualism. Like the mechanics, they wanted the "old order" of a harmonious society of yeoman content with a competence and independence, and morality in the pursuit of them. Yet they were in a quandary. Their ideal society and their ideal yeoman were not really distinct from the aims and values held by the villains, the business and professional men who seemed to be taking advantage of the wage earner. The audiences addressed by the reformers were either, like the established spokesmen, taking millionaires as exemplars or else were so far removed from the possibility of traditional success that to offer it was a cruelty. Many, like the Channings, tried to make the yeoman dream fit the proletariat at a time when marketing, financing, and production were becoming separate functions; others, like Andrew Carnegie, tried to make the rich fit the yeoman dream.[65] The reformers wanted self-sufficiency, but they lamented materialism; they desired independence, but they condemned individualism; they praised the moral pursuit of wealth, but they decried the effect of that wealth on morality. Increasingly, they began to admit that in America the race went to those who started first, the battle to the strong, and the money to the cunning.

Moral: that our welfare depends on ourselves. . . . A quick prying eye, and sharp
face,—the most expressive possible of one on
the lookout for gain,—of the most disagree-
able class of Yankees.

American Notebooks, 1838

. . . It is the curse of prosperity that it takes
work away from us, and shuts that door to
hope and health of spirit.

The Rise of Silas Lapham, 1885

4

FANSHAWE TO GRIMSHAWE

✦

PERHAPS ONE of the differences between subliterature and literature is that the former is uncritical in reflecting a culture's trends of thought while literature seems to deal critically with those configurations, revealing an artistic mind at work examining and impressing form on the culture's assumptions. At least with Nathaniel Hawthorne and the yeoman dream, such is the case. In light of the long tradition of viewing Hawthorne as a novelist who probes the dark corners of the introspective soul, the assertion of his concern with the yeoman dream may seem surprising. But as seen in such stories as "My Kinsman, Major Molineaux" and "The Maypole at Merrymount," he was vitally interested not only in man's relation to himself or to his God, but also to his society. Moreover, this relation was not always depicted by Hawthorne in a pessimistic manner; despite a one-sided view, beginning perhaps with Melville's comments in "Hawthorne and His Mosses," that he rejected Enlightenment or Romantic optimism for a Puritanical gloom, a few recent studies dealing with his social themes and his interest in the public conscience have brought an awareness of his ambivalent attitude toward American society.[1] Hawthorne is as divided in his view of man's social future as man is personally divided between possibility and limitation, and quite often for Hawthorne, man's moral promise and his social future were conceived in the terms of the yeoman dream. The shifting feelings about traditional success seen in the preceding chapters, the mixture of hope and fear, of optimism and pessimism about the destiny of the American yeoman, was perceived by Hawthorne and reinforced by his aware-

131

ness of the promise and shortcomings mixed in the individual's soul. Knowing, from his struggles for a competence, the necessity of a material income wrought from a competitive world, he also understood, from his long isolation and Puritan introspection, the personal moral dangers of that materialism and competition. As an artist, he placed form upon his feelings and beliefs, and the result was a continuing struggle in all but one of his novels to resolve contemporary social problems within the framework of traditional success.

Like so many other figures considered in previous chapters, Hawthorne was descended from an early New England colonist. Brought up among the mercantile life of Salem, related to the owners of a prosperous stage line, and son of a respected sea captain, Hawthorne was born to a position of community respect if not of wealth. With this inheritance came a belief in traditional success, and, at first, the idea was not analyzed by him; it was one of the givens of his universe, either to be ignored for explorations of the individual soul, or to be accepted as a value system within which other ideas were measured and by which they were colored. But gradually the conventions began to lose their certainty for him as they did for his peers, and his sensitivity to America's increasing materialism brought into focus the assumptions of the yeoman dream. Forced by what he recognized as the brute facts of survival to join the drift to materialism, and logically and practically though not emotionally unable to react by withdrawing from it, he could not countenance that drift. Though he did not starve to serve his muse, or join a crusade for phalanxes or abolition, temperance or peace, in his own way he did try to retain the values he considered necessary for true success in America: the mixture of idealism and materialism that made up the old yeoman dream. But finally, after much search, after futilely struggling with the same related themes in his late novels (*The Ancestral Footstep, Septimius Felton, Doctor Grimshawe's Secret,* and *The Dolliver Romance*), he found no solution which would make traditional success viable for the mid-nineteenth century. Like so many others, Hawthorne did not visualize the breadth of impact of the industrial revolution in America, and his attempt to solve its problems with traditional concepts resulted in a now-familiar type of perplexity when faced with the new urban-industrial world. Only *The Scarlet Letter* maintains lasting general appeal based on its unity of concern. In that novel the "private" moral conflicts and the "public" social conflicts are separate; the "Custom House Sketch" treats the persistent theme of success in Hawthorne's society, while the novel itself is primarily dedicated to studying the effects of sin on three souls in a world distant in time and spirit from Hawthorne's own. The result was a focus and timelessness of subject matter that he was unable to achieve in other novels. But if, in these other novels, Hawthorne's answers are incomplete for our own time, his formulation of them still has meaning for us.

Some insight into his use of traditional success is found in the early short stories where he seems to assume the values of that success almost without reflection. There are, it is true, a few in which he grapples with the idea; [2] but it was not until his marriage and the subsequent numerous attempts to find economic security for his family that his concern intensified. Then, like bones in the sand, the underlying assumptions emerged and took on the more definite outline of a theme. Representative of the earlier attitude is *Fanshawe;* although the work is in part Gothic, its characters and plot make use of many of the themes of traditional success seen in the juvenile and labor periodicals already discussed. While offering only the slightest promise of later greatness, the book reveals Hawthorne's early and uncritical acceptance of the familiar conventions of the yeoman dream. They work, as conventions often do, in the manner of a symbolic shorthand in which the very typicality of the actors readily explains both their characters and the novel's statement to readers familiar with the conventions. And, when used uncritically, these conventions spare the author the pain of real artistic effort. Reliance on such characters tends, of course, toward the trite; and it was probably recognition of this triteness which caused a more mature Hawthorne to recall the novel from circulation. But for the purpose of limning cultural or sub-cultural archetypes, for determining the outlines of a period's romance, these conventions and the author's assumptions about their acceptability are vital.

The most salient theme in Hawthorne's first novel is, perhaps, the contrast between a retired, other-worldly scholasticism and this-worldly activity. While a cursory familiarity with Hawthorne's life reveals the importance of this theme for him personally, it also has its more public aspect which is seen in the type-characters used to develop the idea. Dr. Melmoth and his friend Mr. Langdon present the theme on one level, and Fanshawe and Edward Walcott on another. The two older men are slight, familiar figures; here, as in later stories, Hawthorne uses the older generation as an example of failure which the younger generation can avoid, provided it learns from history. Content to live without fame or fortune, the doctor has retired to the realm of study and, though materially poor, is spiritually content. But this retirement is not perfect; he is married, and his termagent wife laments their poverty long and loud. The implication is clear that a bit more material security would quiet the wife and place Melmoth's spiritual retirement on a more solid basis. The conventionality of the doctor's opposite, Mr. Langdon, is readily admitted by Hawthorne when he describes him as one who "in the words of the old ballad, 'set his heart on gold,' and to his absorbing passion had sacrificed his domestic happiness."[3] Neither avaricious nor cruel, he is the familiar unsuccessful rich man that, like the merchant in the *Youth's Companion* (page 59, above), was blinded by his materialistic pursuits to the spiritual values of a truly successful life. The younger men, while pictured with more complexity perhaps because Hawthorne could project himself into their characters, are also conventions drawn from the lore of traditional success. Fanshawe, already half in the other world from his non-physical and consequently sickly scholarly labor, is less typical in that he also represents one of Hawthorne's own themes, the effects of spiritual monomania. Only once, when he is brought to earth by his love for Ellen Langdon, does his dedication waver, and he is tempted to compromise his dream. But by then it is too late, and perhaps here is where the novel's tragedy is supposed to lie. As Langdon had sacrificed his happiness for exclusive materialism, so Fanshawe sacrifices life, fertility, and love for goals which are exclusively non-material. "Where," he laments, is the "happiness of superior knowledge?" The answer, embodied in Fanshawe's young antagonist Edward Walcott, is that true happiness is the familiar mixture of material and spiritual reward found in the yeoman dream. Walcott, like Langdon, illustrates the shortcomings of solely material success in his denial of the non-material in life. Like Langdon, he is also an admitted convention, "the fine gentleman of the little community . . . , a character which generally leads its possessor to follies that he would have otherwise avoided."[4] In the terms of traditional success, Hawthorne presents the reader with both types of unvirtuous wealthy, the secular materialist and the morally underdeveloped inheritor of wealth. However, like Fanshawe, Walcott undergoes a rather abrupt change for the better, which change reveals an early and lasting theme in Hawthorne's writings: a concept of morality defined by one's sensitivity to the feelings of others. Whereas the scholar learns first how destructive his monomania can be, and secondly how unfit he is for the physical world of which Ellen is so much a part, Walcott has his pride chastened and his spirit elevated by recognizing his own foolish recklessness and Fanshawe's exemplary nobility. In showing humility and magnanimity (and respect for Fanshawe's feelings) by withdrawing from the competition for the girl's hand, Walcott gains in spiritual nobility. This spiritual gain is Hawthorne's equivalent of the moral element of traditional success—an elevation equal to that found in the riches-to-rags motif. But the story demands a husband for Ellen—she too deserves her traditional success—and Fanshawe has demonstrated his material unsuitability for such a role. Walcott, through his moral elevation, has overcome the burden of inherited wealth and ends up properly located between Langdon and Fanshawe. Neither entirely material nor exclusively spiritual, he becomes as truly successful a gentleman as ever struck a pose in *Godey's Lady's Book*.

This affinity with Godey's scribbling women may have soured Hawthorne on the novel, but he did not give up the theme of true success. What he did develop in time was a critical eye for its conventions; Ellen, Fanshawe, Walcott—as well as the theme—all reappear portrayed with the complexity of a mature Hawthorne in *The House of the Seven Gables*. This novel has been well read on the level of "private conscience" for its study of the effect of guilt on succeeding generations, but it is also a major attempt to defend the idea of traditional success against the competitive and exclusive materialism that seemed to be changing the yeoman dream in the 1850s. As in *Fanshawe*, and in the numerous early stories he wrote for Peter Parley, Hawthorne works with the conventions of traditional success, mixing materialism and idealism, emphasizing concurrent attainment of wealth and morality. In light of this reading, the novel is direct and economic, and the controversial ending is seen to be carefully anticipated; it is a romance of traditional success in which various alternatives to that success form the work's structure, and the right kind of success forms its happy resolution. Perhaps this use and control of the conventions of traditional success led Hawthorne to differ so much from his later critics in calling *The House of the Seven Gables* his best novel.[5]

Hawthorne often pictured life to be a mixture of, as he said, "marble and mud," and *The House of the Seven Gables* is no exception. He saw the contemporary American's life as bound, on the one hand, by exclusive materialism, and, on the other, by exclusive other-worldliness. The former destroyed the spiritual in man and reduced him to an animal level, while a total rejection of the material world led to the danger of separation from the necessary quotidian life. Man should live neither by bread nor by spirit alone, but by a proper mixture of the two.

Judge Pyncheon and his cousin Clifford are placed in opposition to represent these extremes of materialism and otherworldliness. Like Langdon and Dr. Melmoth, neither the judge nor his cousin is truly successful. The avaricious Judge Pyncheon, very much typifying the mid-nineteenth-century world, embodies material success without concomitant moral elevation. Hawthorne repeatedly stresses the grossness of his manners, appearance, and mind. He was of that class of "men to whom forms are of paramount importance" and whose "field of action lies among the external phenomena of life."[6] Conventionally, his is the false success of mere wealth, and his materialism has reduced him to the level of a sensual animal dominated by a will to the ownership of "things." Clifford is the man of sensibility whose imprisonment by the judge has removed him from the everyday world. His realm is the gloomy solitude of the House as contrasted with the worldliness of the judge, and his exclusive spirituality, like the poet to whom he is compared, leads him to a "poor and impalpable enjoyment of existence." Like the judge, he is "selfish in . . . essence"; however, it is the non-material selfishness of a Fanshawe, though Clifford is a lover of ideal beauty instead of ideal truth. For example, he is drawn to Phoebe's spiritual attractiveness as much as the judge is lured by her more material charms. However, Phoebe's reaction to the former is not one of fear or revulsion, for Clifford's artistic selfishness and spirituality are far better than the selfishness and materialism of the judge. But in a world of marble and mud, Clifford, the embodiment of refined sensibilities, can not survive without help. Having been starved of worldly and sensual development perhaps by his Puritan heritage or nineteenth-century materialism—certainly by his isolation—Clifford no longer has "the heart, and will, and conscience, to fight the battle with the world."[7] He lacks the capability to earn the material competence and independence necessary to true success. Hawthorne is careful to show the dangerous psychological effect of this separation from the material realities of life, and here his personal fear of isolation reinforces the social dimension of the theme. The death of the judge causes Clifford to believe that he is a free spirit, and he leads Hepzibah on a flight into a dream-like euphoria.

Clifford finally exercises his will, but the exercise leads to a success that, for him, can only be a delusion. They board, for the first time in their lives, that major symbol of material progress, a train. Peering through the windows of this new world, Clifford discovers that the effect of contemporary science and technology is to unfix everything from its "age-long rest." In the train, the recluses are "in the midst of life" where material invention hurtles America along the rails of progress. And at last the lover of beauty has joined the industrializing society, bringing a vision of the future which resembles the Virgilian Golden Age. With soaring cadence the delirious Clifford paints an Arcadian picture of freedom from the common burdens of life, of escape from past afflictions, of entrance into a future where science and art harmoniously unite to liberate mankind for spiritual as well as physical development. However, for him it is only a dream; he cannot embrace the rough competitive materialism of American life, "These railroads—could but the whistle be made musical, and the rumble and the jar got rid of—are positively the greatest blessing that the ages have wrought out for us." The shriek of the whistle and the lurch of the road-bed remain; as the cold, common sense replies of the old gentleman passenger reveal, science and technology will not transcend the material realm, with or without the aid of Clifford's artistic vision. The evaporation of his dream is depicted in the two fugitives' return to earth. When they alight, the world is cold, sullen, bleak. His will—weak because it has not been properly exercised in the real world—fades in the face of this hostile environment. It sinks and pulls his vision down with it; he is again dependent upon the Hepzibah of the old decayed gentility. And she, no longer under the spell of Clifford's mania, driven from the light and warmth of the train, alone in a dark world whose sky is invisible and whose landmarks are strange, finally turns to her only resource: "Oh God . . . are we not thy children? Have mercy on us!"[8] At the end of the novel, her first sincerely humble prayer is rewarded.

Two other aspects of success are opposed in the characterizations of Phoebe and Hepzibah. The former represents the "new Plebianism" of American democracy—a female yeoman; the latter is the decadent artificial aristocracy of the past. Hepzibah is characterized by the Pyncheons' "absurd delusion of family importance" based upon ancient empty claims to greatness (the lost Eastern Tract). With ironic detachment, Hawthorne measures this false aristocracy against a scale of traditional success and finds it lacking, "In the better specimens of the breed this peculiarity threw an ideal grace over the hard material of human life, without stealing away any truly valuable quality. In the baser sort, its effect was to increase the liability to sluggishness and dependence, and to induce the victim of a shadowy hope to remit all self-effort."[9]

If the "better specimens" approach this traditional success despite their inherited wealth, it is because, in their combination of "ideal grace" and "hard material," they are at home in both the abstract and concrete realms. The "baser sort" are conventional failures: lazy, dependent, and falsely proud; they may enjoy a competence and even independence, but their lack of self-effort denies the morality necessary for true success. In the lore of traditional success the idle rich man who contributes nothing to—or who actually harms—human progress is commonly contrasted with the industrious yeoman. Hepzibah, for example, when beginning her spiritual climb through self-effort in the material world, asks about one of her peers, "for what good end . . . does that woman live?"[10] Hepzibah clarifies Hawthorne's attack on false success by offering, as might be expected of Hawthorne's multi-faceted mind, gradations of the thematic ideas. Because of her redeeming love for Clifford, Hawthorne does not damn her as he does the entirely materialistic judge; the pattern of her salvation is the convention of riches-to-rags: a reversal of material fortune which humbles the falsely proud and awakens them to an awareness of their moral shortcomings and to a consequent spiritual rise. This archetypal pattern is classically portrayed in William Dean Howell's *The Rise of Silas Lapham*, and with less ability in numerous nineteenth century books, plays, and stories. Unlike Howells, Hawthorne could assume an audience more familiar with the conventions and consequently begins the theme in *medias res*, at the nadir of Hepzibah's material fortune and the beginning of her moral rise. She is forced to open the penny shop, a humiliating act caused both by her poverty and by her love for Clifford. A clear indication of Hawthorne's attitude toward Hepzibah's previous state and toward her coming regeneration occurs at the first sale when Hepzibah begins to earn her own way: "The healthiest glow that Hepzibah had known for years had come now in the dreaded crisis, when, for the first time, she had put forth her hand to help herself. The . . . copper coin . . . had proved a talisman, fragrant with good, and deserving to be set in gold and worn next to her heart."[11] Money, but money morally earned, is here depicted as good. It is, in other words, not in wealth

itself, but in the attitude toward the pursuit of wealth that its curse
or blessing lies. Hepzibah in contrast to Judge Pyncheon must learn
this lesson through material misfortune, "she [Hepzibah] had been
enriched by poverty, developed by sorrow, elevated by the strong
and solitary affection of her life, and thus endowed with a heroism,
which never could have characterized her in what are called happier
circumstances."[12]

Hawthorne does more than simply depict the idle rich being
morally rearmed by poverty. In Hepzibah, as in Clifford, he combines the conventions of traditional success with the personal theme
of isolation—that man cannot and most importantly, must not escape
the claims of everyday life. Although she can never reach the heights
attained by Phoebe, the best of Hepzibah's character can be win-
nowed out, for in her plunge into ordinary life is found both sanity
and true success.

Hepzibah's moral regeneration, though begun before Phoebe's
appearance, received impetus and restatement from that natural noblewoman's presence. Phoebe epitomizes the best in New England womanhood which no amount of work can brutify, and like her classical
namesake, like the agrarian yeoman, her realm is Arcadia. Because she
escaped being brought up as an idle and proud Pyncheon, because she
is fresh from the country and radiates sunshine and health and the
smiling aspects of democracy, Phoebe's environment has overcome
any hereditary taint to make her the ideal American woman, "the
example of feminine grace and availability combined." Her work in
the store shows Hepzibah and the reader the morally refining aspect
of the Protestant Ethic, which is in contrast, of course, to the Pyncheon burden of sin symbolized in the tainted inheritance. Like the
"gold talisman" that Hepzibah's first coin becomes, gold is used again
as a positive image when Hawthorne pictures Phoebe's joy in work,
"[She had] the cheeriness of an active temperament, finding joy in
its activity, and, therefore rendering it beautiful; it was a New England trait,—the stern stuff of Puritanism with a gold thread in the
web."[13] In support of his observations on Phoebe, Hawthorne then
demonstrates the golden Plebian's moral pursuit of wealth. Her first
day in the store, which includes a contest between "wrinkled slyness
of craft pitted against native truth and sagacity," results in "an enor-
mous heap of copper!" But such competitive money-making does not
threaten Phoebe; the storekeeping occupation "that might so easily
have taken a squalid and ugly aspect—had been made pleasant, and

even lovely, by the spontaneous grace with which these homely duties seemed to bloom out of her character. . . ."[14] Like the Lowell factory women celebrated in the previous chapter, Phoebe brings to the pursuit of wealth the virtues of a yeoman upbringing; but unlike those women whose work was becoming ominously degrading, she is not threatened. Rather, her yeoman character is strong enough to transcend the material threat and make the pursuit of money function as part of traditional success.

In addition to demonstrating the virtuous pursuit of wealth, Phoebe underscores the idea that true success is to be found in the real world and not in isolation or dreams. She is not only the natural noblewoman contrasted with an idle and false aristocracy, but is also a natural and independent poetic force which is contrasted with the dependent and contrived artistry of Clifford. She brings, as does the golden bough of the Pyncheon elm that reaches for the house at the end of the story, nature's light and life to the isolated Clifford, who now can only absorb them. Like Milton's Eve, Phoebe's spirit is linked to fruitful nature; she tends the garden and makes it grow, greeting each dawn with a simple prayer. Unlike Hepzibah, she does not need a trauma to shock her into the child-like faith she already has; unlike Clifford, she does not need the incantations and magic of artistry to create beauty. But Phoebe is not a static character like so many heroines of romance; she undergoes change as a result of challenges first from Judge Pyncheon, then from Holgrave. At the beginning, she is pictured as among the class of people who might, if given knowledge of the world's hypocrisy, be "tumbled headlong into chaos." But in the chapter aptly entitled "Phoebe's Goodbye," when she learns of earth's sadness and death, the result is neither incurable pessimism nor black despair. Rather, it is a moral maturity. Like Hester Prynne, like Hepzibah, she finds that adversity strengthens her will and she becomes a more adult person thereby. But because—unlike Hester—Phoebe is a major component of the moral society, her virtues make her eligible for the traditional reward of that society's womankind: independent "huswifery."

Repeated references to Uncle Venner as the "old Philosopher" indicate his role as commentator on society's aims and values. Though condemned by the commonality as "rather deficient . . . in his wits" because he does not try for "such success as other men seek," he has —more than Clifford—"something tough and vigorous about him." At the same time, there is "something like Poetry in him." The toughness results from his ability for survival in the world of wharves and street corners; the poetry is the distilled wisdom and serenity won by studying that world. In the manner of Dr. Melmoth, Venner rejects the struggle to "heap up property" and moves in the realm of philosophical meditation, but his wisdom is less an abstract reasoning and more a practical knowledge based on everyday life. His advice to Hepzibah about supplying the shop, for instance, is borne out by the customers' demands and by Phoebe's observations. His clothing—that outside form which presents itself to the world—had been "patched together . . . of different epochs; an epitome of times and fashions." But this harlequin appearance is not meant by Hawthorne to be the same restlessness and variety of occupation characteristic of Holgrave. Venner's clothes might reflect different philosophical fashions, but the person within them and the essential wisdom he represents remain the same. Unlike the judge, Venner's interest was in essences and not external forms, and his heart had "not a drop of bitter essence at the bottom."[15] This picture of Venner as philosopher places Hawthorne in that broad, ill-defined stream of American philosophical thought eventually called Pragmatism. Like William James, Hawthorne was aware of the material necessities of human existence and he desired a system of thought which would be practical in everyday life. Again, like James, he was dissatisfied with being forced to choose either materialism or idealism and tried to find a synthesis of the two. And, again as in James, the truth of an observation was often relative to the conditions surrounding that observation; Venner's symbolic clothing shows that Hawthorne credited "truth" to philosophies that "worked." As earlier times and fashions needed their "suitable" beliefs, a different philosophy was called for in mid-nineteenth-century America.[16] Nevertheless, an absolute underlies all this change: each philosophy represented by Venner's clothing is but a different expression of the common aim of increasing man's happiness. Venner's heart (the common yearning behind those various shreds of philosophy) is filled with the same benevolence toward mankind that Holgrave found in Fourierism; Venner's constant aim is to render life "sweet, bland, and gently beneficent." But the methods of attaining this beneficence, bland or not, must be defined by each generation for itself and must avoid the dogmatism of a Fourier. For Hawthorne, though man's happiness might be the unchanging goal, the relationship between method and environment had to be pragmatically considered. He would return with more careful consideration to this theme in *The Blithedale Romance* and *Doctor Grim-shawe's Secret*, but *The House of the Seven Gables* was to be an op-timistic portrayal of the survival of the yeoman dream, and Venner's role was not to serve as a start to speculation about that dream's value, but was to fit the mosaic of traditional success.

The "blandness" of Venner's philosophy, despite the practical-ity of his business advice, is related to the old belief in philosophical retirement. Just as this retirement had not been compatible with the Puritan advocation of unceasing Fruitfulness, neither did it now fit the energetic demands of an expanding nineteenth-century America; consequently, Hawthorne does not present it as a viable alternative to traditional success, for Venner's philosophy lacks material fruit-fulness. Although not isolated like Hepzibah from mankind, his con-tribution to general social progress is just as nil, and the constant references to his future as a ward of society underline his unyeo-manly dependence, "It does seem to me that men make a wonderful mistake in trying to heap up property upon property. If I had done so, I should feel as if Providence was not bound to take care of me; and, at all events, the city wouldn't be!" His riches, he argues, are not in the material realm, "infinity is big enough for us all—and eternity long enough." But as Hawthorne had pointed out with Melmoth and his wife, Venner's immaterial success is not enough for this world; Phoebe argues that a more secular success is also necessary: "for this short life of ours, one would like a house and a moderate garden-spot of one's own."[17] For busy, growing, mid-century America, it is Phoebe's more material involvement with life rather than Venner's contemplation of eternity which wins Hawthorne's approval. She has, as Holgrave points out to the reader, an "intuitive sympathy" for understanding the true nature of man's happiness; and in the story, her pursuit of that happiness—the house and garden-spot of one's own —is eminently practical. Though Venner eventually receives his re-ward of classical retirement, it is not through his own efforts but is the gift of the heirs of the New World, Holgrave and Phoebe. At the rejuvenated estate in the country, Venner's cottage is placed a scant "five minutes saunter from Clifford's chair," and Art and mellow Philosophy find a home in the utopia built by "real men."

As demonstrated in preceding chapters, social change was not disapproved of in the ethic of traditional success, for it often con-tributed to the self-responsibility so necessary for individual inde-pendence. But such change was to be by safe evolution rather than by dangerous revolution. Whereas other believers in traditional success often feared the effects of revolution on their property, Hawthorne's primary concern with social disorder emphasized its dangers to the soul. In "Old News," (1834), for example, he wrote that the results of a revolution "or anything that interrupts social order . . . are pernicious to general morality." The same belief is apparent in "My Kinsman, Major Molineaux," in *Septimius Felton*, and in "Chiefly About War Matters." In *The House of the Seven Gables*, the idea of social change appears, as A. N. Kaul has noted, in Maule's curse—the lower class progeny that represents the leveling democracy in America.[18] As Maule's descendant, Holgrave elicits Hawthorne's admiration for his industrious self-reliance and Hawthorne's fear for his threat to America's soul. In order for Holgrave to be morally worthy of material reward, he must evolve through spiritual refinement and have the threat of his revolutionary bent laid to rest. In contrast to Venner, the daguerreotypist is a social rather than a moral philosopher, and a major part of his role in the novel is that of a reformer of social institutions. At first Holgrave was concerned more with the flesh than with the spirit; and his way of life, the "rude struggle of man with man" which he had been involved in since boyhood, was, in mid-nineteenth-century America, a morally ambivalent environment that could easily have made him into another Judge Pyncheon. For, like the judge, Holgrave had a naturally strong "force of will," and—at the beginning of the novel—he was as determined to witness his revenge as the judge was determined to invade the house. On the social level, the danger that Holgrave posed was that, as often depicted in the lore of traditional failure, his attributes could become socially destructive; his self-reliance, independence, will, and egocentricity could, if not governed by a strong personal morality, make a monster of him. Despite being a Yankee, his potential defect was not the excessive materialism of Judge Pyncheon, but the self-delusion of an over-weening will; he was caught up in his own law of the self-made man which endangered old and life-giving institutions: social order, peace, and the home. Phoebe, with traditional reverence for stability, was "startled . . . and sometimes repelled . . . by a sense that his law differed from her own" in being so much more ambitious. And Hawthorne, sharing Phoebe's bias, indicates that Holgrave's law was presumptuous. He steps forward in Chapter XII to tell the reader that although he approved of much of Holgrave's liberation from the past, there were two things he disliked in the young man: the delusion that the past could be totally rejected, and the radical substitution of a new Fourierist social system which would eventually be just as petrifying as the past orders of society. Although the belief that the world could be improved was a vital, admirable, and necessary virtue, the improvement was to be effected not by man in a single day, but by God over a long period of time. Hawthorne further promises that Holgrave, though right in his optimism, will learn, as Hepzibah did, to submit to an humble, child-like faith in Providence, and that he will develop a less blasphemous and self-mesmerized faith in man's ability to create his own progress. "The haughty faith, with which he [Holgrave] began life, would be well bartered for a far humbler one at its close, in discerning that man's best directed effort accomplishes a kind of dream, while God is the sole worker of realities."[19] Thus, the daguerreotypist-mesmerist-radical would learn to reject visionary man-made dreams for the belief in gradual divine progress in which the best of the past would survive and the best of the future would come about.

Just as Hawthorne is careful to portray the gross materialism of the conventionally evil Judge Pyncheon, so he is careful to show the development in Holgrave's character that serves to redeem him and the American society he represents. The redemption is within the framework of "real" progress that Hawthorne advocated, and its reward is in the familiar tradition. True reform, Holgrave learns, must come through man's heart, for "All other reform and renovation . . . will prove to be no better than moonshine."[20] The morally converting agent is Phoebe, but it is for Holgrave alone to forswear the mesmeric powers which tempt him to repeat Maule's sin. Fortunately, Holgrave, despite his upbringing in a dangerous environment, had—like Phoebe—an innate moral strength. He "never violated the innermost man, but had carried his conscience along with him."[21] This conscience—this innate nobility found by Jefferson, Emerson, and Thoreau to be in the hearts of all men—leads Holgrave to respect the spiritual element of humanity and to purge himself of the sinful desire to manipulate other humans. The purging takes place, of course, at the telling of the story of Alice Pyncheon and Matthew Maule, the subject of which is pride and lust. Matthew, no less material and ignoble than the Pyncheons, had used his mesmeric powers to destroy the pride of Alice, and in doing so, had destroyed her soul. Holgrave, though sorely tempted to "acquire empire" over Phoebe's mesmerized spirit—and the slightly veiled analogy to her body—voluntarily breaks the spell and thus turns from the morally reprehensible revenge of his ancestor. Further along in mankind's moral progress than was his ancestor, Holgrave advances one more step; he subsequently feels rejuvenated by his sympathy for another human soul, and this rejuvenation blossoms into love for Phoebe.[22] Of thematic importance, his love combines the judge's love for Phoebe's flesh with Clifford's love for her spirit; and thus, like Edward Walcott, Holgrave becomes the proper man to receive the lady's hand.

Though Holgrave is described as an artist and a man more interested in making reforms than in making money, his art is more of a craft and the subject of his tinkering is society. The artistic aspect of Holgrave's character indicates his spiritual refinement, but unlike Clifford or Venner, Holgrave is deeply involved in the everyday material world. Thus, rather than an art of intellectual abstraction or inspired genius, Holgrave's art is in the area of technical craft.[23] A good part of what Hawthorne admires about Holgrave is this involvement in life, this practicality, this economic and moral self-reliance. Even the rapid change of occupation and location, while dangerous and dizzying, is not—for Holgrave and many other Americans—necessarily bad. Numerous contemporary biographies of successful men demonstrate that this flexibility strengthened those attributes of character which Hawthorne praised in his ideal Yankee. As a representative American, Holgrave partakes of this same development; as a heroic archetype in a romance of traditional success, he embodies the virtues of the yeoman and serves to point the way for society to achieve that success. Real reform, Hawthorne told us, comes through the heart. Holgrave's moral elevation takes place with the rejection of Maule's revenge, and what remains is for his view of society to be reformed too. This occurs in conjunction with his love for Phoebe. Without her, death makes the world appear to him as a "strange, wild, evil, hostile" place; but nature's life force brings "hope, warmth, and joy." In other words, death makes the new Adam and Eve conscious of the immortality of love and regeneration. The earthly fecundity represented by Phoebe convinces Holgrave of the necessity of a stable institutional framework to protect both her and the home—matrices within which all that is good will develop for the future. Indeed, as he thinks of the Pyncheon country seat, he wishes that it had been built of stone rather than wood in order to accommodate both change and stability, "Then, every generation of the family might have altered the interior, to suit its own taste and convenience; while the exterior . . . might have been adding venerableness to its original beauty, and thus giving the impression of permanence which I consider essential to . . . happiness. . . ."[24]

Here, Hawthorne, unlike many of his contemporaries, is not nearly as certain that an elevated soul will result merely from the moral pursuit of wealth; the catalyst of Phoebe's love must be added. Her "poise"—the solid rock of nature upon which man's fundamental institution, the home, is built—turns out to be more powerful than Holgrave's tendency to oscillate between social responsibility and irresponsibility (a tendency which seemed to be so much a part of the character of restless American democracy). Phoebe is justly startled at his rapid change in attitude toward social institutions. So is the reader, for despite the character development, Hawthorne here manipulates Holgrave to meet the conventional demands of the romance of success. He is made to illustrate the venturous conservatism of traditional success; his realm is now to "set out trees, to make fences . . . in a word, to conform myself to laws, and the peaceful practice of society."[25] The social danger of the new American has been averted, and Holgrave turns out to be a conservative in the same vein that many Jacksonian Democrats—Hawthorne among them—were conservative in the face of the radical capitalism and materialism that threatened the yeoman dream. This desire for permanent fundamental laws based upon nature, within which there would be justified mobility for each generation, offered assumptions about society on which Hawthorne could build the social level of his allegory. And it is into the utopia of traditional success that he pushes his morally regenerated characters.

The novel's ending has been called, among other things, an example of Hawthorne's conscious irony. According to this view, the ending is only apparently happy; Judge Pyncheon's wealth in reality will enable Hepzibah and Clifford to return to their old ways, as well as ultimately corrupt and isolate Holgrave and Phoebe.[26] This reading, it seems to me, overlooks the carefully built social representativeness of Holgrave's entourage as well as the individual changes of character undergone by the major actors. In their moral refinement, these figures and the society they represent are not endangered by the Pyncheon fortune. Rather, in much the same way that Phoebe's innate natural nobility and Puritan industriousness elevated store-keeping and made profit taking both honorable and moral, the inheritance is seen in the light of the "competence" element of traditional success.

The wealth is the reward for moral endeavor and contributes to the continued improvement of the individual and his society. Apparently, Hawthorne intended the utopia to represent a fulfillment of both material and moral needs; each character, incomplete in the body of the tale, reaches fulfillment in the utopian conclusion. The ethic of traditional success had its evil rich, as Judge Pyncheon personifies, but it also had its virtuous wealthy: those with independence and morality, but whose competence had grown to riches. Because Holgrave's will was strengthened by his independence, because he attained virtue in the course of the novel, his utopia is, indeed, without evil. Moreover, the conversion of the judge's wealth into a positive agent—through an act of God—is but another instance of Hawthorne's belief in the mysterious workings of Providence which turns man's petty drives into general good. Holgrave's presentiment that "a man's bewilderment is the measure of his wisdom" is borne out.

Still, the novel's ending is, as Mattheissen argues, unsatisfactory.[27] But the reader's feeling of dissatisfaction comes not from any intentional ironic twist of statement nor from an intense and all-embracing pessimism in Hawthorne's work. Rather, it comes from Hawthorne's commitment to a particular set of conventions while, at the same time, implicit questions are raised about those conventions. Like Huck Finn, Holgrave is forced to "light out for the territory ahead" if his achievement is to be preserved; but his utopia, rather than being a rejection of civilization, is the familiar hope for a society in which competitive materialism is replaced by spiritual and material progress and by social harmony. While Holgrave's new role is to "build fences," to actively contribute to the progress of society in contrast to the more indolent Uncle Venner or the rapacious Judge Pyncheon, the entire society itself is separated from the world of the House of the Seven Gables. Perhaps the cavalier tone pervading the last chapter implies Hawthorne's attitude that, after all, the story is a romance and need not restrict itself to "the probable and ordinary course of man's experience." Indeed, one of the overlooked frames of reference for the characters involves, as I have tried to show, the by now romantic conventions of the yeoman dream. Yet, though the ending is appropriate for such a romance, it seems shallow. Not only is there a conflict in the reader's mind between leaving history behind yet bringing society along, but also the escape conflicts with Hawthorne's stated doubts about man's ability to deny the harsh realities of life. That is, though Holgrave leads society into the utopia envisioned by

Clifford on the train, the suspicion remains that the "rumbles and jars" cannot be so easily gotten rid of. What enabled Hawthorne (if not the twentieth-century reader) to accept the ending was his faith in Providence and the controlling conventions of traditional success.

The Blithedale Romance is Hawthorne's longest adverse comment on American society, and a good part of its disillusion is based on his perception of the failure of the yeoman dream. Like William Henry Channing, Hawthorne scores that element of the middle class caught in the drift toward competitive materialism; but he also distrusted the visionary reformers who denied man's earthly needs. Traditional success influences this novel less as an allegory which aligns representative types and more as a thematic problem whose attempted resolution reveals human character. That is, the focus this time is not upon defining true success for America by personifying its various conventions and basing the story's plot on the familiar stages of the attainment of that success. Rather, it is more a study of the human nature which makes that success impossible. The opposing poles of human nature are familiar—the exocentric versus the egocentric—but these poles are described in economic as well as in moral terms, terms provided by the yeoman dream. Hawthorne seems to be echoing William Perkins in saying that man is inescapably selfish, yet paradoxically only insofar as he overcomes that self-interest will he be truly successful. At the story's end, he poses a dilemma which is, in fact, the novel's resolution. Akin to the Puritans' early attempt to balance economic self-interest and a moral, selfless love of fellow man, this dilemma is stated in terms much less optimistic than those of their God-centered universe. And if, as Ihab Hassan argues in *Radical Innocence*, there is a relationship between an ironic view of the world and an "open" form in the novel, then Coverdale's traditional dilemma in a secular and confusing world points up the basis of the novel's irony as well as its centrifugal structure: on the one hand his happiness is traditional success; yet on the other hand, he is too competitive and selfish to be satisfied with such an humble goal until that goal is irretrievably lost.

The narrator and protagonist, Coverdale, describes the intent of the Blithedale colonists to flee "the weary tread-mill of the established system" for the "sake of showing mankind the example of a life governed by other than the false and cruel principles, on which society has all along been based." Like the Pilgrims to which Coverdale compares them, they wished to find a new world, to leave behind the "system of society that shackled" them, and to establish a "blessed state of brotherhood and sisterhood."[28] However, the "blessed state" is a chimera; while God may work wonders, man cannot, for he is a fallen animal whose sin and punishment are blind self-interest. The first night of Coverdale's residence reveals a familiar threat to their Arcadia. The practical, sturdy yeoman, Silas Foster, needs to buy pigs, and Coverdale begins to realize the inability of escape; unlike Holgrave, the Blithedale adventurers have not moved out of time and space, but are still part of the competitive world "[standing] in a new position of hostility, rather than new brotherhood." The group's inability to avoid competition is reflected by a similar inability in its individual members as hostility born of self-interest soon separates the members of the colony from each other. Hollingsworth's self-interest was his monomaniacal dedication of himself and others to an idea. The sexually provocative Zenobia used her charms in a competitive attempt to dominate men in general and Hollingsworth in particular. Coverdale is also a victim of self-interest; his desires, like Zenobia's, are on the two levels of nature and intellect, the first being his more or less felt love and jealousy, the second a less pardonable "cold tendency between instinct and intellect, which made me pry with a speculative interest into people's passions and impulses. . . ."[29] The word "speculative" has, in the context of theme and period, an extended meaning: like the economic speculator of literary convention, Coverdale's speculation in human passions was something selfish and evil which, as it did for Ethan Brand, "unhumanized" Coverdale's heart.

Minor figures, too, illuminate the theme of self-interest. Westervelt, as materially avaricious and totally lacking in heart as Judge Pyncheon, sees Zenobia's suicide only as the loss of twenty years' revenue. "He was," snarls Coverdale, "altogether earthy, worldly, made for time and its gross objects, and incapable . . . of so much as one spiritual idea."[30] Moody, the shadowy, ruined materialist who sired both Zenobia and Priscilla, is the vision of failure and poverty that, though it exists, seems somehow to stay just out of sight in bounteous America. Born as "Fauntleroy," he had the conventionally weak character and shared the conventionally miserable fate of those who never had to labor to support themselves. But poverty, as the riches-to-rags story would have it, affects his character for the better, and the two sides of his moral life are seen in his children. The unnatural Zenobia, an offspring of his materially prosperous but morally empty life, is dominated by those traits and is rejected by the reformed Moody. He loves the child of his morally worthwhile but poverty-stricken phase, Priscilla. Embodying the traits of this period of Moody's life, she represents a natural life of labor which can, like Phoebe's of the *House of the Seven Gables,* infuse the world's necessary materialism with an elevating spirituality. Deceptively a "poor, pallid flower" of purity, she is contrasted with Zenobia of the alluringly jewelled but false flower. Unfortunately, the misguided world, like the book's narrator, is more attracted to the glitter than to the gold. Too late, if at all, does the world realize that Phoebe is natural, Zenobia unnatural; that one is a home-maker, the other fatally divided between the fecundity of her sex and the destruction of the home inherent in her desire to compete with mankind. It is no coincidence that the product of Priscilla's industrious fingers are homely emblems of frugality, silken purses, for through industry and frugality Priscilla has the ability to make silken purses in a sow's-ear world. Long overshadowed by Zenobia, her homely virtues eventually become beautiful while Zenobia's unnatural artistic beauty leads to conflict and death.

Priscilla's selflessness enables her to transform life's materialism into spirituality, and Hawthorne is at pains to indicate that she is the only character who is not selfish. Her love for Zenobia, freely given since childhood, resembles worship "both in its earnestness and its humility," and this idealistic love "gave her soul the refreshment of a purer atmosphere." Hawthorne emphasizes that Priscilla's feelings for her sister were not jealousy but selfless love.[31] Although such an unearthly love gave her a spiritual quality which weakened her resistance to the materialistic Westervelt, the outcome is victory for the spirit. The final confrontation between them takes place in a New England village hall where the villain seems to be in complete control of the maid; however, to believe that the selfishly material aspect of life was stronger than the spiritual power of selfless love and contentment would make man an apostate. As Coverdale, in another step of his education, learns, "the individual soul was virtually annihilated, and all that is sweet and pure in our present life debased, and . . . the idea of man's eternal responsibility was made ridiculous, and immortality rendered at once impossible, and not worth accepting."[32] Fortunately, Priscilla's selfless love was able to transcend Westervelt's hypnotic power, and just as fortunately, the object of that love was in the audience, "the true heart-throb of a woman's affection was too powerful for the jugglery that had hitherto environed her."[33] Love becomes the agent of salvation for her and for Hollingsworth.

The punishments suffered by the characters for their selfish qualities are various. Zenobia, defeated in life by men, is defeated by them even in the manner of her death; her suicide, finely ironic, illustrates a social facet of the individually reprehensible trait of selfishness. Its shock lies less in the fact of the death and more in the recognition of the power of conventions; she dies fulfilling the social demands of that same "masculine egotism" which narrowed the area in which a woman could be called a failure or success in life.[34] The careful artistry of Zenobia's funeral gown—indeed, the very conventionality of the funeral itself—shows how completely vanquished she was not only by Hollingsworth but by the masculine view of the world. Hollingsworth's fate is less ingeniously portrayed. Made aware of the ruin done to Zenobia's heart by his monomania, he gained love and wealth, but lost his proud independence. His competitive will is emasculated, replaced by a "self-distrustful weakness, and a childlike or childish tendency to press close" to the side of Priscilla. The loss of this village blacksmith's self-reliant manliness is his punishment, but because his sin was thoughtless rather than premeditated, it is a milder punishment, the humiliation of which makes him morally deserving of Priscilla. Although the fiery reformer cannot lead society into a utopia as his cousin Holgrave had done, Hollingsworth does get the mid-century sanctuary of home and wife—a refuge from the savage competition of the world. More painfully than Holgrave, Cloverdale learns that "man proposes but God disposes"—that the evolution of human institutions is a slow and often painful progress of the soul and will not be aided by radicals or revolution.

For his cold prying and premeditated act of revenge, Coverdale suffers the harshest punishment of any of the major characters. He is cursed by the aching awareness of his isolation from the warmth of human love and by the loss of any illusion of perfectability. Whereas he once sweated in the fields to earn his bread, and through this yeomanly endeavor "established my claim to be on earth, and my fellowship with all the sons of labor," that fellowship is severed, leaving in Coverdale's voice a tone of nostalgia and a sense of loss. He is fated to remain forever a homeless bachelor and a dilettante, unfruitful both in offspring and in productive labor. Though independent and possessing a competence, Coverdale is not happy, for the immorality of his acts leaves him a life without purpose. Heretofore blinded by competitive jealousy and self-interest, he reveals in the novel's last paragraph that he had truly loved Priscilla and that she was now beyond reach. Keeping in mind that the narrator tells the tale after the action has been completed, the unstated conclusion is, evidently, that despite Coverdale's new awareness, he still torments himself with his inescapable human selfishness: voluptuous Zenobia, for whom he and Hollingsworth had competed, was dead; now Hollingsworth had Priscilla, and Coverdale realizes with a mixture of despair and longing that pallid Priscilla was the true object of his love. Aware of his faults, aware of the cause, his punishment is intensified because he nevertheless cannot rid himself of the selfishness that condemns him to the futility of further longing.

The escape from self-interest, as represented by the spiritual Priscilla, is through purely selfless charity. To illustrate her selflessness, Hawthorne not only paints her in self-abnegating colors, but also contrasts her with several false alternatives. Benevolence such as Hollingsworth's, which is tainted with selfish pride, seems to lead to heaven but is really a by-way to hell. However, self-interest without human kindness or the Christian casuistry of economics leads to the godless materialism of a Westervelt. A third, and the most complex alternative, is Coverdale—the "normal" human who discovers and is doomed to live a sterile life with mankind's major weakness of self-interest. Although the dream of brotherhood may not work, Coverdale sadly tells us, man is still elevated for having had the dream, "More and more I feel that we had struck upon what ought to be a truth." But "ought" is not "is," and Coverdale is left to study his feet of clay, "One still retains some little consideration for one's self."[35] If the novel is read in this way, its conclusion, attacked as "awkward" almost as much as the final scene of *The Seven Gables*, is justified because it implies humanity's (and Coverdale's) final ironic predicament of being placed between the inescapable material love of self and the spiritual need for love of others. Events, like the characters, illustrate this theme; despite the punishments, some good ensues. Hollingsworth *did* have the dream and unwittingly brought happiness to Priscilla thereby; Zenobia's suicide is not without its lesson that Providence can create good out of evil; nor did Coverdale's heart turn into a lump of marble. Although isolated from humanity he has the knowledge he searched for and can teach it to the reader: the moral element of true success must include not only selfless love for fellow man but also the strength derived from recognizing man's basic motivating force of self-interest.

As in *The House of the Seven Gables*, many of the conventions of the yeoman dream are found in *The Blithedale Romance*: the avaricious man, the riches-to-rags theme, the concept of success as competence, independence and morality, and ideas about competitive self-interest. It is Hawthorne's talent that enabled him to make these conventions transcend the stereotyped treatment they received in many of the popular magazines of the period. However, Hawthorne was increasingly uneasy with the conventions. At the same time that he was aware of the necessity of self-interest and competition, he was suspicious of the tendency to equate man's will with God's. Such spokesmen as Goodrich used the morality of traditional success to defend their social hegemony in the drift to competitive materialism; Hawthorne believed in the idealism of the yeoman dream and was thus out of touch with the new use of the image. He did not believe that God should be defined by what a given group of men considered the good to be, nor did he believe that there was no evil in man. This tended to make him skeptical of the two principal poles forming the field of thought that surrounded him: the romantic idealism which sought to transcend the material, and the materialist's rejection of the spiritual. As part of this skepticism, he attempted to maintain the traditional combination of spirituality and materialism found in true success at a time when these two beliefs had become antagonists. There are, however, indications that he was unhappy with his own formulation and resolution of the conflict between the material and the spiritual. In *The House of the Seven Gables*, the conclusion was couched in such conventionally sentimental diction that many readers suspect irony. If this is so, it is a contradictory and vague irony indicating ill-defined dissatisfaction rather than a meaningful analysis. The dissatisfaction might have come from his yearning for a utopia while at the same time distrusting any utopia—even the one dictated by the conventions within which he was working.

The resolution of *Blithedale*, on the other hand, though scarcely as formal, is far more impressive. In this novel, the only character to find true success is Priscilla, but she was an unearthly figure, and Coverdale constantly reminds us that as long as man treads the earth, he will share base elements. Consequently, at the novel's end the dreamers find their own sad truths, and the staunch Silas Foster feeds the pigs. Coverdale concludes that the proper balance between worldliness and spiritualism reflected in the structure of society and in the mind of man will always be a precarious one, one without formal resolution in either life or art, "The yeoman and the scholar—the yeoman and the man of finest moral culture, though not the man of sturdiest sense and integrity—are two distinct individuals, and can never be melted or welded into one substance."[36]

Nevertheless, the idea of true success still plagued Hawthorne. Actual living Americans did seem to earn both spiritual and material reward at the same time—his friend Franklin Pierce was one of them —and in contrast to Europe, America seemed a long march ahead on the road to new harmony. Many Americans, however, were in danger of growing more material, of forgetting the lessons of the past, of forgetting definitions of right and wrong in the celebration of competition. And, a casualty of this drift, the yeoman dream was also being forgotten.

It was while he was in Europe, Hawthorne wrote, that he saw most clearly the American character; he would perhaps have been more accurate if he said that the distance highlighted traits he had already noticed. The trip also gave him the material wealth he longed for as well as a sudden knowledge of the realities of poverty, and it was with these experiences in mind that he was drawn again to American success and to the vectors which troubled him. This time he sought their outlines by contrasting American and English societies, by confronting the dynamic, materialistic American character with the venerable, stable English past. This theme runs through the unfinished works of his last period: *The Ancestral Footstep*, *Doctor Grimshawe's Secret*, *The Dolliver Romance*, and *Septimius Felton*.

Because the best documented manuscript is *Doctor Grimshawe's Secret*, it is possible to study the isolated but vital passages of this unfinished work which show the direction of the novel. The statements receiving most attention here will be those which were repeated in the various drafts of the novel, and those which were in the last draft. The story concerns a young American who, having won fortune and fame in the competitive world of national politics, visits England to find out the truth about his mysterious past. This secret, given to him by the not wholly benevolent Dr. Grimshawe, is that he may be the rightful heir to a large English estate. There is, of course, a love interest, but it is undeveloped and almost extraneous to the main line of the story; the central theme is not the taming of masculine competitiveness by feminine love, but the contrast between the American and the English male culture, the former being characterized by competitiveness, the latter by stability and rigid class distinctions. According to Hawthorne's notes, he wanted to show the

"feelings of the Democrat and the Aristocrat." "The great gist of the
story," he continued, "ought to be the natural hatred of men—and the
particular hatred of Americans—to an Aristocracy; at the same time
doing a good deal of justice to the aristocratic system by respecting
its grand, beautiful, and noble characteristics."[37] The novel was thus
predicated upon a patriotic commitment to demonstrate the superiority of democracy, and to make that way of life have stronger appeal
to the protagonist and to the reader than did a stable English aristocracy. The good and bad of both forms of society were to be portrayed with the balance being in America's favor. And, as might be
expected, the character opposed to the false nobility of the English
aristocrat was the naturally noble yeoman who had so long ago found
refuge on American shores.

It was necessary for Hawthorne to sketch in the character of
that new man, the American, and to place him in immediate relation
to the "good," "[He] shall be a boy of the workhouse perhaps, at
any rate a self-made man, and yet the sense of high birth and long
descent shall be clear within him. He shall be the rightful heir, but
still the gist of the story shall be not to install him in possession of
the property."[38] This representative American's mentor in the first
draft, the kindly Dr. Etherege, had close ties to England and may
have been intended to represent the early English immigrants to
America. In the later draft, an attempt to answer one of the demands
of fiction and give "deeper life" to the doctor is met by portraying
him as the revenge-twisted Dr. Grimshawe. This latter figure may
symbolize the spirit of the defeated Roundheads, the jealousy of nineteenth-century America toward England, or even the threat to the
American yeoman of inherited wealth. In any case, the implication is
clear that the American is heir to English history and traditions,
while at the same time possessing a character of his own which stems
from the new democratic society of yeoman endeavor. The elements
of character which distinguish this representative self-made man from
his English cousins are aggressiveness, self-reliance, and adaptability;
these are tempered by a love for democracy and the virtues of traditional success. Redclyffe, the protagonist, enters England as a man
who, though young, has already attained independence, competence,
and even fame. Although without mechanic or agrarian background,
he has won part of his success; the novel traces the strengthening of
his virtue and the concurrent justification of his choice of American
democracy over English aristocracy on the grounds of its moral

superiority. The hospital warden who cares for the wounded American is at first impressed by the amount of Redclyffe's bank draft and the title "Honorable" before his name; "it showed no ordinary ability and energy for so young a man to have acquired a title of honor or held such a position as this title denoted in the fiercely contested political struggles of the new democracy."[39] Later, the warden is moved by the hero's virtue which is shown in the reason for his withdrawal from active politics—the "virulence of party animosity, the abusiveness of the press, had acted much upon a disposition naturally somewhat too sensitive for [politics]." American political life, like its business life, was becoming a savage race in which immoral tricks were winked at if great wealth could be won. Fortunately, Redclyffe, like the earlier Holgrave, had guarded the innermost man, and his morality is seen in his naturally noble bearing and manners: "I doubt not," the warden muses, "that you can look back upon a line of ancestry. . . ."[40] While this ancestry is, because of the demands of plot, true, Hawthorne comes forward to indicate that the American's manners are based upon the natural nobility of a democratic system rather than any aristocratic heredity:

> Often, you would not know the American ambassador from a duke. —This is often merely external; but in [Redclyffe], having delicate original traits in his character, it was something more; and, we are bold to say, when our countrymen are developed . . . as they ought to be, they will show finer traits than have yet been seen. We have more delicate and quicker sensibilities; nerves more easily impressed; and these are surely requisites for perfect manners. . . .[41]

Our American, then, is a natural nobleman whose innate but characteristic sensibility softens the competitive half of his personality. Importantly, for Hawthorne's nationalistic theme, the form of government—if not the style of politics—has a lot to do with liberating this inner nobility by giving all individuals both freedom and responsibility. He goes on to carefully distinguish between false manners based upon a sense of superiority to other men, and manners which are truly noble because they derive from a feeling of shared humanity found in the equalitarianism of the democratic system: "the courtesy that proceeds on the ground of perfect equality is better than that which is a gracious and benignant condescension—as is the case with the manners of the aristocracy of England."[42] Redclyffe, well on the way to fulfilling the yeoman dream, needs only to be alerted to that dream's spiritual value for his moral fibre to be strengthened and his final goal attained.

But the reader must see the protagonist's promise come true, and in seeing, believe. For psychological depth, Redclyffe is given an internal conflict between the competitiveness learned from American life and the inherent respect for the individual which is the basis of his identification with the best of American democracy. More personal to Hawthorne, Redclyffe is strongly attracted by the lure of England's serene permanency in the face of America's ever-restless change. The central theme of the novel lies in the resolution of these related conflicts.

The first conflict is not treated in great detail. Unlike the inhabitants of Blithedale, Redclyffe must, for various reasons, already be materially successful. Instead, like the earlier Holgrave, Redclyffe's conflict is one of moral rather than economic survival; he must erase the rough morality born of competitive strife in American business and politics. This is dramatized by the confrontation between Redclyffe and the Old Pensioner, a philosopher whose physical aspect resembled Bronson Alcott.[43] The Pensioner was at first to be a speculator of the "Nicholas Biddle stamp," as harsh a description as the ardent Jacksonian could generate, who had fled America after having ruined himself and his investors by manipulating his ill-gotten financial and political power.[44] It is possible, however, that Hawthorne believed Redclyffe's materialism could not be effectively countered in his readers' minds by the sour grapes preaching of an unlucky materialist. At any rate, later drafts depict the Pensioner as a Transcendentalist whose highly sensitive spiritual nature spurs Redclyffe's moral change; Hawthorne would not consider the presence of such an American in England to be impossible, for while consul at Liverpool he had listened to the preaching of the now-expatriate William Henry Channing. In an early display of the harshly aggressive side of the American character, Redclyffe asserts that in practical affairs a "highly cultivated conscience . . . would be a nuisance to one's self and one's fellows," and goes on to defend the Will:

> the efficient actors—those who mould the world—are the persons in whom something else is developed more strongly than conscience. There must be an invincible determination to effect something; it may be set to work in the right direction, but after that it must go onward, trampling down small obstacles—small con-

siderations of right and wrong—as a great rock, thundering down a hillside crushes a thousand sweet flowers. . . .

The reader is quickly told that this doctrine, representing the worst of a Hollingsworth or even a Westervelt, is not endemic to the American; it "was not naturally his, but . . . the inculcation of a life hitherto devoted to politics." The solemn gaze of the Pensioner, Redclyffe's uncomfortable feeling of being "under the eye of omniscience," made him suddenly aware of "the ugliness and indefensibleness of what he said." Thus he discovers, like the earlier Hawthorne's young Ben Franklin, that the end does not justify the means, that the act which harms any individual is forever morally culpable.[45] It is the reassertion of democratic theory: the sanctity of the individual regardless of his place in society and of the individual's responsibility to fellow man rather than to destiny. However, Hawthorne's continual awareness of the material realities of life and his new knowledge of the depths of English poverty result in the reply that a complete surrender to the dictates of a very tender conscience would stifle progress by "shutting out the possibility of action."[46] What is wanted is a balance between material competitiveness and spiritual selflessness; but whereas Holgrave—who found this balance—was allowed to escape nineteenth-century America, and Coverdale—who yearned for the balance—failed because he could not escape, Redclyffe is supposed to demonstrate the viability of the balance in contemporary American life. The interview, like the novel, is not resolved; the reader is offered only Redclyffe's half-hearted admission that selfishness is morally wrong.

The yeoman dream had advocated an individualism in which, though material gain and its moral pursuit were highly personal, the social ramifications had conventionally been governed by the ethics of charity and virtue while the goal was open to all men in the democracy. Now, however, Hawthorne saw the influence of materialism driving the ethical aspect out of the yeoman dream by means of a doctrine of harsh and ceaseless competition; and because the struggle was so difficult, the earthly reward was inflated in size and limited to the victors in the race of life. Redclyffe's epiphany concerning this traditional conflict between selfishness and selflessness inclined him in favor of the latter, but an entirely secular resolution is made difficult, if not impossible, by Hawthorne's relating self-interest with material opportunity in America, with individual rights, and with democracy

—all of which he heartily approved. Because of the nationalistic theme, Redclyffe had to turn his back upon the peaceful retirement of England for the fierce competition and consequent high promise of self-made American life; unfortunately, as Hawthorne saw, the fierce competition did not always promise highly, and the self-made man was not always a model of virtue. A further complication, masked in the *House of the Seven Gables* by the conventional ending but salient in *Doctor Grimshawe's Secret*, is Hawthorne's skepticism about man's ability to attain perfection in either goal or means. Yet the latter novel was supposed to be both realistic and optimistic, one which without the aid of a deus ex machina proved the superiority of democracy for the moral improvement of all Americans and the progress of humanity in general. In trying to depict the successful American, Hawthorne was caught up in the long-standing dilemma between selfish and public interest, as well as in the newly disquieting shift in the meaning of mid-century success toward material opulence as a reward for harsh competition. Apparently, the only resolution he could find was a dual faith: that in the best Americans an innate sensibility would insure the eighteenth-century hope of an identity between individual interest and public interest, and that God would insure that the best Americans became the leaders of the democratic society.

Related to the dilemma of individual versus public interest is the conflict between England's aristocratic stability and democracy's restless opportunity. This theme receives more detailed discussion in the second draft of the novel, the last pages making palpable the appeal of repose and stability. The warden's quiet library symbolizes the contrast between America and an England "where the strife, novelties, uneasy agitating conflict, attrition of unsettled theories, fresh-springing thought, did not obtain. . . . How unlike what he had hitherto known, and was destined to know; the quick violent struggle of his native country. . . ."[47] But Redclyffe has to turn his back on England's appeal. America, uncomfortably restless and demanding, nevertheless offered the only opportunity to Redclyffe—as an every-man, a boy of the workhouse—for the morally sanctioned traditional success:

> "What prospects—what rewards for spirited exertion—what a career, open only to an American, should I give up, to become merely a rich and idle Englishman, belonging (as I should) no-

where, without a possibility of struggle, such as a strong man loves, with only a mockery of a title. . . . What has any success in English life to offer . . . to balance the proud career of an American statesman?" [48]

And later Redclyffe argues to himself:

"I am not fit to be here—I so strongly susceptible of a newer, more stirring life than these men lead; I, who feel, that whatever the thought and cultivation of England may be, my own countrymen have gone forward a long, long march beyond them, not intellectually, but in a way that gives them a further start. If I come back hither, with the purpose to make myself an Englishman . . . of rank and hereditary estate—then for me America has been discovered in vain, and the great spirit that has been breathed into us is in vain; and I am false to it all!" [49]

Such a betrayal of his fellow Americans' ideals was impossible; the major advantage of America over Europe (the true progress of America in history) was manifest in its government and in its material opportunity: the equal chance for every individual to attain the yeoman dream. It is with pride that Redclyffe speaks of an America where, like all white male voters, he finds "no man above me—for my ruler is only myself . . .—nor any below me."[50]

As the novel stands, Redclyffe's goal in life is not the final attainment of assured reward, yeomanly or otherwise. Rather he must return to continue the struggle for wealth and position in America. He has already won much, and it is the opportunity to immediately take gentlemanly retirement which makes the English squire's life so appealing. Yet, as Redclyffe repeats somewhat desperately, it is the struggle which gives real value to the material goal by making the possession of it morally justified. But here the dilemma is acute, for America has amply demonstrated to Hawthorne that the struggle can easily be a moral catastrophe both for the individual who succeeds and for the masses that don't. Somehow the inherited morality must be sustained and the hope of democracy must continue in an America radically different from the preceding century. But the only means Hawthorne offers is through the industry, frugality and perseverance which made up the virtuous pursuit of the old yeoman dream. Because the novel's purpose was to convince readers of the value of a "real" American life over a "false" English life, Redclyffe had to re-join—

and rejoice in—the continuing struggle for success, a struggle which was becoming increasing amoral, a struggle which was becoming increasingly elitist. As with most profound losses, the home of traditional success was also the arena of its defeat.

The implication is strong that the Hawthorne of mid-century came to view the moral pursuit of wealth as Franklin had viewed it a century before: a means of material and spiritual elevation for the individual and for society. The manner of Redclyffe's rise in the world epitomized the virtues in which mid-century Americans found their superiority to sophisticated Europeans: self-reliance, equality, and, newly intensified, the competitive spirit. In the truly successful man's character, the harsher aspects of these virtues were depicted as being somehow tempered by a form of morality based upon a democratic respect for the individual. In the finest example of the new man, the pursuit was personally moral and contributed to the social and moral progress of the nation and the world. But though Hawthorne had come full circle, his country had not; exactly why the pursuit should be moral is, except for the explanation of inherent worth, left vague. The apparent shortcomings of democracy—the injury done to others by strong-willed and selfish men, the heavy emphasis upon materialism—these were apparently part of Providence's plan, and from them would come good. But such a resolution offered little to a Hawthorne who had wrestled with the same problems in two previous novels, who identified the old yeoman dream with the virtues of American democracy, who in this novel found less reason for optimism than was allowed by the nationalistic commitments and the attempts at a realistic presentation. He discovered that the aspects of American society which were superior to Europe were in great part the same aspects which made America inferior. The result was a situational irony at odds with the "closed" novelistic structure demanded by a definite choice for America. Sensitive to the literary importance of the conflict between the yeoman dream and the industrial revolution, Hawthorne was unable to offer an artistic resolution viable for his times. In start after start, in groping note after note, he struggled for a statement which would bring to mid-century competitive materialism the virtues of the old yeoman dream. Not only was such a resolution impossible, but there was also an incompatibility between his romantic approach and the realism demanded by his sociological theme. Unable to find an answer, he was also unable to form a method.

✸

In his life as well as in his fiction, Hawthorne was divided between two realms. The subjects of his own *Il Penseroso* and *L'Allegro* were, roughly, the realm of the mind and the realm of "real men." Forced by life to be acutely aware of the economic necessities in America, he defined and pursued his material well-being as sedulously as any other member of his society. Yet, at the same time, he considered his calling to be opposed to the materialism around him and dependent upon isolation and retirement. Intensely concerned with independence and a competence, he accepted the competitive methods by which they must be won, yet he feared and fought the moral effects of that competition. This particular conflict in Hawthorne's mind and life, while intensely personal and autobiographical, also received a literary expression which used, at least on the level of social criticism, the imagery and logic of the yeoman dream. Many of the values he defended, many of the goals his characters sought, much of that which he condemned in American life, and many of the symbols and conflicts in his stories were based upon the idea of success as independence, competence, and a particular form of morality. It was a fact for him that there could be no material success without a moral success to support it; nor could one reject materiality and retire to some utopia. These social "facts" coincided with his personal antipathy toward exclusive intellectuality and exclusive materialism to drive him in search of some mid-range between the two.

In his *The House of the Seven Gables*, the plot and its concluding promise of a modest utopia are formed from the truisms of traditional success. *The Blithedale Romance* is an anti-utopian reaction, showing that an idyllic escape from the brute facts of humanity and the world is impossible. In these two novels, he tried to work out resolutions to the personal and public conflicts that he felt in his own as well as in his fellow Americans' search for success. His unfinished *Doctor Grimshawe's Secret* returned to the problem after a hiatus of moral and artistic exploration in *The Marble Faun*. But by now, the successful life was not based on the establishment of a separate society. Rather, it was pictured as an individual choice between a harsh, active world in which a competence and independence were to be wrested from other men, versus the soft, green shades of meditation, art, and pastoral retirement that was so valuable to him as a writer. Hawthorne was never entirely comfortable with America's drift toward harsh competition and opulent materialism; although he was subject to material concerns himself, his acute awareness of its dangers to the sanctity of the individual made him portray materialists with the utmost scorn and to fear the effects of America's trends on himself and others. Yet his protagonist was, from the inception of the novel, committed to the promise of an America realistically portrayed. The essence of that promise for the rest of the world was still equal economic opportunity even though it now entailed competitive strife; indeed, in the yeoman tradition, the reward was unworthy without the struggle to achieve it. Hawthorne honestly pictured the harsher aspects of his American, then softened them with Redclyffe's natural nobility which, when reinforced by conscience-prodding discoveries, would refine those harsh characteristics. Hawthorne seemed to be working toward Franklin's belief that morality resulted from a sanctified pursuit of material goals; and in completion of a circle, this student of the Puritans voiced a familiar statement of the dilemma between the egocentric struggle and an exocentric Christian casuistry of economics. But, ironically, the several attempts to write a novel portraying that resolution failed to make the conventions fit the mid-century America he perceived; Hawthorne was trying to vivify an old idea in a new world whose industrial changes he sensed but could not comprehend.

For most other Americans, the old yeoman dream moved into the realm of nostalgia, while the new, harsh competition and its material promise moved toward identification with God's Plan. The identification lacked only some empirical evidence, evidence which the yeoman's descendants were to find soon in Social Darwinism.

I say, then, you ought to have money. If you can honestly attain unto riches in Philadelphia, it is your Christian duty to do so. It is an awful mistake of these pious people to think you must be awfully poor in order to be pious.

"Acres of Diamonds," Russell Conwell

At the same time she cooked for the men, took care of the children, washed and ironed, milked the cows at night, made the butter, and sometimes fed the horses and watered them while her husband kept at the shocking. No slave in the Roman galleys could have toiled so frighteningly and lived, for this man thought himself a free man, and that he was working for his wife and babes.

"Under the Lion's Paw," Hamlin Garland

5

THE LATER NINETEENTH CENTURY

※

By the last third of the nineteenth century, the dominant concept of success was one of opulent materialism competitively won. The widely read biographies of "Kings of Fortune" or "America's Millionaires," and the vastly popular "Acres of Diamonds" lecture by Russell Conwell readily indicate the emphasis upon this belief. However, the idea of traditional success did not die out entirely. Though subject to change, it persisted both as an excuse for and in opposition to competition and opulent materialism; and many of the popular writers of the period built their fame on adaptations of the old concepts to the new environment.

The imagery and idiom of traditional success were often used in the more or less conscious attempt to justify the competitive aggressiveness of Social Darwinism. One of the most important spokesmen of this belief was Andrew Carnegie. Son of a Scot hand-loom weaver forced out of work by the new factory system, Andrew was twelve years old when his impoverished family moved to Pennsylvania in 1847. Forty years later, his steel empire alone was worth over two hundred million dollars; and, in 1901, U.S. Steel finally bought him out for $250 million. In semi-retirement for a number of years, he propagandized success in familiar terms which echo the thought of the Enlightenment (*Triumphant Democracy*, 1886) and of Calvin (*The Gospel of Wealth*, 1889). The latter essay became phenomenally popular and was reprinted, collected, and translated in numberless copies; and Carnegie practiced—albeit by his own light—what he preached by donating over $350 million to education, research, and public libraries.

In his eyes, as in the eyes of most of his countrymen, Andrew Carnegie epitomized American Success; as the advice literature of his childhood promised, the rewards of work and knowledge had become his.
Now he saw it his duty to offer those same opportunities to other
striving lads.

He described his rise for those lads in, as might be guessed, the
Youth's Companion, 23 April 1896: "How I Served My Apprenticeship." A word with connotations of the yeoman mechanic, "apprenticeship" indicated not only that Carnegie's success was decorous and
moral, but also that in our democracy, it could come to any working
class boy who had drive and ability. As a youth, he states, he "had,
fortunately, to perform some useful work in the world . . . in order to
earn an honest livelihood." That useful work for twelve-year-old Andrew was to be placed as a bobbin-boy in a cotton factory; when he
received his first week's pay of $1.20, he had a taste of achievement
which he remembered in terms that combine the old yeoman dream
and the new business world, "[I was] no longer entirely dependent
upon my parents" but had become a contributing member to the
"family partnership." His work in the factories was, he admits, terribly
hard, but he had the courage not to complain. Besides, poverty and
hard work were the only moral beginnings for a multi-millionaire;
there was "more genuine satisfaction, a truer life, and more obtained
from life in the humble cottages of the poor than in the palaces of the
rich." Poverty, in the familiar convention, was a "precious heritage"
which generated industry, which in turn produced the "virtues which
enable our race to reach a still higher civilization." Obviously, for the
mature Carnegie, the progressive evolution of man and nation depended on the exertion of its individual members; and, just as obviously, without need there would be little exertion.

But like so many other wage earners in pre-Civil War American industry, young Andrew soon learned that the factory laborer had
no future. Writing somewhat inconsistently of his fear of the "wolf
of poverty," he found a new job as a runner for a Pittsburgh telegraph
office. He speaks of this occupation, apparently without punning, as a
"deliverance," and it may help explain his later penchant for building
libraries as the principal means of self-help for ambitious lads, "There,
amid books, newspapers, pencils, pens and ink and writing-pads, and a
clean office, bright windows, and the literary atmosphere, I was the
happiest boy alive." While we may smile wonderingly at the "literary
atmosphere" of a telegraph office, the felt relief in that description

indicates how oppressive in so many ways was his previous factory labor. Presumably had he not been literate in English, there would have been no escape.

Despite this atmosphere, Carnegie's memory of poverty spurred him to ceaseless industry for his employer. He was equally industrious in the pursuit of useful knowledge. A self-taught understanding of telegraphic code won him a promotion to operator and gave him some leisure time to "do a little business," which he defined as doing something beyond one's task for pay beyond one's salary. The exact nature of this business is left vague in the article, possibly because it had little to do with a physical product. But it led him to work for the Pennsylvania Railroad where, thirteen years and one war later, he became superintendent of the Pittsburgh division. In this administrative capacity and among inventor-engineers, he received a tip about a new invention; and, spurred by the voice of Providence at his ear, he made his first speculation with capital raised from within his family. He had moved from factory worker to administrator to technological entrepreneur; and the first dividend convinced him that the man who could really profit from technical knowledge was neither the craftsman nor the inventor, but the entrepreneur whose capital and ability combined new technological knowledge with specific needs of industry. He invested further in oil, sleeping cars, iron bridges, and, finally in 1873, the Bessemer process. He was no longer an apprentice millionaire; now he had his own shop: "I was no longer merely an official working for others upon a salary, but a full-fledged business man working upon my own account. . . . I always liked the idea of being my own master, of manufacturing something and giving employment to many men." He was truly independent, and though his speculative manner of achieving wealth may have been suspect in an earlier period, few were arguing with it now. He and many Americans saw his struggle for great wealth not only as proper, but also in line with God's plan; his rise contributed to the growth of the nation and made "our country . . . the greatest producer of iron in the world." As for the competence aspect—well, $350 million or so should be competence enough for any man.

The Gospel of Wealth was both an answer to socialism and a reaffirmation of faith in old values reinterpreted. It also reveals the period's celebration of competition and opulent materialism. Civilization depended, Carnegie wrote in the mood of Peter Parley, "upon the sacredness of property."[1] But unlike Goodrich and so many other spokesmen for the yeoman dream, Carnegie was no longer interested in maintaining a balance between competition and social harmony; rather, like other Social Darwinists, he saw no tension between competition and harmony. Indeed, the progress of civilization was seen as dependent upon a law of competition which was "not only beneficial, but essential to the future progress of the race."[2] Anything that promised to lessen the competitive struggle of one individual against the other was seen as evil; communism, for example, was "not evolution, but revolution. It necessitates the changing of human nature itself." As the latest science had shown him, human nature was—like all nature—competitive and self-interested; and as his own experience had clearly demonstrated, only the best of the species survived the struggle to the top.

Given these basic facts about human nature and evolution, Carnegie continued, man's philosophy had to be Pragmatism, "Our duty is with what is practicable now." The ultimate goal was "to bend the universal tree of humanity a little in the direction most favorable to the production of good fruit under existing circumstances." But this "fruitfulness" was different from that of William Perkins or the early nineteenth century defenders of traditional success: ". . . Individualism, Private Property, the Law of Accumulation of Wealth, and the Law of Competition . . . are the highest result of human experiences, the soil in which society, so far, had produced the best fruit."[3] The highest form of man, therefore, was the most competitive and accumulative individual who almost automatically would serve society as well as self. Inheritance taxes were one means of insuring this service, and Carnegie heartily supported this idea as a way of sharing the acquisitive man's wealth with society and of forcing the scions of the rich (including his own) to moral labor. But the best manner of service was, in the tradition of Mather and Franklin, voluntary; the rich were to organize "benefactions from which the masses of their fellows will derive lasting advantage, and thus dignify their own lives."[4] Carnegie apparently believed, as did Franklin, that the virtues exercised in the struggle for wealth would refine the character as well as fatten the pocketbook. But Carnegie's world was different from Franklin's; multi-millions and boundless power over regiments of industrial laborers were alien to his Physiocratic economic theory. And, unlike Franklin, Carnegie saw no gentlemanly retirement for the acquisitive man: "It becomes the duty of the millionaire to increase his revenues. Then he labors not for self, but for others; not to hoard, but to spend.

The more he makes, the more the public gets."[5] The old yeoman was to become a prince, and the useful product was no longer goods but money.

Carnegie's practical advice on investment was only that he relied on his "business instinct" and knew a good deal when he saw it. His main interest in writing was to justify the morality of the big money makers and to explain the natural and divine basis of that undertaking. The frame of reference for that justification was traditional success, but he added radical changes wrought by Social Darwinism and the Industrial Revolution. Now the successful man rose to the top through savagely competitive business practices rather than the independent production of goods; now, supported by claims of scientific morality, success no longer meant a competence and independence, but vast riches and dominant power.

※

Different inheritors of the yeoman dream believed that traditional success was being corrupted by the Carnegies and Sumners. To them, the inordinate wealth of soulless trusts and unvirtuous (or even virtuous) millionaires, as well as the increasing restlessness of a proletariat forbidden traditional success, threatened to pull society apart. Laissez-faire economics and the competitive philosophy which justified opulent materialism were blamed for creating a society of two giant antagonists: capital and labor. However, these heirs, too, tended to change the yeoman dream. Because of their hatred for competitive individualism, they found it difficult to defend the independence element of traditional success in other than general terms. And, indeed, many were willing to sacrifice it for the universal competence and moral society which they saw to be the promise of socialism.

The "soul of the Social Gospel" was Walter Rauschenbusch. A Baptist minister and professor of theology, Rauschenbusch was born in Rochester, New York, in 1861, the son of a German Baptist minister who had answered the call to serve among the immigrants to the New World. Like his father and grandfather and great-grandfather, Rauschenbusch early decided on the ministry; and, after study in Germany as well as in America, he soon found himself working among poor Germans in the Hell's Kitchen area of New York City. The misery which he saw there, intensified by the depression of 1893, convinced the young man that the church—indeed, all Christianity—should not only save souls but also improve society so that those souls would have something to live for while they were in this world. Synthesizing his reading of Tolstoi, Mazzini, Bellamy, Henry George, and Fabian socialism, he began writing essays and newspaper columns calling for rejection of the competitive spirit and a regeneration of the spirit of love and sharing. But unlike the brotherly love called for by the young William Henry Channing, Rauschenbusch's call was immediately translated into economic theory. And whereas the later Channing had tried to regenerate the moral consciousness of the middle class, Rauschenbusch assumed that the middle class would be ineffectual in the growing contest between capital and labor. Consequently, he could begin where Channing had surrendered. No longer clinging to all the elements of the yeoman dream, no longer believing in the efficacy of the middle class or the value of yeomanly independence, Rauschenbusch could call for reforms which were far more fundamental to the social structure than were those entailed in Channing's Associationism. Rauschenbusch wanted laws which would not only restrict competitive individualism and give a fair chance to labor, but which would also elevate the rights of a collective public over those of a few individuals or corporations. For example, he called for the public ownership of natural resources, of public services, and railroads: those businesses which made inordinate profits out of the basic needs of the people—profits which would not exist without the presence of those same people.

Whereas Channing had advocated "wedding church and state" to reform the world, Rauschenbusch wanted the separation of church and state in order to protect the larger spiritual concerns that were the responsibility of religion. At the same time, he rejected the materialism if not the insights of Marx, and argued for a faith in human possibilities rather than a surrender to Marx's sense of inevitable cataclysm. Such beliefs led him to support Henry George's single-tax idea as well as the Populist Party, and he thought of himself as a "gradualist socialist" and argued consistently against the secularizing of the church advocated by many of his fellow social gospellers.[6] It is not surprising to read of him being called "radical but Christian" by the *New York Times*.[7]

In proposing the Kingdom of God on Earth, Rauschenbusch was both loud and eloquent, and he soon won prominence not just in New York but throughout the United States and in England, too, as a prophet of the Social Gospel. Among his several works, perhaps *Christianity and the Social Crisis* (1907) is the most famous.[8] Here, he wrote that love, not the survival of the fittest, brought society to higher levels. But contemporary society suffered under a deleterious spirit of competitiveness which frustrated the force of that love. This fault, however, was only in part attributable to human nature; competitiveness was also the result of new business ethics. The corruptions of capitalism had combined with the rise of industrialism to destroy the yeoman dream:

> Hitherto each master of a handicraft, with his family and a few apprentices and journeymen about him, had plied his trade in his home, owner of his simple tools and master of his profits. His workmen ate at his table, married his daughters, and hoped to become masters themselves when their time of education was over. . . . They had no hope of millions to lure them, nor the fear of poverty to haunt them. They lacked many of the luxuries accessible even to the poor today, but they had a large degree of security, independence, and hope. And man liveth not by cake alone.
>
> Then arrived the power-machine, and the old economic world tottered and fell like San Francisco in 1906. . . . If the guilds had been wise enough to purchase and operate machinery in common, they might have effected a cooperative organization of industry in which all could have shared the increased profits of machine production. As it was, the wealthy and enterprising and ruthless seized the new opening, turned out a rapid flow of products, and of necessity underbid the others in marketing their goods. The old customs and regulations which had forbidden or limited free competition were brushed away. New economic theories were developed which sanctioned what was going on and secured the support of public opinion and legislation for those who were driving the machine through the framework of the social structure.[9]

Rauschenbusch's litany is familiar: technological entrepreneurs, financiers, stock-market speculators had taken control of the industrial society and taken away the yeoman status of the worker. But whereas Channing believed that society could reestablish the yeoman dream, Rauschenbusch believed that industrialization had made obsolete the old figure and with it the independence that had been so elemental to it. Independence, even the Enlightened Self-Interest which since

Franklin's time had been viewed as moral, had been changed into a destructive and ungoverned competition by changes in production, distribution, and ownership:

> This individualistic philosophy was worked out at the end of the eighteenth century in order to cut away the artificial restraints inherited from a by-gone period of industry. The noblest thinkers enthusiastically believed that the unfettered operation of self-love would result in happy conditions for all. Experience has proved this a ghastly mistake. . . . Yet as long as competitive commerce continues and is the source of profit in the business world, competitive selfishness will be defended as the true law of life.[10]

The answer was not a call for a return to some Golden Age of the Virgilian Husbandman, but a recognition and melioration of the impact of industrialism:

> One of these futile efforts is the attempt to make economic development revert to earlier stages. . . . But it is safe to say that no such return would be permanent. . . . Our effort must rather be to preserve all the benefits which the elaboration of the productive machinery has worked out, but to make these benefits enrich the many instead of the few. Reform movements arising among the business class are often reactionary; they seek to revert to outgrown conditions and turn the shadow on the dial backward. Socialism is almost unique in accepting as inevitable and desirable the essential achievements of the industrial organization, but only as halfway stages toward a vaster and far juster social system.[11]

Socialism and communism, that which had been anathema for Bradford, condemned by Goodrich, laughed at by Jacksonian Democrats, peeked at by Channing, and lamented by Hawthorne in his struggle for a balance between traditional success and the new competitive materialism, was now seen as the refuge for humanity faced with the profound upheavals wrought by the Industrial Revolution. Now the church must make Americans see that the new Christian casuistry of economics called for the deemphasis of individualism, a lessening of independence in order to strengthen the sense of collectivity:

> If production would be organized on a basis of cooperative fraternity; if distribution could at least approximately be determined

by justice; if all men could be conscious that their labor contributed to the welfare of all and that their personal well-being was dependent on the prosperity of the commonwealth; if predatory business and parasitic wealth ceased and all men lived only by their labor, if the luxury of unearned wealth no longer made us all feverish with covetousness and a simpler life became the fashion; if our time and strength were not used up either in getting a bare living or in amassing unusable wealth and we had more leisure for the higher pursuits of the mind and the soul— then there might be a chance to live such a life of gentleness and brotherly kindliness and tranquillity of heart as Jesus desired for men.[12]

If only society gave a fair share to every industrious member, a competence and morality would result. These elements of the yeoman dream were still basic to Rauschenbusch's view of a successful life. But his horror at the effects of unrestrained individualism in an industrialized economy led him to reject as outmoded the picture of the average man isolated on his own fee-simple threshold. Now independence meant freedom from wage-slavery, not from wage-earning; under the new economic configurations, the idea of ownership was no longer individual but communal. Rauschenbusch and those who shared his ideas saw the new yeoman, the twentieth-century yeoman, to be one whose ownership and profits would not be the result of legal title but of input of labor. The new independence was based on being part of a producing collectivity which, perhaps ironically for a Baptist minister, would have the virtues of the pre-Reformation church:

For fifteen centuries and more it was the common consent of Christendom that private property was due to sin, and that the ideal life involved fraternal sharing. . . . Protestantism especially, by its intimate alliance with the growing cities and the rising business class, had been individualistic in its theories of Christian society. The question is now how quickly Christian thought will realize that individualism is coming to be an inadequate and antiquated form of communistic organization, and how thoroughly it will comprehend that this new communism will afford a far nobler social basis for the spiritual temple of Christianity.[13]

The old yeoman was lost in the masses of the new proletariat; his independence was submerged under the fear and condemnation of a savage individualism which had caused so much despair for so many Americans. In the coming upheavals of the twentieth century, the yeoman's ghost would be heard, but faintly and uneasily, and—like the flute music in *Death of a Salesman*—with a sense of profound loss.

✿

In *Christianizing the Social Order*, Rauschenbusch admitted that "the great mass of our nation, with the exception of the monopolists and the socialists, is anxious to get back from the fire of monopoly into the cool and refreshing frying pan of competition." This mass included the middle class, a group which Rauschenbusch believed was doomed by the coming dominance of capital and labor; and a large portion of that doomed mass still adhered to the values of traditional success. One of the later nineteenth century's most popular advocates of just this belief was Horatio Alger, Jr.

A year before *Parley's* was born, Horatio was born in what is now Revere, Massachusetts, in 1832. He was the eldest son of a Unitarian preacher who held profound hopes that Junior would also follow the path to the pulpit.[14] In his secular way, Alger did minister to a vast congregation of readers, offering them a vision of a success that fell somewhere between the titanic competition of Carnegie and the Christian socialism of Rauschenbusch. Apparently, to judge from the early and wide acceptance of Alger's message, it was a vision shared by hundreds of thousands of Americans throughout the nation. The boys and girls who read him may have done so primarily for his eventful story-line, comparatively realistic dialogue, and realism of city setting; but they could not miss the homily that was the foundation of each adventure. Nor did their parents, and for decades Alger's name was synonymous with "uplifting reading" in countless homes and libraries.[15] Rapid and prolific, Alger turned out 109 complete novels and a large collection of shorter works in fifty years of writing. His first best-seller came in 1868 with his eighth book, *Ragged Dick;* and this adventure set the formula which—with slight variations—became the structure for another hundred novels. Generally, the hero was a lad in his early or mid-teens, "swarthy" and determined, either an orphan or supporting his mother. The plot, actuated by chance events and rigid characterization, centered on the boy's struggle for a position of respect and occasionally wealth in the commercial life of New York City. Often, the hero had been dispossessed of his rightful inheritance by a scheming relative, and the story ends with the revelation of a mysterious letter or witness, and with the guilty punished and the hero rewarded. Most often, the protagonist had no secrets concerning his birth but was required to earn his own way. In either case, the reward was justified by the hero's virtuous behavior. Take, for example, *Silas Snobden's Office Boy*, wherein the young man must overcome calumny, extortion, loss of his job, assault, kidnapping, and charges of poker-playing.

The line dividing the novel's protagonists from its antagonists is the familiar one of virtuous behavior. The object of both parties is similar—money—but there are two ways of pursuing it: honestly and dishonestly. As in so many of the earlier tales in the nineteenth century, Alger's moral division of society runs through the various social levels. Snobden, the rich but crusty employer, worked his way up to become the owner of his own business (its exact nature, as in most of the novels, is not clear). The rich benefactor, a banker, likewise began poor but earned his money through hard work and, consequently, is also classed among the virtuous rich. The virtuous poor include Snobden's office boy, Frank Manton, as well as Frank's mother and a scattering of secondary characters not destined for good fortune. There is even a representative of the virtuous middle-class, Mr. Duncan, Frank's landlord. In opposition to the cast of virtuous characters is the roster of villains: John Carter, Snobden's nephew who—in the familiar riches-to-rags manner—squandered his $30,000 inheritance and now schemes to get money from his wealthy uncle. The evil middle-class is seen in a figure common to many Alger books, the sly subordinate who plots to get the hero's job for a young relative who lacks the gumption to find work for himself. And the undeserving poor is represented by Frank's step-father, Luke Gerrish, who would "rather live without work." It is this theme of being willing or unwilling to do honest work which usually divides the society of Alger's novels into the virtuous and the unvirtuous. Rarely is the possibility admitted that there might be no work available; and though admitting occasional exploitation by a penurious employer, Alger clearly indicates that the worthy lad will quit that job for one which pays better for his labor. In this case, Frank wins Mr. Snobden's approval by not returning to work for him despite Snobden's raising the wages.

Frank threads his way with determination and luck through a series of adventures to be rewarded with $10,000 and a white-collar job. When the reward comes, the reader is left with no doubt that it is deserved. Like most of the rewards in the Alger stories, Frank's is not the great riches of a Carnegie or even a Snobden, but a competence and greater opportunity. He becomes, in short, a virtuous member of the middle class;[16] and though he may not have achieved a yeomanly independence, Alger indicates that such a goal is not entirely forgotten. In commenting on Snobden's long hours, Frank states:

> "I would be willing to do the same if I had a business of my own."
>
> "If I had a business of my own" [said John Carter] "I'd hire others to do the work, and have a good time."
>
> "I dare say you would," thought Frank. "That isn't the way to succeed." [17]

Yet Alger's heroes very seldom attain this full independence as part of their immediate reward, and it is here that he—like Carnegie and Rauschenbusch—reveals a major change in the yeoman dream.

Frank and most of the other Alger protagonists win freedom from the demands of poverty rather than ownership of their own shop. The virtues needed for this freedom are the traditional ones of industry, frugality, sobriety, honesty, etc. And with good reason, Alger has been seen as celebrating the individual entrepreneur rather than the organization man. However, the independence depicted in Alger's stories is tied more to the laissez-faire struggle than to economic independence. Indeed, as a bootblack or a news hawker, the boy was more his own boss than at the end of the novel when he became a clerk or junior partner. What he of course lacked at the beginning of the story were the symbols, though not the fact, of respectability, and a competence. Only the heirs to wealth attain immediate independence; for the others, there is a loss of independence in exchange for a better position in life's race.

Alger consistently describes his protagonists as superior in mind and body, self-confident and—while properly modest—able to act decisively when occasion demands (as it often does). Frank Manton, for instance, outwits two bullies by tossing a raw egg into the eyes of one and outsprinting the other. He is equally cool and alert when John Carter tries to trick him out of an important letter, or when Luke Gerrish attempts a swindle. Another Frank—the Cash Boy, Frank Fowler—begins his adventures as the natural leader on a local baseball team. Both his prowess on the field of competition and his forthrightness are quickly sketched by Alger to justify the other boys' natural acquiescence to his leadership.

Athletics, it should be mentioned briefly, crop up over and over again as an explanation for and justification of the dominance of some men or boys over others. Far from being condemned, sports serve to train the individual for the competitive world; a good left hook punishes more than one Alger villain. Indeed, the villain seldom, if ever, participates in sport or is a member of an athletic club. This use of sport is quite different from the non-competitive exercises advocated so much earlier in the century; by Alger's time, sport is frankly combative, and the object is to beat others, "The ambition of the boys was aroused . . . they wanted to win local reknown [sic] . . . ."[18]

A key point in comparing Alger's view of competition with those of Rauschenbusch and Carnegie is that while Alger shared the belief in the elevating effect of the struggle, he also saw faults in competition. But these were individual rather than social, personal rather than public. The characters in his books are kept down by individual weaknesses and not by faulty economic or political structures. For the villains, it was an aversion to honest labor; for the lesser characters who do to fill a scene or two, a weaker competitive drive or lesser abilities. The forces that the hero must overcome are also individual rather than built into the social framework—a rich boy or superior who takes unfair advantage of wealth or position to keep the hero down. In short, Alger admits the problems of competitive individualism, but he does so in terms of Jacksonian Democracy: that rich and powerful individuals are preventing the otherwise satisfactory society from giving all deserving people a fair chance at life's rewards. Once the unfair competitors are removed—once the game's cheaters are exposed—then the rules can be followed, and the naturally superior hero will move to the front in the race of life. It is, of course, a return to the "frying pan of competition" that Rauschenbusch saw obviated by the Industrial Revolution.[19]

As has been often indicated, Alger's heroes are not unaided in their struggles. Luck, usually in the form of an accident which brings the lad to the attention of a good rich man, plays a major role. This luck is not the religious Providence of earlier success formulas, but is entirely secular.[20] The good fortune—the "break"—offers avenues which lesser boys ignore, but which the hero can and does take advantage of. It is also evidence of a shadow in the usually sunny endings of the novels: it *can* happen outside the novel, but it isn't certain that it *will.* The use of luck brings in an element of selectivity—some factor beyond the possibilities of the original myth—which shows how far Alger and his readers have moved from faith in the broad applicability of traditional success. Not only has independence changed its role, but the guaranteed right to a competence and respect has also become the prize in some ill-defined lottery. Chance, fortune, luck—heretofore, such an explanation had been seen as violating the justice of the universe, had been linked with the evils of gambling and speculation. Now, it was a major factor in the poor-but-honest boy's rise to the middle class. While this luck helped make the Alger hero properly modest, it also singled him out from the majority of poor-but-honest boys and gradually moved him beyond the realm of believable myth into that of entertaining fable. Apparently, a competence and respect could be found in the city; but it would take luck as well as pluck, and it would cost the yeoman his independence.

🏵

The predictions of Marx and Rauschenbusch were wrong, or their timetables were off. In the United States, as in most Western countries, the cataclysm has not yet come nor has the middle-class disappeared—though predictions of both occurrences abound. But the middle class's yeoman no longer stands tall in the nation; the essential configuration of a competence, independence, and morality could not withstand the assaults of the Industrial Revolution or the seductions of opulent materialism. And while echoes of traditional success are heard here and there—efforts to subsidize the family farm for the nation's moral health, to improve the sense of individual responsibility and morality in mid-range executives, to involve the production line worker in "his" product through stock incentives or "team assembly techniques"—those who tend to hold to the original yeoman dream seldom identify with the American middle class of the late twentieth century.

Perhaps even this ghost will fade. Given the various means for redistributing wealth, the competence may no longer be the individual's responsibility; and given the inflating expectations of many for whom a competence once seemed sufficient, it now may be too little. Even the independence so vital to the dream may prove too expensive under the impact of shrinking space and natural resources. And perhaps the increasing pressure to form collectivities of one kind or another will ultimately bring changes to the concepts of morality.

LIST OF ABBREVIATIONS

BM	*Boston Mechanic*
DAB	*Dictionary of American Biography*
JM	*Juvenile Miscellany*
MA	*Mechanic's Advocate*
MechM	*Mechanic's Magazine and Register of Inventions and Improvements*
MFP	*Mechanic's Free Press*
MM	*Merry's Museum*
NYSM	*New York State Mechanic*
PM	*Parley's Magazine*
SA	*Spirit of the Age*
Vol	*Voice of Industry*
WMA	*Working Man's Advocate*
YAM	*Young American's Magazine*
YC	*Youth's Companion*

NOTES

INTRODUCTION

1. For a concise discussion of the history of the eighteenth-century yeoman, see A. Whitney Griswold, *Farming and Democracy* (New York, 1949), especially chapter two. Henry Nash Smith, in *The Virgin Land* (New York, 1962), traces the agrarian yeoman into the "garden" of the Midwest during the nineteenth century.

2. Max Weber, *The Protestant Ethic and the Spirit of Capitalism*, trans. Talcott Parsons (New York, 1958); R. H. Tawney, *Religion and the Rise of Capitalism* (New York, 1926); E. M. W. Tillyard, *The Elizabethan World Picture* (New York, 1959); Perry Miller, *The New England Mind*, 2 vols. (Boston, 1953).

3. Jeannette Tawney, ed., *Chapters from a Christian Directory*, by Richard Baxter (London, 1925), p. xii.

4. William Perkins, *Works* (Cambridge, 1605), p. 904.

5. William Bradford, *History of the Plimoth Plantation*, in *The Puritans*, ed. Perry Miller and Thomas H. Johnson (New York, 1963), rev. ed., 1: 105. For studies of Elizabethan middle class attitudes, see Louis B. Wright, *Middle-Class Culture in Elizabethan England* (Chapel Hill, 1935), and Christopher Hill, *Society and Puritanism in Pre-Revolutionary England* (London, 1964).

6. Maren Sophie Røstvig, *The Happy Man: Studies in the Metamorphoses of A Classical Ideal*, 2 vols. (Oslo, 1962). Also, Edwin H. Cady, *The Gentleman in America: A Literary Study in American Culture* (Syracuse, N.Y., 1949).

7. Alexander Pope, *Essay on Man*, Epistle 4, ll. 77–80.

8. J. Hector St. John Crevecoeur, *Letters from an American Farmer* (New York, 1904), p. 72.

9. Cotton Mather, *Two Brief Discourses. One Directing a Christian in his Gen-*

eral Calling; Another Directing him in his Personal Calling (Boston, 1701), p. 42.

10. Pope, Epistle 3, ll. 317–318.

11. Benjamin Franklin, *Autobiography*, ed. Leonard W. Labaree et. al. (New Haven, 1964), p. 146.

12. "To Messieurs the Public," in *The Works of Benjamin Franklin*, ed. Jared Sparks, 10 vols. (Boston, 1840), 2:358–59.

13. *Works*, 2:92.

14. *Works*, 2:97.

15. Quoted in Lewis Carey, *Franklin's Economic Views* (New York, 1928), p. 207.

CHAPTER I

1. The standard guide to magazines of the period is Frank L. Mott, *A History of American Magazines*, 2 vols. (New York, 1930–57); more specialized studies are: Ruth Elson, *Guardians of Tradition: American Schoolbooks of the Nineteenth Century* (Lincoln, Neb., 1964); Sheila A. Egoff, "Children's Periodicals in the Nineteenth Century," *Library Association Pamphlet Number Eight* (London, 1951); Bess Porter Adams, *About Books and Children: Historical Survey of Children's Literature* (New York, 1953); William B. Cairns, "On the Development of American Literature from 1815 to 1833, with Especial Reference to Periodicals," *Bulletin of the University of Wisconsin Philology and Literature Series*, 1 (Madison, 1898), pp. 1–87; F. J. Harvey Darton, *Children's Books in England; Five Centuries of Social Life* (Cambridge, Engl., 1958); Alice M. Jordon, *From Rollo to Tom Sawyer* (Boston, 1948). An extensive but by no means exhaustive list of my primary sources may be found in the bibliography below.

2. *Juvenile Miscellany* 4 (Mar. 1830): 25–29. (Cited hereafter as *JM*.)

3. *JM* 3 (Nov. 1829): 120–128.

4. "Happiness," *JM* 2 (May 1827): 94.

5. "Benjamin Franklin" *JM* 2 (Mar. 1827): 18.

6. *JM* 3 (Nov. 1829): 187. For the optimistic view of farm life, see Anne L. Kuhn, *The Mother's Role in Childhood Education: New England Concepts, 1830–1860* (New Haven, 1947).

7. *JM* 2 (May 1829): 185–198.

8. "Walter Armstrong," *JM* 3 (Nov. 1829): 170.

9. "Rich and Poor," *JM* 1 (Jan. 1829): 170. The author is probably Ann Maria Wells. Other frequent contributors were Sara J. Hale ("S.J.H.") and Lydia Huntley Sigourney ("L.H.S.").

10. *JM* 6 (Aug. 1831): 318.

11. "Alvan the Poor Little Burnt Boy," *JM* 3 (Sept. 1829): 23.

12. "Imprisonment for Debt," *JM* 6 (June 1831): 210.

13. "Infant Schools," *JM* 3 (Sept. 1829): 88–89. Despite frequent references to religion, the *Miscellany's* God is less imminent for those who are not among the poor than He was for Cotton Mather or Benjamin Franklin. The *Miscellany* studiously avoided denigrating anyone, though the poor of the stories are often Irish, and during this period it was common to blame Roman Catholicism for the Irishman's failure to follow the Protestant Ethic. For Mrs. Child, stress upon prudential virtues comes less from divine fiat than from secular morality; industry and charity are inculcated because they benefit man and society. Perhaps one major reason for the relative silence of the magazine on religious doctrine was an attempt to avoid alienating subscribers through sectarian controversy; most juvenile periodicals with any longevity soon became non-denominational. But whatever the cause, there is less emphasis upon goodness for God's sake and more upon goodness for the sake of man; heaven is occasionally the reward for good children, but more often the reward is earthly: money, mother's approval, or the feeling of contentment.

14. Samuel G. Goodrich, *Recollections of a Lifetime*, 2 vols. (New York, 1857), 1:418 (cited hereafter as "*Recollections*"). Trumbull, the more well known of the three, was an ardent Federalist; Percival was perhaps the most popular romantic poet before Bryant, and continued publishing poems well into the 1840s; John Brainard, who died in 1828 at age 32, wrote in the "pre-romantic" mode.

15. Ibid., 2:167. Miss More was by this time better known for her contributions to the Religious Tract Society, and for authorship of the didactic novel *Coelebs in Search of a Wife* (1809), than for her earlier plays.

16. Ibid., 2:309.

17. Ibid., 2:308. Horace Mann saw public school education as a "great equalizer" of human conditions and a means to social harmony through the instillation of a universal set of moral values. Borrowing from Pestalozzi and phrenology, Mann taught a behavioristic pedagogy that entailed the exercise of desirable faculties and the disuse of the undesirable ones. (See Lawrence A. Cremin, *The Transformation of the School* [New York, 1961], esp. pp. 8–13.) Carter advocated Pestalozzi's pedagogic principle of discovery rather than memory. Goodrich seems to have been more influenced by Carter's emphasis on geography than by his Pestalozzian theories.

18. Ibid., 2:321.

19. Egoff, "Children's Periodicals," p. 9.

20. "Billy Bump," *Merry's Museum* 16 (1848). Cited below as *MM*.

21. "Life and Adventures of Robert Merry," *MM* 4 (July 1842). This serial was published in 1844 as the book *Wit Bought*.

22. *MM* 16 (Oct. 1848): 122.

23. "English Farmers," *MM* 8 (Aug. 1844): 55.

24. *MM* 9 (Mar. 1845): 78.

25. Ibid., pp. 79–84.

26. "Cheerful Cherry," *MM* 3 (1842): 49.
27. *MM* 2 (1841): 40–42.
28. "Cheating the Indians," *Parley's Magazine* 5 (1834): 123.
29. *Recollections*, 1:414–415.
30. "The Choice of a Profession," *MM* 10 (Sept. 1845): 270.
31. *Recollections*, 1:119–21n.
32. Ibid., 2:361; "The Brahmins," *MM* 13 (June 1847): 164–66.
33. "Philip Brusque," *MM* (1842). Published as a book in 1845.
34. "Equality," *MM* 36 (1859): 190.
35. "The Beggar," *MM* 24 (1852): 16.
36. Peggy Betsey, "Two Sides of a Picture," *MM* 17 (1849): 142.
37. "The Flying Horse," *MM* 18 (1849): 15–18.
38. "The Famine in Ireland," *MM* 14 (July 1847): 55.
39. "Rent Day," *MM* 16 (Nov. 1848): 145.
40. "Romance of Manufactures," *MM* 11 (Jan. 1846): 4–12.
41. George W. Cutter, "The Song of Steam," *MM* 17 (1849): 23–24. This poem was second in popularity only to Cutter's "Buena Vista," which commemorated that fight in the Mexican War. Both poems were used as book titles by this "western poet": *Buena Vista and Other Poems* (1848) and *Song of Steam and Other Poems* (1857), an indication that the title poems' circulation in magazines was wide enough to support sales in book form.
42. *Recollections*, 1: 317–19.
43. Victor S. Clark, *History of Manufactures in the United States* (New York, 1929), 1: 397.
44. *Recollections*, 1: 317–19.
45. See Arthur A. Ekirch, "The Idea of Progress in America, 1815–1860," *Studies in History, Economics, and Public Law, no. 115; Columbia University* (New York, 1944), esp. pp. 192–250.
46. *Recollections*, 1: 318.
47. Ibid., 1: 95–96.
48. "Try, Try Again," *MM* 35 (1858): 172.
49. "I Like to Beat," *MM* 13 (1847): 65–66.
50. "Go Ahead," *MM* 37 (1859): 21. The poem was submitted by a "Buckeye Boy of Ohio," and indicates an adoption of Davy Crockett's war cry to the frontier of economic struggle.
51. "Wealth and Its Wings," *MM* 30 (1855): 141–43.

CHAPTER 2

1. Goodrich, *Recollections*, 2: 269n.
2. *Youth's Companion* 31 (1 Oct. 1857): 160. Cited below as *YC*.
3. Henry A. Beers, *Nathaniel Parker Willis* (Boston, 1885), p. 11; see also *DAB*, 20: 305. Compare the father's description with that of his son Nathaniel: "He is a tall dashing looking fellow, dressed rather in the extreme of fashion, yet

in good taste, and with an air of fashionable languor about him. . . . But time and the pen have left their traces on his face; evidently he cultivates the Graces, although the enemy has thinned his curling locks, which are jauntily disposed over a fine forehead. . . . The cheeks . . . have a yellowish tinge, which travel or good living might have caused." George W. Bungay, *Off-hand Takings* . . . (New York, 1854), pp. 47–48.

4. Mott, *History of American Magazines*, 2: 266.

5. "The Hooseroons," *Parley's Magazine* 1 (Mar. 1833): 143.

6. *YC* 4 (11 Aug. 1830): 46; "Conscience," *YC* 4 (15 Mar. 1831): 172.

7. *YC* 1, 2 (6 June 1827): 8.

8. "Advice to Young Men," *YC* 22 (15 Feb. 1849): 167.

9. "A Good Trade a Good Fortune," *YC* 32 (30 Sept. 1858): 155.

10. "Benefits of Apprenticeship," *YC* 26 (23 Sept. 1852): 87.

11. "Two Rich Men," *YC* 12 (22 Feb. 1839): 161–62.

12. "The Two Brothers," *YC* 31 (16 July 1857): 115.

13. "Business Life," *YC* 32 (21 Jan. 1858): 12.

14. Editorial, *YC* 30: (24 Dec. 1857): 108.

15. "How to Get Rich," *YC* 23 (1 Nov. 1849): 106.

16. Cited in Irvin G. Wyllie, *The Self-Made Man in America: The Myth of Rags to Riches* (New Brunswick, 1954), p. 8.

17. "Self-Made Men," *YC* 22 (12 Oct. 1848): 96.

18. "Advice for Young Men," *YC* 22 (15 Feb. 1849): 167.

19. "Hoarding Wealth," *YC* 24 (27 Mar. 1851): 192.

20. This convenient distinction between "coercive" and "assimilative" reform is made by Joseph R. Gusfield, *Symbolic Crusade* (Urbana, 1963). See also Clifford Griffin, *Their Brother's Keepers* (New Brunswick, 1960) and William H. and Jane H. Pease, "Antislavery Ambivalence: Immediatism, Expediency, Race," *American Quarterly* 17 (Winter 1965): 682–95.

21. Lydia Maria Child, *An Appeal in Favor of . . . Africans* (Boston, 1833), pp. 77–108, 211.

22. *Proceedings of the Anti-Slavery Convention of Philadelphia, December 4, 5, and 6, 1833* (New York, 1833), p. 19.

23. Child, *The Right Way the Safe Way* . . . (New York, 1860), pp. 5–6.

24. Louis Filler, *The Crusade Against Slavery, 1830–1860* (New York, 1963), pp. 93–107.

25. "The Contraband's Ethics," *YC* 37 (29 Jan. 1863): 19.

26. "The Contrabands," *YC* 37 (8 Jan. 1863): 19.

27. "A Young Contraband," *YC* 36 (1 May 1862): 70.

28. *YC* 38 (5 Feb. 1864): 22.

29. John Allen Krout, *The Origins of Prohibition* (New York, 1925).

30. George F. Clark, *History of Temperance Reform in Massachusetts, 1813–1883* (Boston, 1888), pp. 35–36; *DAB*.

31. Ernest H. Cherrington, *The Evolution of Prohibition in the United States* (Westerville, Ohio, 1920), p. 123.

32. Augustus F. Fehlandt, *A Century of Drink Reform in the United States* (New York, 1904), p. 89.
33. Clark, *History of Temperance Reform*, p. 38.
34. "The Confectioner," *YC* 1 (9 Nov. 1827): 96.
35. *YC* 10 (10 Mar. 1837): 175, 182.
36. *YC* 16 (2 Feb. 1843): 156.
37. *YC* 24 (17 Apr. 1851): 203.
38. "The Seduced," *YC* 6 (5 Dec. 1831): 144; "The Unfaithful Husband," *YC* 10 (16 Sept. 1836): 71; *YC* 18 (28 Mar. 1844): 196.
39. Editorial, *YC* 21 (12 Feb. 1857): 28. Arthur Tappan, in fact, went bankrupt twice, the first time following the panic of 1837, the second time, in 1842, through speculation in real estate. Having sat under the pulpit of William Ellery Channing as a youth, Tappan resolved that when he had wealth he would "reflect seriously upon his obligations as a STEWARD of the Lord." His stewardship led him to support various societies from Sunday Schools to militant abolitionism. *DAB*.
40. "Obituary," *YC* 1 (18 Apr. 1828): 187.
41. *YC* 9 (18 Dec. 1835): 124.
42. *YC* 17 (24 Aug. 1843): 64.
43. "Charity Children of England," *YC* 26 (24 Mar. 1853): 190.
44. "The Emigrants," *YC* 17 (3 Aug. 1843): 50.
45. "The Log Cabin," *YC* 18 (31 Oct. 1844): 102–3.
46. Henry Nash Smith argues that the yeoman image died out in the South as it came to be associated with anti-slavery attitudes (*Virgin Land*, pp. 160–64). However, not all Southern apologists were willing to give up the idea, for in their eyes, the small freeholders of the South constituted a class between the aristocratic plantation owners and the slaves. As the war talk grew, some argued that the South's stalwart soldiers would be drawn from her yeomanry. Even the pro-slavery George Fitzhugh, used by Smith to show the rejection of the yeoman idea, reveals support for it both in his taunts at Northern industrial society for losing its yeomanry, and in his view of the future South as a proud yeoman mechanic among nations: "States must live by hand-work or head-work. The production of books . . . , the manufacture of fine silks, woolens, calicoes, shawls, the making of exquisite porcelain, the building of ships, and steamboats, the construction of machinery. . . . A nation chiefly engaged in such pursuits, follows head-work within doors, labors lightly, and makes five times as much as one engaged in the coarsest occupations of mere hand-work. . . . The hand-work men and nations are slaves in fact. . . ." *Sociology for the South* (reprint ed., New York, n.d.), pp. 172–73.
47. "A Lowell Girl," *YC* 16 (6 Apr. 1843): 192.
48. "Working Girls," *YC* 21 (13 Apr. 1848): 200.
49. "Song of the Shirt," *YC* 19 (6 Nov. 1846): 108.
50. "Tammany Hall," *YC* 13 (2 Aug. 1939): 46.

51. "The Strawberry Woman," *YC* 21 (9 Sept. 1847): 73.
52. "The Newsboy," *YC* 21 (5 Mar. 1857): 37.
53. "The Merchant's Dream," *YC* 18 (11 July 1844): 37.
54. By 1878, the *Youth's Companion* had one of the leading circulations in the country, ahead of *Harper's Weekly*, with 141,420 sales per issue, a substantial number for that time. Cited in Mary Noel, *Villains Galore . . .* (New York, 1954), p. 120.

CHAPTER 3

1. James Montgomery, *A Practical Detail of the Cotton Manufactures in the United States . . .* (Glasgow, 1840); Vera Shlakman, "Economic History of a Factory Town" (Chicopee, Mass.), *Smith College Studies in History* 20 (Oct. 1934–July 1935); Elwin H. Powell, "The Evolution of the American City and the Emergence of Anomie: A Culture Case Study of Buffalo, N.Y.: 1810–1910," *British Journal of Sociology* 13 (June 1962): 157–63; William Sullivan, *The Industrial Worker in Pennsylvania, 1800–1840* (Harrisburg, Pa., 1955); Rowland T. Berthoff, *British Immigrants in Industrial America, 1790–1950* (Cambridge, Mass., 1953).
2. Timothy Claxton, "Memoir," *Boston Mechanic* 1 (Nov. 1832): 167.
3. *BM* 1 (Jan. 1832): 1–2.
4. "James Brindley," *BM* 1 (Feb. 1832): 28–29. Brindley (1716–72) was also admired for having designed viaducts and steam engines in his head without drawings or written calculations, perhaps thereby suggesting to would-be technological entrepreneurs that they did not need much formal schooling.
5. "Everyone to His Trade," *BM* 3 (Sept. 1834): 284–85.
6. "Habits," *BM* 3 (Feb. 1834): 64.
7. John Neal, "Education," *BM* 3 (June 1834): 184–86. A prolific hack, Neal was attuned to his audience's likes and dislikes, and his topics serve as an index to that taste.
8. *BM* 1 (Apr. 1832): 61.
9. "A Stitch in Time Saves Nine," *BM* 3 (Dec. 1834): 373.
10. "Essay on the Mechanic Arts," *BM* 1 (Mar. 1832): 34–35.
11. "Mechanics," *BM* 2 (Oct. 1833): 169.
12. "Respectability of Mechanics," *BM* 4 (Nov. 1835): 205–6.
13. *BM* 1 (June 1832): 94–96.
14. Timothy Claxton, *Memoir of a Mechanic* (Boston, 1839), p. 161.
15. "A Plea for the Laboring Classes," *BM* 4 (Dec. 1835): 238.
16. "On the Division of Labor," *BM* 4 (Oct. 1835): 190–91. For a detailed discussion of the "mechanic" versus the "organic" in major American thinkers, see Leo Marx, *The Machine in the Garden* (New York, 1964).
17. "Address to Mechanics," *BM* 4 (Nov. 1835): 199–201.
18. "Evils of Machinery and their Remedy," *BM* 4 (Sept. 1835): 154.

19. "Measuring Time," *BM* 4 (June 1835): 87.
20. "A Plea for the Laboring Classes," *BM* 4 (Dec. 1835): 236.
21. "Education Among Mechanics," *BM* 4 (Mar. 1835): 9.
22. "Information Relating to Industry," *BM* 4 (May 1835): 63–65.
23. "Trust Yourself," *BM* 2 (Nov. 1833): 176.
24. *Young American's Magazine* (Jan. 1847), pp. 17–24; *YAM* (Jul. 1847), pp. 15–16.
25. "Thought and Reading," *YAM* (Jan. 1847), p. 21.
26. George Light, *Keep Cool, Go Ahead, and a Few Other Poems* (Boston, 1851), pp. 15–16.
27. *Mechanics' Magazine and Register of Inventions and Improvements* 1, 5 (May 1833): 219, 272; 5 (Feb. 1835): 63. McCoy began his successes in 1870 with machine lubrication.
28. *MechM* 5 (Feb. 1835): 68–79.
29. David S. Edelstein, "Joel Munsell: Printer and Antiquarian," *Columbia Studies in History . . . No. 560* (New York, 1950), p. 362.
30. Benjamin Grieg, "Address," *New York State Mechanic* 1, no. 2 (10 Sept. 1842): 126.
31. "Associationism," *NYSM* 1 (28 May 1842): 6.
32. "Riot in Philadelphia," *NYSM* 1 (1 Oct. 1842): 154.
33. S. T. Austin, "Address," *NYSM* 1 (16 Jan. 1842): 58.
34. "The Laboring Classes," *NYSM* 2 (15 Apr. 1843): 163. Ephraim G. Squier apparently shared Munsell's antiquarian interests, for his later fame derived from his archeological studies of the Midwest. He seemingly believed his doctrine of individualism; having been caught in the panic of 1837 and forced to turn from engineering to journalism, he was by the date of this article well into a second career largely self-taught.
35. Ralph Waldo Emerson, "Social Agitation," *NYSM* 2 (4 Mar. 1843): 115.
36. *NYSM* 2 (15 Apr. 1843): 164. Hunt, an itinerant publisher and self-made man, previously published the *Juvenile Miscellany* and shared Mrs. Child's abolitionism. He was also an ardent supporter of Andrew Jackson.
37. *NYSM* 1 (21 May 1842): 207; 1 (11 Jan. 1842): 19; 1 (16 July 1842): 63; 1 (23 July 1842): 71; 1 (17 Sept. 1842): 131, 139; 1 (1 Oct. 1842): 154, 155; 1 (19 Nov. 1842): 206.
38. "Daughters of the Poor," *NYSM* 2 (20 May 1843): 204.
39. The theoretical assumption underlying my statement is one familiar to students of public opinion, that audiences practice selective perception and retention. Consequently, because of feedback from an editor's audience, one can guess a rough correlation between an audience's interests and the publications it reads, the television it watches, the legislation it supports. See, for further discussion, *The Process and Effects of Mass Communication*, ed. Wilbur Schramm (Urbana, 1954); *Public Opinion and Propaganda*, ed. Daniel Katz (New York, 1954), esp. pp. 435–46; and Joseph T. Klapper, *The Effects of Mass Communications* (Glencoe, Ill., 1960).

40. "Free and Independent," *Mechanic's Advocate* 1 (25 Sept. 1847): 333.
41. "Mechanic's Song," *MA* 1 (9 Oct. 1847): 337.
42. Eli Moore, "Address delivered before the General Trades' Union of the City of New York . . . December 2, 1833," in *Social Theories of Jacksonian Democracy*, ed. Joseph L. Blau (New York, 1954), pp. 289, 299–300.
43. *Mechanic's Free Press* 1 (24 May 1828): 2.
44. *MFP* 3 (9 Jan. 1830): 1.
45. Ibid., 3. The Provident Society, established 1824, originally taught the poor to support themselves through learning such trades as candle-dipping and weaving. Apparently, the recipients were less appreciative of the training than were the society's managers. By 1854, the Society—now more concerned with unclaimed children—was melded in the general consolidation of charitable organizations in Philadelphia.
46. *MFP* 4 (5 Mar. 1831): 2.
47. *MFP* 4 (2 Apr. 1831): 3.
48. F. W. Young, "Address," *Voice of Industry* 1 (5 June 1845): 2.
49. *Vol* 2 (8 Jan. 1847): 1.
50. "Industry and Integrity," *Vol* 1 (10 July 1845): 4.
51. "The Lowell Offering," *Vol* 1 (2 Jan. 1846): 2.
52. John Allen, "Letters to . . . Abbott Lawrence," *Vol* 2 (25 Sept. 1846): 2.
53. "A Word . . . ," *Vol* 3 (14 Apr. 1848): 2.
54. *Working Man's Advocate* 1 (6 Apr. 1844): 2.
55. *WMA* 1 (13 July 1844): 2.
56. *WMA* 1 (6 Apr. 1844): 2.
57. William Henry Channing, *The Life of William Ellery Channing, D.D.*, 6th ed. (Boston, 1899), p. 477.
58. Ibid., p. 482.
59. Channing, "Elevation of the Laboring Portion of the Community," *Western Messenger* 8 (May 1840): 35–41.
60. *The Spirit of the Age* 1 (7 July 1849): 8.
61. "New York Regiment," *SA* 1 (7 July 1849): 14.
62. "A New Heaven and a New Earth," *SA* 1 (21 July 1849): 35.
63. "The Middle Class," *SA* 1 (15 Sept. 1849): 169–71.
64. Channing, in Newell D. Hillis, *Right Living as a Fine Art* (New York, 1899), p. 8.
65. Carnegie's charities were designed to give help to those able to help themselves through self-education. In rejecting the idea of bequeathing his wealth to his family, he echoed the riches-to-rags motif: " 'I would as soon leave my son a curse as the almighty dollar.' " In Joseph F. Wall, *Andrew Carnegie* (New York, 1970), p. 807.

CHAPTER 4

1. Van Wyck Brooks, for example, in *The Writer in America* (New York

1953), tends to see Hawthorne's philosophy as concerned with metaphysics. A. N. Kaul in *The American Vision* (New Haven, 1963) examines Hawthorne's attitudes toward contemporary society. Frederick Crews's *The Sins of the Fathers* (New York, 1968) argues that Hawthorne raises social questions and then leaves them without solving them. Other critics indicating Hawthorne's pessimism about social progress are Darrel Abel, "Hawthorne's Skepticism About Social Reform," *University Review* 19 (1953): 181–93; and Arlin Turner, "Hawthorne and Reform," *New England Quarterly* 15 (1942) 1: 700–714. My argument is that Hawthorne defined many social questions within the framework of the yeoman dream and tried—albeit unsuccessfully—to resolve the problems with the conventions of that dream. He was certainly not alone among major writers in his concern with American concepts of success. Before him, Washington Irving expressed dislike for the new American standards of success (Stanley T. Williams, *The Life of Washington Irving*, New York, 1935, 1: 143–44); and after him, the established materialism of American success was a dominant topic for Twain (George M. Spangler, "*Pudd'nhead Wilson*: A Parable of Property," *American Literature* 42 [1970]: 28–37). Hawthorne comes at a time in the development of this motif when American romantics were becoming aware of nascent sociological concepts, and his later novels reveal a growing incompatibility between his romantic mode of writing and the realistic mode demanded by sociological themes.

2. The biographical sketches which Hawthorne did for Freeman Hunt's *American Magazine of Useful and Entertaining Knowledge* (Mar.–Aug. 1836) focused on Americans notable for their personal and consequent civic virtues. The familiar moralizing tone and picture of traditional success also marked Hawthorne's *The Grandfather's Chair* (1841) and especially *Biographical Stories* (1842), both of which drew on his earlier work for Samuel Goodrich.

3. Nathaniel Hawthorne, *Fanshawe* (Athens, Ohio, 1964), pp. 338–39.

4. Ibid., p. 343.

5. Edward Wagenknecht, *Nathaniel Hawthorne: Man and Writer* (New York, 1961), p. 57.

6. *Complete Works of Nathaniel Hawthorne*, 12 vols. (Cambridge, Mass., 1883), 3:273. A substantial portion of this section on *The House of the Seven Gables* appeared in *Texas Studies in Literature and Language* and is copyrighted by the University of Texas Press, Fall 1970.

7. Ibid., p. 134.

8. Ibid., pp. 300–316.

9. Ibid., p. 33.

10. Ibid., p. 75.

11. Ibid., p. 71.

12. Ibid., p. 162.

13. Ibid., p. 99.

14. Ibid., pp. 102–6.
15. Ibid., pp. 81–83.
16. The temporal relativism of practical advice is seen in Hawthorne's biography of Franklin, where the narrator remarks that Poor Richard's proverbs "were suited to the condition of the country" in Franklin's time, though not to the more refined nineteenth century—when such writers as Thoreau and Hawthorne used Franklin as the epitome of crass materialism. *Works*, 12: 202.
17. *Works*, 3: 188.
18. Kaul, pp. 191–94.
19. *Works*, 3: 211–16.
20. Ibid., p. 255.
21. Ibid., p. 212.
22. Ibid., pp. 252–61.
23. For a view which sees Judge Pyncheon as a Jacksonian Democrat and Holgrave as entirely unconcerned with materialism, see H. N. Smith, "The Morals of Power: Business Enterprise as a Theme in Mid-Nineteenth-Century American Fiction," in *Essays on American Literature in Honor of Jay B. Hubbel*, ed. Clarence Gohdes (Durham, 1967), pp. 90–107.
24. *Works*, 3: 372.
25. Ibid., p. 363.
26. William B. Dillingham, "Structure and Theme in *The House of the Seven Gables*," *Nineteenth Century Fiction* 14 (June 1959): 59–79; Philip Young, ed., *The House of the Seven Gables* (New York, 1965), p. xv.
27. F. O. Matthiessen, *American Renaissance* (New York, 1966), pp. 331–35.
28. *The Blithedale Romance* (Columbus, Ohio, 1964), pp. 13–20.
29. Ibid., p. 153.
30. Ibid., p. 241.
31. Ibid., pp. 182–88.
32. Ibid., p. 198.
33. Ibid., p. 203.
34. Ibid., p. 241.
35. Ibid., p. 245.
36. Ibid., p. 66.
37. Reprinted by permission of the publishers from Edward H. Davidson, *Hawthorne's Doctor Grimshawe's Secret*, Cambridge, Mass.: Harvard University Press, copyright, 1954, by the President and Fellows of Harvard College, p. 22.
38. Ibid., p. 23.
39. Ibid., p. 289.
40. Ibid., pp. 70–71.
41. Ibid., p. 85.
42. Ibid., pp. 85–86.
43. Ibid., pp. 197–234n. It is possible, too, that Hawthorne had in mind William Henry Channing.

44. Ibid., pp. 26–27.
45. *Works*, 12: 199. In the *Autobiography*, Franklin wrote simply, "several of us were corrected by our Fathers; and tho' I pleaded the Usefulness of the Work, mine convinc'd me that nothing was useful which was not honest" (*The Autobiography of Benjamin Franklin*, ed. Leonard W. Labaree et. al., New Haven, 1964, p. 54). Hawthorne embellished the note: "There is no more terrible mistake than to violate what is eternally right for the sake of a seeming expediency. Those who act upon such a principle do the utmost in their power to destroy all that is good in the world. . . . No act . . . can possibly be for the benefit of the public generally which involves injustice to any individual."
46. *Grimshawe*, pp. 112–13.
47. Ibid., p. 292.
48. Ibid., pp. 141–42.
49. Ibid., pp. 160–61.
50. Ibid., p. 80.

CHAPTER 5

1. "The Gospel of Wealth," in *The Gospel of Wealth and Other Timely Essays* (New York, 1900), p. 7.
2. Ibid., p. 4. See also William G. Sumner, "Reply to a Socialist," which is based upon the same Social Darwinism. Carnegie spoke to an audience inclined to agree with Sumner, as indicated by the popularity of his essay.
3. Ibid., p. 7.
4. Ibid., p. 16.
5. "The Advantages of Poverty," ibid., p. 75.
6. Dores R. Sharpe, *Walter Rauschenbusch* (New York, 1942), p. 92.
7. Ibid., p. 95.
8. As evidence of the wide acceptance of Rauschenbusch's first book, my edition notes, "Published March, 1907. Reprinted October, November, 1907; April, September, December, 1908; December, 1909; January, June, 1910; January, March, May, November, 1911; February, 1912; March, October, 1912; March, 1913; November, 1914; August, 1915; March, 1916; September, 1917." His popularity received a heavy blow when he publicly argued that England should share the blame for World War I.
9. Ibid., p. 215.
10. Ibid., p. 313.
11. Ibid., p. 345.
12. Ibid., pp. 340–41.
13. Ibid., pp. 389–90.
14. "Alger studies" may be divided into two broad areas: Freudian and cultural. The former has been based on Herbert R. Mayes's suspect biography, *Alger:*

A Biography Without a Hero (New York, 1928). Several scholars have accepted Mayes's distortions and factual errors, with the result that a sound psychological study of Alger has yet to be made. The view that Alger's stories and popularity result from their foundation in the Protestant Ethic has been advanced by: Robert Falk, "Notes on the 'Higher Criticism' of Horatio Alger, Jr.," *Arizona Quarterly* 19 (Summer 1962): 151–67; Rychard Fink, "Horatio Alger as a Social Philosopher," in *"Ragged Dick" and "Mark the Match Boy,"* by Horatio Alger, Jr. (New York, 1962), pp. 5–31; and John G. Cawelti, *Apostles of the Self-Made Man* (Chicago, 1965), pp. 101–23. The corrective to Mayes's work is Frank Gruber, *Horatio Alger, Jr.: A Biography and Bibliography* (Los Angeles, 1961). The best short study of Alger criticism is John Seelye, "Who Was Horatio? The Alger Myth and American Scholarship," *American Quarterly* 17 (Winter 1965): 749–56. The most reliable biography of Alger, though wanting in scholarly paraphernalia, is Ralph D. Gardner, *Horatio Alger, or the American Hero Era* (Mendota, Ill., 1964).

15. Estimates of the number of Alger books in print from the late 1850s to the 1920s vary from one to four hundred million, according to Ralph D. Gardner in *"Silas Snobden's Office Boy" by Horatio Alger* (Garden City, N.Y., 1973), pp. 14–15. This does not include the serialization of the novels in such vastly popular periodicals as the *Golden Argosy, Student and Scholar, Young Israel.*

16. Apparently, Frank's ten thousand dollar white-collar job represents the average reward for Alger heroes. See Cawelti, *Apostles of the Self-Made Man,* p. 109.

17. *Snobden,* p. 33.

18. Alger, *The Cash Boy* (Chicago, n.d.), p. 4.

19. Alger's titles indicate only two books devoted to the tribulations of factory boys. In these novels, as in his other works, the reward includes establishment in commerce rather than manufacturing.

20. Cawelti, *Apostles of the Self-Made Man,* pp. 103–4.

SELECTED BIBLIOGRAPHY

PRIMARY

Alcott, William A. *The Young Man's Guide.* 3rd ed. Boston, 1834.

Alger, Horatio Jr. *The Cash Boy.* Chicago: W. A. Donohue, n. d.

——. *Ragged Dick and Mark the Match Boy.* Intro. by Rychard Fink. New York: Collier Books, 1962.

——. *Silas Snobden's Office Boy.* Intro. by R. D. Gardner. Garden City, N.Y.: Doubleday, 1973.

American Magazine of Useful and Entertaining Knowledge. Edited by Freeman Hunt et al. Boston, 1834–37.

American Quarterly Review. Edited by Robert Walsh. Philadelphia, 1827–32.

Annals of Cleveland. Vols. 9–43 (1826–60). Cleveland, Ohio: WPA Project 16823, 1938.

Apprentice's Companion. Edited by D. K. Minor. Boston, 1835.

Baxter, Richard. *The Practical Works of Richard Baxter.* Edited by William Orme. 23 vols. London, 1830.

Boston Mechanic. Edited by George W. Light. Boston, 1832–36.

Boy's and Girl's Magazine. Edited by Mrs. S. Coleman. Boston, 1843–?

Brother Jonathan. Edited by Park Benjamin and Rufus W. Griswold. New York, 1842–43.

Bullock, William. *Virginia Impartially Examined . . . Advising People of All Degrees . . . How Suddenly to Raise Their Fortunes.* London, 1649.

Channing, William Henry. *Life of William Ellery Channing, D. D.* 6th ed. Boston, 1899.

Child, Lydia M. *The American Frugal Housewife.* 16th ed. Boston, 1836.

——. *An Appeal in Favor of that Race of People Called Africans.* Boston, 1833.

——. *The Right Way the Safe Way, Proved by Emancipation in the British West Indies and Elsewhere.* New York, 1860.

195

Child's Friend and Family Magazine. Edited by Eliza L. Follen, Boston, 1843–49.

Child's Newspaper. Edited by Thomas Brainard. Cincinnati, 1834.

Claxton, Timothy. *Memoir of a Mechanic.* Boston, 1839.

Constitution of the American Anti-Slavery Society. New York, 1838.

Cotton, John. *The Way of Life.* London, 1641.

———. *Two Brief Discourses. One Directing a Christian in His General Calling; Another Directing Him in His Personal Calling.* Boston, 1701.

Crevecoeur, St. John de. *Letters From an American Farmer.* London, 1782.

DeFoe, Daniel. *The Complete English Tradesman.* Anonymous editor. 2 vols. Oxford, 1841.

Education Reporter and Weekly Lyceum. Boston, 1830–31.

Farmer and Mechanic. Edited by W. H. Starr et al. New York, 1847–49.

Fitzhugh, George. *Sociology for the South or the Failure of Free Society.* 1854. Reprint. New York: Burt Franklin, n. d.

Forrester's Boy's and Girl's Companion. Edited by Henry V. Degan et al. Boston, 1851–57.

Franklin, Benjamin. *Autobiography.* Edited by Leonard W. Labaree et al. New Haven: Yale University Press, 1964.

———. *The Works of Benjamin Franklin.* Edited by Jared Sparks. 10 vols. Boston, 1840.

Friend of Youth. Edited by Margaret L. Baily. Washington, D.C., 1849–50.

Goodrich, Samuel G. *Recollections of a Lifetime.* 2 vols. New York. 1857.

Harbinger, Devoted to Social and Political Progress. Edited by George Ripley. Boston and New York, 1845–49.

Hawthorne, Manning. "Hawthorne Prepares for College." *New England Quarterly* 11 (1938): 66–68.

Hawthorne, Nathaniel. *The American Notebooks.* Edited by Randall Stewart. New Haven: Yale University Press, 1932.

———. *The English Notebooks.* Edited by Randall Stewart. New York: Modern Language Association of America, 1941.

———. *Fanshawe.* Centenary ed. Columbus, Ohio: Ohio State University Press, 1964.

———. *Hawthorne's "Doctor Grimshawe's Secret."* Edited by Edward H. Davidson. Cambridge, Mass.: Harvard University Press, 1954.

———. *Life of Franklin Pierce.* Boston, 1852.

———. *The Scarlet Letter.* Centenary ed. Columbus, Ohio: Ohio State University Press, 1962.

———. *The Complete Works of Nathaniel Hawthorne.* Edited by G. P. Lathrop. 15 vols. Boston: Houghton Mifflin, 1882.

Hesperian, or Western Monthly Magazine. Edited by William D. Gallagher and Otway Curry. Columbus, Ohio, 1838–39.

Hundley, D. R. *Social Relations in Our Southern States.* 1860. Reprint. Ann Arbor, Mich.: University Microfilms. American Culture Series 134:2.

Hungerford, Edward B. "Hawthorne Gossips About Salem." *New England Quarterly* 6 (1933): 445–69.

Hunt's Merchant's Magazine and Commercial Review. Edited by Freeman Hunt. New York, 1839–70.

Juvenile Miscellany. Edited by Lydia M. Child. Boston, 1826–34.

Letters of Hawthorne to William D. Ticknor, 1851–1864. Reprint. 2 vols. Ann Arbor, Mich.: University Microfilms, 1961.

Light, George W. *Keep Cool, Go Ahead, and a Few Other Poems*. Boston, 1851.

Lowell Mercury and Massachusetts Gazette. Lowell, Mass., 1831.

Mather, Cotton. *Bonifacius. An Essay Upon the Good* . . . Boston, 1710.

———. *Essays to Do Good*. Edited by George Burder. Boston, 1808.

Mechanic's Advocate. Edited by John Tanner. Albany, N.Y., 1846–48.

Mechanic's Magazine and Register of Inventions and Improvements. Edited by D. K. Minor et al. New York, 1833–37.

New England Farmer. Edited by Thomas G. Fessenden et al. Boston, 1823–47.

New York Mirror and Ladies' Literary Gazette. Edited by Samuel Woodworth et al. New York, 1830–57(?).

North American Magazine. Edited by Sumner L. Fairfield. Philadelphia, 1832–38.

People's Magazine. Boston: Lilly, Wait, & Co., 1833–1835.

Philadelphia Liberalist. Edited by Zelotes Fuller. Philadelphia, 1832–36.

Philadelphia Mirror. Philadelphia: Makin & Holden, 1836–37.

Present. Edited by William H. Channing. New York, 1843–44.

Rauschenbusch, Walter C. et al. *Conservation of National Ideals*. New York: Fleming H. Revell, 1911.

Robert Merry's Museum. Edited by Samuel G. Goodrich et al. Boston, 1841–72(?).

Sentinel and Star in the West. Edited by J. Kidwell et al. Cincinnati, 1829–37.

Spirit of the Age. Edited by William H. Channing. Boston, 1849.

Stewart, Randall. "Hawthorne and Politics: Unpublished Letters to William B. Pike." *New England Quarterly* 5 (1932): 237–63.

Voice of Industry. Edited by W. F. Young et al. Fitchburg and Lowell, Mass., 1845–47.

Western Messenger. Edited by James F. Clarke et al. Cincinnati and Louisville, 1835–41.

Western Monthly Magazine. Edited by James Hall. Cincinnati, 1833–35.

Western Quarterly Review. Cincinnati: J. S. Hitchcock, 1849.

Working Man's Advocate. Edited by George H. Evans. New York, 1829–45.

Young American's Magazine of Self-Improvement. Edited by George W. Light. Boston, 1847.

Young People's Book. Edited by John Frost. Philadelphia, 1841–42.

Youth's Cabinet. Edited by Francis Woodworth. New York, 1846–48.

Youth's Companion. Edited by Nathaniel P. Willis et al. Boston, 1827–1929.

Youth's Magazine: A Monthly Miscellany. New York: T. Mason & G. Lane, 1838–39.

SECONDARY

Abel, Darrel. "Hawthorne's Skepticism About Social Reform." *University Review* 19 (1953): 181–93.

Abele, Rudolph von. *The Death of the Artist: A Study of Hawthorne's Disintegration.* The Hague: Nijhoff, 1955.

Adams, Bess Porter. *About Books and Children: Historical Survey of Children's Literature.* New York: Holt, Rinehart & Winston, 1953.

Allen, F. R. et al. *Technology and Social Change.* New York: Appleton-Century, 1957.

Anderson, Louis F. *History of Manual and Industrial School Education.* New York: Appleton, 1926.

Arvin, Newton. *Hawthorne.* Boston: Little, Brown, 1929.

Bailyn, Bernard. *The New England Merchants in the Seventeenth Century.* Cambridge, Mass.: Harvard University Press, 1955.

Banner, Lois W. "Religion and Reform in the Early Republic: The Role of Youth." *American Quarterly* 23 (1971): 677–95.

Barnes, Gilbert H. *The Anti-Slavery Impulse, 1830–1844.* New York: Appleton-Century-Crofts, 1933.

Baxter, Annette F. "Independence vs. Isolation: Hawthorne and James on the Problem of the Artist." *Nineteenth Century Fiction* 10 (1955): 225–31.

Beach, Seth C. *Daughters of the Puritans.* Boston: American Unitarian Association, 1905.

Beck, Robert H. *A Social History of Education.* Englewood Cliffs, N.J.: Prentice-Hall, 1965.

Becker, Carl. *The Heavenly City of the Eighteenth-Century Philosophers.* New Haven: Yale University Press, 1959.

Beebe, Maurice. "The Fall of the House of Pyncheon." *Nineteenth Century Fiction* 2 (1956–57): 1–17.

Beers, Henry A. *Nathaniel Parker Willis.* Boston, 1885.

Bendix, Richard, and Lipset, Seymour. *Class, Status and Power.* Glencoe, Ill.: Free Press, 1953.

Benson, Lee. *The Concept of Jacksonian Democracy: New York as a Test Case.* New York: Atheneum, 1964.

Berthoff, Rowland T. *British Immigrants in Industrial America, 1790–1950.* Cambridge, Mass.: Harvard University Press, 1953.

Best, John Hardin, ed. *Franklin on Education.* New York: Bureau of Publications, Teachers College, Columbia University, 1962.

Bestor, Arthur Jr. *Backwoods Utopias.* Philadelphia: University of Pennsylvania Press, 1950.

Blau, Joseph L. *Social Theories of Jacksonian Democracy*. New York: Liberal Arts Press, 1954.

Bode, Carl. *The Anatomy of American Popular Culture, 1840–1861*. Berkeley: University of California Press, 1959.

——. "Hawthorne's *Fanshawe*: The Promise of Greatness." *New England Quarterly* 3 (1950): 235–42.

Brawley, Benjamin. *A Social History of the American Negro*. New York: Macmillan, 1921.

Bridenbaugh, Carl. *Cities in Revolt: Urban Life in America, 1743–1776*. New York: Knopf, 1955.

Brown, Herbert R. *The Sentimental Novel in America, 1789–1860*. Durham, N.C.: Duke, 1940

Brown, Robert E. *Middle Class Democracy and the Revolution in Massachusetts, 1691–1780*. Ithaca, N.Y.: Cornell University Press, 1955.

Cady, Edwin H. *The Gentleman in America: A Literary Study in American Culture*. Syracuse, N.Y.: Syracuse University Press, 1949.

Cain, Norman, and Carlson, Eric T. "Moral Insanity in the United States, 1835–1866." *American Journal of Psychiatry* 8 (1962): 795–801.

Cairns, William B. *On the Development of American Literature from 1815 to 1833, with Especial Reference to Periodicals*. Bulletin of the University of Wisconsin Philology and Literature Series, vol. 1. Madison, 1898.

Campbell, Mildred. *The English Yeoman Under Elizabeth and the Stewarts*. The Hague: Kripps Reprint Co., 1960.

Cantwell, Robert. *Nathaniel Hawthorne: The American Years*. New York: Rinehart, 1948.

Carey, Lewis J. *Franklin's Economic Views*. New York: Doubleday, 1928.

Carter, Henry. *The English Temperance Movement*. London: Epworth, 1933.

Cassirer, Ernst. *The Philosophy of the Enlightenment*. Boston: Beacon, 1962.

Cawelti, John G. *Apostles of the Self-Made Man*. Chicago: University of Chicago Press, 1965.

Chandler, Elizabeth Lathrop. *A Study of the Sources of the Tales and Romances Written by Nathaniel Hawthorne Before 1853*. Studies in Modern Languages, vol. 7, no. 4. Smith College Library: Northampton, Mass. 1926.

Cherrington, Ernest H. *The Evolution of Prohibition in the United States*. Westerville, Ohio: American Issues Press, 1920.

Clark, George F. *History of Temperance Reform in Massachusetts, 1813–1883*. Boston, 1888.

Clark, Harry H., ed. *Transitions in American Literary History*. Durham, N.C.: Duke University Press, 1953.

Clark, Victor S. *History of Manufactures in the United States, Volume I: 1607–1860*. New York: McGraw-Hill, 1929.

Clement, N. H. "Nature and the Country in Sixteenth and Seventeenth Century French Poetry." *PMLA* 44 (1929): 1005–47.

Cochran, Thomas C. "The Historian's Use of Social Role." In *Generalizations in the Writing of History*, edited by Louis R. Gottschalk. Chicago: University of Chicago Press, 1963.

————. "Role and Sanction in American Entrepreneurial History." In *Change and the Entrepreneur, Postulates and Patterns for Entrepreneurial History*. Research Center in Entrepreneurial History, preface by Arthur H. Cole. Harvard University Press, 1949.

Crawford, Ingeborg Haavik. "Hawthorne and Childhood." Master's thesis, University of Minnesota, 1942.

Crews, Frederick. "A New Reading of the Blithedale Romance." *American Literature* 21 (1957): 147–70.

Crump, P. E. "The Theme of Solitude." *French Quarterly* 7 (1925): 158–69.

Curti, Merle. *The Growth of American Thought*. 2nd ed. New York: Harper & Row, 1951.

Darton, F. J. Harvey. *Children's Books in England: Five Centuries of Social Life*. 2nd ed. Cambridge, Engl.: University Press, 1958.

Davidson, Frank. "Toward a Re-Evaluation of the *Blithedale Romance*." *New England Quarterly* 25 (1952): 374–83.

Denny, Margaret, and Gilman, William H., eds. *The American Writer and the European Tradition*. New York: Haskell House, 1968.

Dillingham, Wlliam B. "Structure and Theme in *The House of the Seven Gables*." *Nineteenth Century Fiction* 14 (1959): 59–70.

Donald, David H. *Lincoln Reconsidered*. New York: Knopf, 1956.

Dorfman, Joseph. *The Economic Mind in American Civilization, 1606–1933*. Vols. 1 and 2. New York: Viking, 1946–59.

Douglas, Paul H. *American Apprenticeship and Industrial Education*. Columbia University Studies, vol. 95. New York: Columbia University Press, 1921.

Edelstein, David S. *Joel Munsell: Printer and Antiquarian*. Columbia University Studies, vol. 560. New York: Columbia University Press, 1950.

Egoff, Shiela A. *Children's Periodicals in the Nineteenth Century*. Library Association Pamphlet Number Eight. London, 1951.

Ekirch, Arthur A., Jr. *The American Democratic Tradition*. New York: Macmillan, 1963.

————. *The Idea of Progress in America, 1815–1860*. Columbia University Studies, vol. 511. New York: Columbia University Press, 1944.

Elson, Ruth. *Guardians of Tradition: American Schoolbooks of the Nineteenth Century*. Lincoln, Neb.: University of Nebraska Press, 1964.

Evans, George H., Jr. *Business Incorporations in the United States, 1800–1943*. New York: National Bureau of Economic Research, 1948.

Fairbanks, Henry G. "Sin, Free Will, and 'Pessimism' in Hawthorne." *PMLA* 71 (1956): 975–89.

Falk, Robert. "Notes on the 'Higher Criticism' of Horatio Alger, Jr." *Arizona Quarterly* 19 (1963): 151–67.

Faulkner, Harold U. *American Economic History*. 7th ed. New York: Harper, 1954.

Fehlandt, Augustus F. *A Century of Drink Reform in the United States.* New York: Methodist Books, 1904.

Filler, Louis. *The Crusade Against Slavery, 1830–1860.* New York: Harper, 1963.

Fink, Rychard. "Horatio Alger as a Social Philosopher." In *"Ragged Dick" and "Mark the Match Boy" by Horatio Alger, Jr.* New York: Collier Books, 1962.

Fisher, Marvin. *Workshops in the Wilderness.* New York: Oxford University Press, 1967.

Gardner, Ralph D. *Horatio Alger, or the American Hero Era.* Mendota, Ill.: Wayside Press, 1964.

Gide, Charles, and Rist, Charles. *A History of Economic Doctrines.* Translated by R. Richards, 2nd Engl. ed. London: G. G. Harrap, 1948.

Greene, Theodore P. *America's Heroes: The Changing Models of Success in America's Magazines.* New York: Oxford University Press, 1970.

Grierson, Herbert. *Cross Currents in Seventeenth Century English Literature.* New York: Harper, 1958.

Griffin, Clifford. "Religious Benevolence as Social Control." *Mississippi Valley Historical Review* 46 (1957): 423–44.

————. *Their Brother's Keepers: Moral Stewardship in the United States.* New Brunswick, N.J.: Rutgers University Press, 1960.

Griffith, Clark. "Substance and Shadow: Language and Meaning in *The House of the Seven Gables.*" *Modern Philology* 51 (1953): 187–95.

Griswold, A. Whitney. "The American Gospel of Success." Ph.D. dissertation, Yale University, 1933.

————. *Farming and Democracy.* New York: Harcourt, Brace, 1948.

————. "Three Puritans on Prosperity." *New England Quarterly* 7 (1934): 475–93.

Gruber, Frank. *Horatio Alger, Jr.: A Biography and Bibliography.* Los Angeles: Grover Jones Press, 1961.

Gusfield, Joseph R. *Symbolic Crusade: Status Politics and the American Temperance Movement.* Urbana, Ill.: University of Illinois Press, 1963.

Habakkuk, H. J. *American and British Technology in the Nineteenth Century.* Cambridge, Engl.: University Press, 1962.

Hall, Lawrence S. *Hawthorne, Critic of Society.* New Haven: Yale University Press, 1944.

Hart, James. *The Popular Book: A History of America's Literary Taste.* Berkeley: University of California Press, 1961.

Hartz, Louis. *The Liberal Tradition in America.* New York: Harcourt, Brace & World, 1955.

Hassan, Ihab. *Radical Innocence: Studies in the Contemporary American Novel.* Princeton, N.J.: Princeton University Press, 1961.

Havens, Teresina Rowell. *Standards of Success.* Pendle Hill Pamphlets, no. 43. Wallingford, Pa.: Pendle Hill, 1948.

Hawthorne, Julian. *Nathaniel Hawthorne and His Wife.* 2 vols. Boston: Houghton Mifflin, 1884.

Heilbroner, Robert L. *The Quest for Wealth: A Study of Acquisitive Man.* New York: Simon & Schuster, 1956.

Hill, Christopher. *Reformation to Industrial Revolution, Vol. I: 1530–1780.* New York: Random House, 1967.

———. *Society and Puritanism in Pre-Revolutionary England.* London: Secker & Warburg, 1964.

History of Wages in the United States from Colonial Times to 1928. Bulletin of the United States Bureau of Labor Statistics, no. 604. Washington, D.C., 1934.

Hoffman, Daniel G. *Form and Fable in American Fiction.* New York: Oxford University Press, 1961.

Hofstadter, Richard. "The Myth of the Happy Yeoman." *American Heritage* 7 (1956): 42–53.

Hollingsworth, Kieth. *The Newgate Novel, 1830–1847.* Detroit: Wayne State University Press, 1963.

Hugins, Walter. *Jacksonian Democracy and the Working Class: A Study of the New York Workingman's Movement, 1829–1837.* Stanford: Stanford University Press, 1960.

Inventions and the Patent System. Washington, D.C.: U.S. Government Printing Office, 1964.

James, Louis. *Fiction for the Working Man, 1830–1850.* London: Oxford University Press, 1963.

Johnstone, Paul H. "In Praise of Husbandry." *Agricultural History* 11 (1937): 80–95.

Jones, Fred M. *Middlemen in the Domestic Trade of the United States, 1800–1860.* Illinois Studies in the Social Sciences, vol. 21, no. 3. Urbana: University of Illinois, 1937.

Jones, Howard M. *Ideas in America.* Cambridge, Mass.: Harvard University Press, 1944.

———. *O Strange New World.* New York: Viking, 1967.

Jordan, Alice M. *From Rollo to Tom Sawyer.* Boston: Horn Book, 1948.

Kesselring, Marion L. *Hawthorne's Reading, 1828–1850.* New York: New York Public Library, 1949.

Kiefer, Monica. *American Children Through Their Books, 1700–1835.* Philadelphia: University of Pennsylvania Press, 1948.

Knowles, Lillian C. A. *Economic Development in the Nineteenth Century.* London: Routledge, 1936.

Krout, John A. *The Origins of Prohibition.* New York: Knopf, 1925.

Kuhn, Anne L. *The Mother's Role in Childhood Education: New England Concepts, 1830–1860.* New Haven: Yale University Press, 1947.

Levin, Harry. *The Power of Blackness.* New York: Knopf, 1958.

Lovejoy, Arthur O. *The Great Chain of Being.* Cambridge, Mass.: Harvard University Press, 1948.

Lynn, Kenneth S. *The Dream of Success.* Boston: Little, Brown, 1955.

McConnell, Donald. *Economic Virtues in the United States.* New York: Columbia University Press, 1930.

McGivern, James G. *First Hundred Years of Engineering Education in the United States, 1807–1907.* Spokane, Wash.: Gonzaga University Press, 1960.

McLoughlin, W. G. "Pietism and the American Character." *American Quarterly* 17 (1965): 163–86.

Main, Jackson Turner. *The Social Structure of Revolutionary America.* Princeton: Princeton University Press, 1965.

Malin, James C. *The Contriving Brain and the Skilful Hand in the United States.* Lawrence, Kans.: University of Kansas Press, 1955.

Marks, Alfred H. "Who Killed Judge Pyncheon?" *PMLA* 71 (1956): 335–69.

Marx, Leo. *The Machine in the Garden.* New York: Oxford University Press, 1964.

Matthews, H. L. "Children's Magazines." *Bulletin of Bibliography* 1 (1899): 133–36.

Mayes, Herbert R. *Alger: A Biography Without A Hero.* New York: Macy-Masius, 1928.

Mayo, Thomas Franklin. *Epicurus in England (1650–1725).* Dallas: Southwest Press, 1934.

Meier, Hugo A. "Technology and Democracy, 1800–1860." *Mississippi Valley Historical Review* 43 (1957): 618–40.

Meyers, Marvin. *The Jacksonian Persuasion: Politics and Belief.* New York: Knopf, 1960.

Miller, Perry. *The New England Mind: Colony to Province.* Cambridge, Mass.: Harvard University Press, 1953.

———. *The New England Mind: The Seventeenth Century.* New York: Macmillan, 1939.

———. *The Raven and the Whale.* New York: Harcourt, Brace & World, 1956.

Mizruchi, Ephraim. *Success and Opportunity: A Study of Anomie.* Glencoe, Ill.: Free Press, 1964.

Mosier, Richard D. *Making the American Mind: Social and Moral Ideas in the McGuffey Readers.* New York: King's Crown, 1947.

Mott, Frank L. *American Journalism.* Toronto: Macmillan, 1941.

———. *A History of American Magazines.* 4 vols. New York: Appleton, 1930–57.

Noel, Mary. *Villains Galore . . .: The Heyday of the Popular Story Weekly.* New York: Macmillan, 1954.

Nordhoff, Ellen von. "The American Frontier as Safety Valve." *Agricultural History* 36 (1962): 123–42.

Nye, Russel B. *The Cultural Life of the New Nation, 1776–1830.* New York: Harper, 1960.

Papashvily, Helen W. *All the Happy Endings.* New York: Harper, 1956.

Pearce, Roy H. "Hawthorne and the Sense of the Past." *Journal of English Literary History* 21 (1954): 237–349.

Pease, William H., and Pease, Jane H. "Antislavery Ambivalence: Immediatism, Expedience, Race." *American Quarterly* 17 (1965): 682–95.

Persons, Stow. *American Minds: A History of Ideas.* New York: Holt & Co., 1958.

Pessin, Edward. "The Workingman's Movement of the Jacksonian Era." *Mississippi Valley Historical Review* 43 (1956): 428–43.

The Philosophy of Individualism. A Bibliography. London: The Individualist Bookshop, 1927.

Pierson, George W. "The M-Factor in American History." *American Quarterly* 14 (1962): 275–89.

Poli, Bernard. "The Hero in France and America." *Journal of American Studies* 2 (1966): 226.

Powell, Edwin H. "The Evolution of the American City and the Emergence of Anomie: A Culture Case Study of Buffalo, New York: 1810–1910." *British Journal of Sociology* 13 (1961): 156–68.

Ramsey, Peter. *Tudor Economic Problems.* London: Gollancz, 1963.

Remini, Robert V. *The Election of Andrew Jackson.* Philadelphia: Lippincott, 1963.

Riegal, Robert E. *Young America, 1830–1840.* Norman, Okla.: University of Oklahoma Press, 1949.

Ringe, Donald. "Hawthorne's Psychology of the Head and the Heart." *PMLA* 65 (1950): 120–32.

Robertson, H. M. *Aspects of the Rise of Economic Individualism.* Cambridge, Engl.: University Press, 1933.

Rokeach, Milton, and Merzei, Louis. "Race and Shared Belief as Factors in Social Choice." *Science* 151 (1966): 167–72.

Rostow, Walter W. "The Take-Off Into Self-Sustained Growth." *Economic Journal* 66 (1956): 25–47.

Røstvig, Marie-Sophie. *The Happy Man: Studies in the Metamorphoses of a Classical Ideal.* Rev. ed. 2 vols. Oslo: Norwegian University Press, 1962.

Ruggiero, Guido de. *The History of European Liberalism.* Translated by R. G. Collingwood. London: Oxford University Press, 1927.

Sabine, George H. *A History of Political Theory.* Rev. ed. New York: Holt, Rinehart & Winston, 1950.

Schlesinger, Arthur A., Jr. *The Age of Jackson.* Boston: Little, Brown, 1950.

Seelye, John. "Who Was Horatio? The Alger Myth and American Scholarship." *American Quarterly* 17 (1965): 749–56.

Sharpe, Dores R. *Walter Rauschenbusch.* New York: Macmillan, 1942.

Shepperson, W. S. *British Immigration to North America.* Oxford: Blackwell, 1957.

Shlakman, Vera. *Economic History of a Factory Town (Chicopee, Mass.).* Studies in History, vol. 20, nos. 1–4. Council of Industrial Studies Series, Study 2. Northampton, Mass.: Smith College, 1935.

Smith, Henry Nash. "The Businessman in Nineteenth Century Fiction." *Essays in Honor of Jay B. Hubbell.* Edited by Clarence Gohdes. Durham, N.C.: Duke University Press, 1967.

————. *Virgin Land: The American West as Symbol and Myth*. New York: Vintage, 1962.

Stanton, Robert. "The Trial of Nature: An Analysis of *The Blithdale Romance*." *PMLA* 76 (1961): 528–38.

Stifler, James M. *The Religion of Benjamin Franklin*. New York: Appleton, 1925.

Still, Bayrd. "The History of the City in American Life." *American Review* 2 (1962): 20–35.

Sullivan, William A. *The Industrial Worker in Pennsylvania, 1800–1840*. Harrisburg, Pa.: Pennsylvania Historical Museum Commission, 1955.

Sunley, Robert. "Early Nineteenth-Century American Literature on Child Rearing." In *Childhood in Contemporary Cultures*, edited by Margaret Mead and Martha Wolfenstein. Chicago: University of Chicago Press, 1955.

Swift, Lindsay. *Brook Farm: Its Members, Scholars and Visitors*. New York: Corinth Books, 1961.

Taft, Philip. *Organized Labor in American History*. New York: Harper, 1964.

Tawney, Jeanette, ed. *Chapters from a Christian Directory, by Richard Baxter*. London: G. Bell, 1925.

Taylor, George R. *The Transportation Revolution, 1815–1860*. New York: Rinehart, 1951.

Tebbel, John. *From Rags to Riches: Horatio Alger, Jr. and the American Dream*. New York: Macmillan, 1963.

Thomas, John L. "Romantic Reform in America, 1815–1865." *American Quarterly* 17 (1965): 656–81.

Tillyard, E. M. W. *The Elizabethan World Picture*. New York: Macmillan, 1944.

Turner, Arlin. *Hawthorne as Editor*. University, La.: Louisiana State University Press, 1941.

————. "Hawthorne and Reform." *New England Quarterly* 15 (1942): 700–714.

Turner, Ralph H., and Killian, Lewis M. *Collective Behavior*. Englewood Cliffs, N.J.: Prentice-Hall, 1957.

Tyler, Moses Coit. *A History of American Literature, 1607–1765*. Ithaca, N.Y.: Cornell University Press, 1949.

United States Patent Law Sesquicentennial Celebration. Washington, D.C.: U.S. Government Printing Office, 1941.

Wall, Joseph F. *Andrew Carnegie*. New York: Oxford University Press, 1970.

Wagenknecht, Edward. *Nathaniel Hawthorne: Man and Writer*. New York: Oxford University Press, 1958.

Ward, John W. *Andrew Jackson: Symbol for an Age*. New York: Oxford University Press, 1955.

Ware, Norman. *The Industrial Worker, 1840–1860*. Boston: Houghton Mifflin, 1924.

Webb, R. K. *The British Working Class Reader, 1790–1848: Literary and Social Tensions*. London: George Allen & Unwin, 1955.

Weber, Max. *The Protestant Ethic and the Spirit of Capitalism.* Translated by Talcott Parsons. New York: Scribner's, 1958.

Welter, Barbara. "The Cult of True Womanhood," *American Quarterly* 18 (1966): 151–74.

Wish, Harvey. *Society and Thought in Early America.* New York: Longman's, 1950.

Wright, Louis B. *The Dream of Prosperity in Colonial America.* New York: New York University Press, 1965.

———. "Franklin's Legacy to the Gilded Age." *Virginia Quarterly Review* 22 (1946): 268–79.

———. *Middle Class Culture in Elizabethan England.* Chapel Hill, N.C.: University of North Carolina Press, 1935.

Wyllie, Irvin G. *The Self-Made Man in America: The Myth of Rags to Riches.* New Brunswick, N.J.: Rutgers University Press, 1954.

Young, G. M., ed. *Early Victorian England: 1830–1865.* 2 vols. London: Oxford University Press, 1951.

INDEX